D1569721

Free Speech and Censorship

Recent Titles in Contemporary Debates

FREE SPEECH AND CENSORSHIP

Examining the Facts

H. L. Pohlman

Contemporary Debates

An Imprint of ABC-CLIO, LLC
Santa Barbara, California • Denver, Colorado

Library of Congress Cataloging-in-Publication Data

Names: Pohlman, H. L., 1952– author.
Title: Free speech and censorship : examining the facts / H.L. Pohlman.
Description: Santa Barbara, California : ABC-CLIO, 2019. | Series: Contemporary
    debates | Includes bibliographical references and index.
Identifiers: LCCN 2019008848 (print) | LCCN 2019014315 (ebook) |
    ISBN 9781440861802 (ebook) | ISBN 9781440861796 (print : alk. paper)
Subjects: LCSH: Freedom of speech—United States. | Censorship—United States.
Classification: LCC KF4772 (ebook) | LCC KF4772 .P64 2019 (print) |
    DDC 342.7308/53—dc23
LC record available at https://lccn.loc.gov/2019008848

ISBN: 978-1-4408-6179-6 (print)
        978-1-4408-6180-2 (ebook)

23 22 21 20 19   1 2 3 4 5

This book is also available as an eBook.

ABC-CLIO
An Imprint of ABC-CLIO, LLC

ABC-CLIO, LLC
147 Castilian Drive
Santa Barbara, California 93117
www.abc-clio.com

This book is printed on acid-free paper ∞

Manufactured in the United States of America

To Thekla, Vera, Moses, and Greta

Contents

How to Use This Book

Free Speech and Censorship: Examining the Facts is part of ABC-CLIO's Contemporary Debates reference series. Each title in this series, which is intended for use by high school and undergraduate students as well as members of the general public, examines the veracity of controversial claims or beliefs surrounding a major political/cultural issue in the United States. The purpose of this series is to give readers a clear and unbiased understanding of current issues by informing them about falsehoods, half-truths, and misconceptions—and confirming the factual validity of other assertions—that have gained traction in America's political and cultural discourse. Ultimately, this series has been crafted to give readers the tools for a fuller understanding of controversial issues, policies, and laws that occupy center stage in American life and politics.

Each volume in this series identifies 30–40 questions swirling about the larger topic under discussion. These questions are examined in individualized entries, which are in turn arranged in broad subject chapters that cover certain aspects of the issue being examined, for example, history of concern about the issue, potential economic or social impact, or findings of latest scholarly research.

Each chapter features 4–10 individual entries. Each entry begins by stating an important and/or well-known **Question** about the issue being studied—for example, "Does freedom of speech protect 'hate speech' that denigrates people on the basis of their race, ethnicity, religion, sex, or sexual orientation?" or "Does a member of an audience at a public speaking event or an attendee at a political demonstration or protest have a free-speech right to 'heckle' a speaker or disrupt the event?"

The entry then provides a concise and objective one- or two-paragraph **Answer** to the featured question, followed by a more comprehensive, detailed explanation of **The Facts**. This latter portion of each entry uses quantifiable, evidence-based information from respected sources to fully address each question and provide readers with the information they need to be informed citizens. Importantly, entries will also acknowledge instances in which conflicting data exists or data is incomplete. Finally, each entry concludes with a **Further Reading** section, providing users with information on other important and influential resources.

The ultimate purpose of every book in the Contemporary Debates series is to reject "false equivalence," in which demonstrably false beliefs or statements are given the same exposure and credence as the facts; to puncture myths that diminish our understanding of important policies and positions; to provide needed context for misleading statements and claims; and to confirm the factual accuracy of other assertions. In other words, volumes in this series are being crafted to clear the air surrounding some of the most contentious and misunderstood issues of our time—not just add another layer of obfuscation and uncertainty to the debate.

Introduction

This volume is part of a series dedicated to examining the facts about controversial claims regarding major issues that Americans are currently debating. Most of the volumes of the series address controversies regarding matters of empirical fact, such as whether global warming is occurring, the status of race relations, or the positive and negative effects of marijuana. The present volume is different in that it addresses controversies regarding two fundamental norms of the United States: what kinds of expression are protected by the constitutional principle of freedom of speech, and what kinds are protected by the corresponding American cultural ideal? Answering these two questions objectively and fairly demands an analysis of facts, but these are facts about norms that govern our legal and cultural existence, not facts about the physical, political, economic, or social world that we live in. This key difference has ramifications for the nature of this study and explains why it is dissimilar in some respects from other volumes in this series.

One important distinction between norms and empirical facts is that the former are rules or principles that an authority has established or created, while empirical facts are discovered by the natural and social sciences utilizing widely accepted methodologies. Regarding the norms linked to the constitutional meaning of freedom of speech, the relevant authority is clear and identifiable: the Supreme Court of the United States. Accordingly, to discuss in a factual and objective manner what freedom of speech means as a constitutional norm requires a fair and evenhanded analysis of the substance of the Court's free-speech decisions. In contrast, any discussion of freedom of speech as a cultural ideal is more complicated because there is no clearly identifiable authority that enforces this ideal. The only relevant authority would appear to be the relatively amorphous one of American public opinion. Since it is next to impossible to justify any factual claims regarding what types of expression Americans in general think are protected by the cultural ideal of free speech and what types are not, the best option is to define a coherent perspective that will function as a baseline to decide when Americans are or are not abiding by an intelligible and justifiable ideal of free speech. Only this level of precision is compatible with this dimension of the topic of free speech.

The fact that norms are created by an authority, whether a clear and identifiable one, such as the Supreme Court, or an amorphous one, such as the American people, does not in any way imply that the authority is infallible or beyond criticism. One of the core principles of the constitutional principle of freedom of speech is that Americans of all stripes have a right to criticize the decisions of the Supreme Court. However, even if most of this criticism is valid, that does not change the reality that the Court's free-speech decisions constitute the current meaning of freedom of speech as a constitutional right. Such criticism, of course, may in time convince the Court to overturn precedent and change the constitutional meaning of free speech, but that simply confirms that the constitutional right of free speech is currently what the Supreme Court says it is, even if it is not yet what it should be.

The situation is somewhat different in terms of the cultural ideal of freedom of speech. There is no clear and authoritative method to ascertain the limits of this societal ideal, but that does not mean that Americans cannot criticize what they take those limits to be. In short, although this book is an attempt to present the reader with facts regarding the constitutional right of free speech and a dispassionate perspective on free speech as a societal ideal, it in no way is meant to insulate the current understandings of this principle and ideal from criticism. However, this book does assume that before you can criticize freedom of speech, whether as a constitutional principle or as a societal ideal, you first have to know what it is. This book is an attempt to make it easier for students to accomplish this latter goal.

The American constitutional principle of freedom of speech and the corresponding cultural ideal do impact each other. Supreme Court decisions limiting government's power to punish or sanction speech can impact how Americans understand what freedom of speech means, both as an ideal and in practice. A good example may be the Court's decisions in the 1970s narrowing the constitutional definition of obscenity, which arguably contributed to today's somewhat blasé attitude regarding what others read or watch on television or what they listen to on their headphones. They may shake their heads in disbelief, but in the end they feel it is none of their business. And there is little doubt that American public opinion about what is or is not permissible speech can have an effect on how the Supreme Court defines what expression the government can punish or sanction. This is so because the Supreme Court does not operate in a political and social vacuum. Supreme Court justices read the newspapers; watch television; and participate in all types of political, economic, and social activities. They are, therefore, not insulated from the evolving values and attitudes of their fellow citizens. Accordingly, the evolving values and attitudes of Americans regarding what speech is permissible and what is not, as a matter of course, will in varying degrees eventually seep into Supreme Court decisions regarding the degree to which government can punish or sanction speech.

This interaction between the constitutional principle and the societal ideal of freedom of speech cannot be measured in any precise way, but that does not mean that it is not a part of our legal, political, and cultural reality. Because it is part of our reality is one reason why both topics are considered in this volume, although the lion's share of the book is dedicated to exploring how the Supreme Court has defined the constitutional principle of freedom of speech. This emphasis on free speech as a constitutional right makes sense for three reasons: first, since this book will examine many controversial claims that are currently being made about freedom of speech, it should explore more deeply those topics that have a factual character. In the context of freedom of speech, that means an exploration of what the Supreme Court has ruled regarding what speech government can punish or sanction and what it cannot. Second, the corpus of the Supreme Court's decisions on freedom of speech is enormous, consisting of thousands of decisions. Accordingly, the slender size of this volume justifies focusing on free speech as a constitutional right, rather than the more nebulous one of free speech as a cultural ideal. Third, and most important, an examination of the constitutional principle of freedom of expression is an excellent—one might almost say a necessary—preliminary to any discussion of freedom of speech as a cultural ideal. For that reason, only the final chapter will address this latter topic. This degree of emphasis in no way implies that the topic of free speech as a cultural ideal is of less importance than free speech as a constitutional principle. Rather, what it means is that some appreciation of free speech as a constitutional principle is a prerequisite for an intelligible discussion of it as a cultural ideal.

This book is structured to provide students with a clear account of the core meaning of the constitutional principle of free speech. The essays featured therein provide concise analyses of majority opinions that show how different dimensions of the principle have legally evolved. Opinions by dissenting justices are typically not discussed, especially if the majority's opinion has become established law. In addition, consistent with the goal of a straightforward, fair, and evenhanded presentation of the constitutional principle of free speech, the essays often include quotations from majority opinions that give students clear insight into the Court's reasoning. Justices who have authored the opinions are identified by name when useful, but other times the majority opinion is referred to as the Court's opinion to underline the opinion's weight as a controlling precedent. Citations for quotations taken from court opinions are consolidated into one parenthetical citation for each decision at the end of the discussion of the case.

The specific topics included within the chapters are those necessary for a basic understanding of the subject as well as those that are linked or associated with various myths and misconceptions about the meaning of free speech. An important goal of the book is to puncture fallacies about freedom of speech that are constantly surfacing and resurfacing in today's popular debates. For example, in 2016 a commentator equated freedom of speech with the freedom to be "polite" and conform to the "rules of public decorum" (Handler, *Sapiens*, www.sapiens.org, January 28, 2016). Such an understanding of the right of free speech overturns its traditional meaning and significance. It converts a right that the individual has against society and government into a duty to conform to one or the other. The fact that such claims about freedom of speech are not all that unusual in today's world is the rationale for this book. Its goal is to give students the knowledge and skills to detect and reject such fallacies and misconceptions about freedom of speech.

1

---◆:◆---

Basic Principles of Free Speech

The First Amendment of the U.S. Constitution includes the constitutional right of freedom of speech. The amendment reads as follows:

> Congress shall make no law respecting an establishment of religion, or prohibiting the free exercise thereof; or abridging the freedom of speech, or of the press, or the right of the people peaceably to assemble, and to petition the Government for a redress of grievances.

The inclusion of freedom of speech in the "First" Amendment is an implicit acknowledgment of the importance of free speech for the U.S. system of government and for American society in general. The meaning of this constitutional right has evolved over the course of American history. It began primarily as a fairly narrow right prohibiting the government from imposing "prior restraints" on publishers. "Prior restraints" were laws that prevented anyone from engaging in publication without a government license. Understood in this way, free speech did not prevent the government from punishing someone for what was published. However, early in the nation's history, in reaction to the Alien and Sedition Acts of 1798, many Americans interpreted free speech to preclude the government from punishing "seditious libel," which was generally defined as any publication that encouraged disrespect of governmental institutions, the law, or public officials. Following the election of 1800, President Thomas Jefferson pardoned those still serving sentences under the Sedition Act, and Congress repaid all fines levied under it. These actions buttressed the emerging view that freedom of speech prohibited not only prior restraints but also the punishment of speech critical of the government or public officials.

Over the course of the next two centuries, the Supreme Court deepened and expanded the right of free speech. It did so in part by expounding on "basic principles" of free speech. These "basic principles" focus on the *why*, the *what*, the *who*, and the *when*: *Why* is free speech a "fundamental" constitutional right? *What* does this right protect? *Who* has this constitutional right? *When* does this right provide protection? *What* limits does free speech place on governmental actions? *What* significance does free speech have as a cultural and societal ideal? A discussion of these general issues is a useful introduction to the more specific questions addressed in later chapters.

Q1. IS FREE SPEECH A "FUNDAMENTAL" CONSTITUTIONAL RIGHT AND, IF SO, WHY?

Answer: Yes. Free speech is a "fundamental" constitutional right because it is a prerequisite for representative democracy, other civil rights and liberties, the effective operation of the marketplace of ideas, and the intellectual growth and development of the individual.

The Facts: Explanations of *why* free speech is a constitutional right in the United States are called justifications. These justifications are important because they have a direct bearing on the scope and resilience of the right of free speech. A broad justification of free speech protects a wide range of expressive activities from governmental prohibitions and regulations. A strong justification produces a right of free speech that is tough and resilient, capable of resisting popular inclinations to limit or restrict it. The four major justifications for freedom of speech are: (1) it is a prerequisite for representative democracy, (2) it is a precondition for other civil rights and liberties, (3) it is necessary for the operation of the marketplace of ideas, and (4) it is essential to an individual's intellectual growth and development. Freedom of speech is a "fundamental" constitutional right because, whether considered individually or in conjunction with one another, these four justifications have substantial weight and intellectual power.

The force of the first justification stems from the fact that the United States is, and for the foreseeable future, will remain a representative democracy. Such a government can function only if its representatives have the right to debate legislative proposals before voting on them. For this reason, the federal Constitution includes a provision that prohibits senators and members of the House of Representatives from being "questioned in any other Place" about "any Speech or Debate in either House" (Art. 1, § 6). More broadly, since representative democracy implies a significant degree of popular control over public policy, citizens must have the right to debate public issues and the qualifications of political candidates. Only if freedom of speech is protected to this extent will citizens have any assurance that their representatives will enact legislation that corresponds to their preferences.

In a comparable way, citizens can assess whether enacted legislation is working as anticipated only if they are aware of the relevant facts and the existence of alternative legislative policies, both of which require free speech. They cannot make an informed choice regarding whether to maintain the status quo or seek additional change through new laws without the opportunity to discuss and debate the issues. Moreover, even if such speech does not lead to changes in current legislative policies, the right to advocate for alternatives gives the opposition a legitimate reason to support the existing system of representative democracy. In this fashion, freedom of speech fosters political stability and legitimacy: the opposition had a fair chance to change the public's mind, but it lost the debate. Lastly, free speech protects a citizen's right to harshly criticize public officials, thereby discouraging abuses of political power. Justice William Brennan firmly embedded this idea into the Constitution with his remark "that debate on public issues should be uninhibited, robust, and wide-open, and that it may well include vehement, caustic, and sometimes unpleasantly sharp attacks on government and public officials" (*New York Times v. Sullivan*, 376 U.S. 254, 270 (1964)). The underlying assumption is that criticism of public officials supports the rule of law by encouraging public officials to perform their public duties and responsibilities lawfully and in ways they would be willing to defend publicly.

However, when freedom of speech is understood as a necessary condition for representative democracy, it arguably only provides protection for speech that is "political" in character. The second justification for freedom of speech broadens the scope of the right by underlining the degree to which it is necessary to protect other constitutional rights and values, including those that relate to our private lives, such as freedom of religion, the right to be free from unreasonable searches and seizures, and the right to privacy in general. As Justice Benjamin N. Cardozo argued in *Palko v. Connecticut*, free speech is "the matrix, the indispensable condition, of nearly every other form of freedom" (302 U.S. 319, 327 (1937)). What Cardozo meant was that at one point in American history "liberty" consisted only of freedom from physical restraint—freedom from being arbitrarily thrown into a dungeon or shackled to a wall. Today, after centuries of evolution, "liberty" includes freedom from oppressive laws, malicious prosecutions, and unfair trials. This expansion of "liberty," according to Cardozo, was possible only because the state over time gradually recognized the right of free speech, the right to express one's opposition to encroachments on freedom and to demand more rights and liberties from the government. Without free speech, it is hard to imagine how we could effectively "preserve" our rights and liberties for future generations or "fight" for those we are demanding for ourselves and our descendants.

The third justification for freedom of speech extends the scope of its protection beyond political issues and constitutional values to include all debates and discussions on matters that can be characterized as either true or false. John Stuart Mill, the 19th-century British philosopher and author of *On Liberty*, crafted the premises of this argument by dividing all such opinions into three categories—what is false, what is true, and what is partly true and partly false—and providing a reason why freedom of speech should be protected for each category. Obviously, false propositions can be overcome only if true propositions are allowed to circulate freely. Not to allow this circulation, according to Mill, is to implicitly assert an infallibility that no human being has a right to claim. On the other hand, even if we assume the received opinion is true, its competition with false ideas should be permitted as a way to clarify what the true opinion means to us as a "vivid conception" and as an "active" principle of our lives. Lastly, regarding opinions that are partly true and partly false, truth requires the "reconciling and combining of opposites" that have to be achieved through "the rough process of a struggle between combatants fighting under hostile banners." This "rough process" sifts through opinions that are partly true and partly false and thereby refines the truth, but no one individual or group of individuals has the intellectual capacities to say when the process of purification is complete. Accordingly, the best assurance of truth, according to Mill, is that the "rough process" remains free and open for all forms of discussion and debate about facts, opinions, and doctrines (Mill, Chap. 2).

In his dissent in *Abrams v. United States* (1919), Justice Oliver Wendell Holmes incorporated Mill's defense of free speech into American constitutional law by invoking the metaphor of a "marketplace of ideas":

Persecution for the expression of opinions seems to me perfectly logical. If you have no doubt of your premises or your power, and want a certain result with all your heart, you naturally express your wishes in law, and sweep away all opposition. To allow opposition by speech seems to indicate that you think the speech impotent, as when a man says that he has squared the circle, or that you do not care wholeheartedly for the result, or that you doubt either your power or your premises. But when men have realized that time has upset many fighting faiths, they may come to believe even more than they believe the very foundations of their own conduct that the ultimate good desired is better reached by free trade in ideas—that the best test of truth is the power of the thought to get itself accepted in the competition of the market, and that truth is the only ground upon which their wishes safely can be carried out. That, at any rate, is the theory of our Constitution. It is an experiment, as all life is an experiment. (250 U.S. 616, 630 (1919))

Holmes's formulation of the "marketplace of ideas" justification of free speech is eloquent, but the force of his reasoning depends on whether Americans in fact believe that "time has upset many fighting faiths" and that the "marketplace of ideas" is the "best test of truth" more than they believe "the very foundations of their own conduct." There is no assurance that all or most Americans accept these premises. For this reason, Holmes describes freedom of speech as a "theory of our Constitution" that is "an experiment." We cannot be certain that the "marketplace of ideas" is the "best test of truth," even if many of us think it is so based on available evidence.

The fourth major justification for freedom of speech is that it is a necessary condition for an individual's intellectual growth and development. The germ of this justification also lies in Mill's *On Liberty*. Mill argued that the free development of individuality is one of the "leading essentials" of well-being, that the human faculties of "perception, judgment, discriminative feeling, mental activity, and even moral preference are exercised only in making a choice," and that the mental and moral powers, "like the muscular powers, are improved only by being used" (Mill, Chap. 3). Individual growth and development, therefore, depend on the ability to make informed choices, which, in turn, requires freedom of speech. Only with free speech, does the individual have the right to choose what to think, what to enjoy, what to feel, what to do, and what to become.

Justice Louis Brandeis underlined the constitutional significance of Mill's argument with the following observation: "Those who won our independence believed that the final end of the State was to make men free to develop their faculties" and "valued liberty both as an end, and as a means" (*Whitney v. California*, 274 U.S. 357, 375 (1927)). Free speech is the means by which individuals can reach their full potential by making decisions that develop their faculties and shape their personalities, an experience that is not just a means to an end, but an end in itself. This justification for freedom of speech delivers the broadest protection for speech. Limits on speech are generally suspect since no one knows beforehand what speech is vital to individual growth and development. This end, however, does not necessarily mean that freedom of speech has no limits. Even if freedom of speech is partly justified as a prerequisite for individual growth and development, the government's interest in placing restraints on certain speech activities can, of course, outweigh the intellectual force of this justification, just as it can, in various contexts, outweigh the force of the arguments that free speech is necessary for representative democracy, the preservation of our liberties, or the discovery of truth.

FURTHER READING

Mill, John Stuart. *On Liberty*. Indianapolis, IN: Hackett Publishing, 1978.

Post, Robert C. *Democracy, Expertise, Academic Freedom: A First Amendment Jurisprudence for the Modern State*. New Haven, CT: Yale University Press, 2012.

Schauer, Frederick. "Free Speech, the Search for Truth, and the Problem of Collective Knowledge." *SMU Law Review* 70 (2017): 231–251.

Sunstein, Cass. *Democracy and the Problem of Free Speech*. New York: Free Press, 1995.

"Symposium: Individual Autonomy and Free Speech." *Constitutional Commentary* 27 (2011): 249–416.

Volokh, Eugene. "In Defense of the Marketplace of Ideas/Search for Truth as a Theory of Free Speech Protection." *Virginia Law Review* 97 (2011): 595–601.

Q2. DOES THE CONSTITUTIONAL RIGHT OF FREE SPEECH ONLY INCLUDE THE RIGHT TO SPEAK AND PUBLISH?

Answer: No. The scope of today's constitutional right of free speech extends well beyond the spoken and written word, to include a wide array of expressive forms of conduct and a number of subsidiary rights logically linked to freedom of speech.

The Facts: The Supreme Court has expanded the scope of freedom of speech beyond speech and the written word throughout the 20th and 21st centuries. It is, however, not always clear which of the four major justifications discussed in Q1 sustains the expansion in specific cases. It is, therefore, a useful exercise to consider whether the extensions can be vindicated in terms of one or more of the four major justifications of freedom of speech. One of the Court's first expansions of free speech occurred in *Stromberg v. California* (1931), a decision that invalidated a state law prohibiting the display of a red flag "as a sign, symbol, or emblem of opposition to organized government." The Court reasoned that such a statute could be construed to apply to conduct that the state could not constitutionally prohibit, such as a "peaceful and orderly" demonstration by a "high minded and patriotic" political party. The statute, therefore, permitted "the punishment of the fair use" of the "opportunity for free political discussion," which in the Court's view violated "a fundamental principle of our constitutional system" (283 U.S. 359, 369 (1931)). This important precedent led to a series of Supreme Court decisions addressing whether other forms of "symbolic conduct" were protected by freedom of speech (see Q21).

In *Thornhill v. Alabama* (1940), the Supreme Court held that "picketing" a place of business during a labor dispute or "loitering" nearby was protected by freedom of speech. In support of this result, the Court argued that "picketing" and "loitering" embraced "nearly every practicable, effective means whereby those interested—including the employees directly affected—may enlighten the public on the nature and causes of a labor dispute." More generally, the Court added that the founders had a "broadened conception" of freedom of speech as a means "to supply the public need for information and education with respect to the significant issues of the times." As the Court remarked, "Freedom of discussion, if it would fulfill its historic function in this nation, must embrace all issues about which information is needed or appropriate to enable the members of society to cope with the exigencies of their period" (310 U.S. 88, 104, 101–102 (1940)). The implication was that the scope of freedom of speech had to adjust to the needs of each generation, a relatively open-ended principle.

In *Burstyn v. Wilson* (1952), the Supreme Court incorporated motion pictures into the scope of freedom of speech. It came to this conclusion in a decision that invalidated a New York law that permitted the banning of a film on the ground that it was "indecent, immoral, inhuman, sacrilegious, . . . [or was] of such a character that its exhibition would tend to corrupt morals or incite to crime." In reaching this decision, the Court argued that motion pictures were "a significant medium for the communication of ideas" that may affect "public attitudes and behavior in a variety of ways, ranging from direct espousal of a political or social doctrine to the subtle shaping of thought which characterizes all artistic expression." It did not matter that one of the purposes of motion pictures was to "entertain" or that they were produced "for profit" or that they have a "greater capacity for evil, particularly among the youth of the community, than other modes of expression" (343 U.S. 495, 497, 501–502 (1952)). The latter factor may be relevant in deciding whether a particular film could be legally censored, but their allegedly "greater capacity for evil," in the Court's view, was no basis for entirely excluding films from the scope of freedom of speech.

The Court extended *Burstyn's* principle to all forms of artistic expression, including photography, painting, and sculpture, in *Miller v. California* (1973), a decision that primarily dealt with the definition of "obscenity," a category of expression that is excluded from the protection of freedom of speech (see Q12). Despite this focus of the decision, the Court announced the following principle: "The First Amendment protects works which, taken as a whole, have serious literary, artistic, political, or scientific value, regardless of whether the government or a majority of the people approve of the ideas these works represent" (413 U.S. 15, 34 (1973)). Although a work must have "serious value" to be entitled to constitutional protection, the scope of free speech encompassed all "literary," "artistic," and "scientific" works of whatever kind. The Court came to a similar conclusion in *Schad v. Borough of Mount Ephraim* (1981): "Entertainment, as well as political and ideological speech, is protected; motion pictures, programs broadcast by radio or television, and live entertainment, such as musical and dramatic works, fall within the First Amendment guarantee" (452 U.S. 61, 65 (1981)).

The lyrics of a song are composed of words and are, therefore, undoubtedly protected by freedom of speech, but what of the instrumental music that accompanies the lyrics? In *Ward v. Rock Against Racism* (1989), the Court resolved this question when it considered whether the sponsor of a concert at the band shell in Central Park could object to New York City's regulations of electronic amplification. In the end, the Court upheld the regulations as neutral time, place, and manner regulations, but it also concluded that music "is one of the oldest forms of human expression." For this reason, the First Amendment protected "the musical aspects of the concert as a form of expression and communication" (491 U.S. 781, 790 (1989)). It was protected speech, though subject to valid time, place, and manner regulations (see Chapter 4).

The Court indirectly confirmed the constitutionally protected status of instrumental music in *Hurley v. Irish-American Gay, Lesbian & Bisexual Group of Boston* (1995). In this decision, the Court determined that "parades" were within the scope of freedom of speech. The sponsors of a St. Patrick's Day parade, in the exercise of their right of free speech, could, therefore, exclude a group from marching in the parade if it advocated ideas the sponsors did not wish to support. "Parades," in the Court's view, are composed of "marchers who are making some sort of collective point, not just to each other but to bystanders along the way." Even if the parade had a wide assortment of "particularized" diverse messages, such as "England get out of Ireland," "Say no to drugs," "Life's too short not to be Irish," it was still constitutionally protected. Otherwise, freedom of speech would not include "the unquestionably shielded painting of Jackson Pollock, music of Arnold Schoenberg, or Jabberwocky verse of Lewis Carroll" (515 U.S. 557, 569 (1995)). In other words, according to the Court, if the opaque and indistinct messages of nonrepresentational art, atonal instrumental music, and nonsense poetry were definitely within the scope of freedom of speech, then so also was a parade, regardless of the parade's generalized and diverse set of messages. Since it was within the scope of freedom of speech, the sponsors could exclude from a parade any "particularized" message they did not wish to convey, such as a message advocating for the rights of gays, lesbians, and bisexuals.

Besides extending free-speech protection to expressive activities beyond the spoken and written word, the Court has also recognized a number of subsidiary rights that are logically associated with freedom of speech. For example, while freedom of speech undoubtedly protects the right to speak, it also implies a right not to speak. The Court came to this conclusion in *West Virginia State Board of Education v. Barnette* (1943), which held that the rights of free speech and the free exercise of religion barred the government from compelling school children to pledge allegiance to the American flag. "To sustain the compulsory flag salute," the Court argued, "we are required to say that a Bill of Rights which guards the individual's right to speak his own mind, left it open to public authorities to compel him to utter what is not in his mind." The goal of national unity would not justify such anomalous reasoning because history has shown that it is futile to achieve unity through compulsion. According to the Court, "Those who begin coercive elimination of dissent soon find themselves exterminating dissenters. Compulsory unification of opinion achieves only the unanimity of the graveyard" (319 U.S. 624, 634, 641 (1943)). The goal of national unity, in short, could not outweigh the individual's right not to speak. The Court reaffirmed this principle that free speech prohibits compelled speech in *National Institute of Family and Life Advocates v. Becerra* (2018), holding that California could not compel crisis pregnancy centers run by organizations opposed to abortion to inform clients that the state provided low-cost abortions to eligible women or that a center was not a "licensed medical provider."

In 1958, the Supreme Court in *NAACP v. Alabama* derived from freedom of speech a constitutional "right of association." This "right of association" was something more than "the right of the people peaceably to assemble, and to petition the Government for redress of grievances." The "right of association" implied the right to organize an identifiable group, with an institutional framework, rules, policies, officers, members, and dues. The Court's reasoning for this extension of the right of free speech was based on the degree to which group association enhanced "effective advocacy."

> Effective advocacy of both public and private points of view, particularly controversial ones, is undeniably enhanced by group association, as this Court has more than once recognized by remarking upon the close nexus between the freedoms of speech and assembly. It is beyond debate that freedom to engage in association for the advancement of beliefs and ideas is an inseparable aspect of the "liberty" assured by . . . freedom of speech. (357 U.S. 449, 460 (1958))

Based on this right of association, the Court rejected Alabama's demand for all the names and addresses of the members of the Alabama chapter of the NAACP. Worried that the disclosure of membership would likely lead to economic reprisals, loss of employment, threats, and other hostile acts, all of which would likely hamper the NAACP's expressive activities, the Court concluded that the "inviolability of privacy in group association may in many circumstances be indispensable to preservation of freedom of association, particularly where a group espouses dissident beliefs" (*Id.* at 462). Accordingly, freedom of speech was the foundation not only for a "right of association," but also for an individual right of privacy regarding one's group affiliations.

Another significant extension of the scope of freedom of speech involved political campaign contributions and expenditures. Can the states and the federal government place limits on the amount of campaign contributions and expenditures as a way to prevent political corruption? When the Court addressed this question in *Buckley v. Valeo* (1976), an initial question was whether campaign contributions and expenditures were within the scope of freedom of speech. The Court gave a strong affirmative answer to this question, arguing that

> virtually every means of communicating ideas in today's mass society requires the expenditure of money. The distribution of the humblest handbill or leaflet entails printing, paper, and circulation costs. Speeches and rallies generally necessitate hiring a hall and publicizing the event. The electorate's increasing dependence on television, radio, and other mass media for news and information has made these expensive modes of communication indispensable instruments of effective political speech. (424 U.S. 1, 19 (1976))

Because money and political speech were so intimately related, the Court concluded any limitations on political contributions and expenditures were not regulations of conduct. In the Court's view, the government's interest "in regulating the alleged 'conduct' of giving and spending money 'arises in some measure because the communication allegedly integral to the conduct is itself thought to be harmful'" (*Id.* at 16). Accordingly, such limitations were regulations of the communication itself and, therefore, were within the scope of free speech. The decision continued the trend of the expansion of the scope of freedom of speech, even though the Court ultimately ruled that reasonable limits on campaign contributions were lawful as a means to prevent political corruption.

FURTHER READING

Bezanson, Randall P. *Art and Freedom of Speech.* Urbana: University of Illinois Press, 2009.

Bresler, Robert J. *Freedom of Association: Rights and Liberties under the Law.* Santa Barbara, CA: ABC-CLIO, 2004.

Post, Robert C. *Citizens Divided: Campaign Finance Reform and the Constitution.* Cambridge, MA: Harvard University Press, 2014.

Tushnet, Mark V., Chen, Alan K., and Blocher, Joseph. *Free Speech Beyond Words.* New York: New York University Press, 2017.

Q3. IS FREE SPEECH AN "ABSOLUTE" CONSTITUTIONAL RIGHT?

Answer: No. The constitutional right of freedom of speech is not an "absolute" right because the Supreme Court has ruled that certain categories of speech are excluded from constitutional protection, and that categories of speech within the First Amendment can be conditionally prohibited or regulated, depending on the circumstances of the speech activity or the intent of the speaker.

The Facts: A significant number of Americans continue to believe that freedom of speech is or should be an "absolute" right. In a 2015 *Huffington Post* YouGov poll, 38 percent of the adults surveyed indicated that students at colleges and universities have "an absolute right to free speech even if that means allowing offensive or racist comments" (Kingkade 2017). This misconception continues to confuse the American public even though the Supreme Court debated and ultimately rejected the notion that free speech was an "absolute" right in a series of decisions during the 1950s and 1960s. On one side of the debate, Justice Hugo Black defended freedom of speech as an "absolute" right. He wrote in *Carlson v. Landon* (1952) "that the First Amendment grants an absolute right to believe in any government system, discuss all governmental affairs, and argue for desired changes in the existing order" (342 U.S. 524, 555 (1952)). Elsewhere, in *Konigsberg v. State Bar of California* (1961), he claimed that the purpose of the free speech clause was "to put the freedom protected there completely out of the area of any congressional control" (366 U.S. 36, 61 (1961)). However, Justice Black applied this categorical rule barring abridgments of freedom of speech only to "speech," not to expressive forms of activity that, in his opinion, did not qualify as "speech." Such expressive activity, according to Black, was "conduct" and could be subject to reasonable governmental prohibitions and regulations. A law "which primarily regulates conduct but which might also indirectly affect speech can be upheld if the effect on speech is minor in relation to the need for control of the conduct" (*Barenblatt v. United States*, 360 U.S. 139, 141 (1959)).

In Black's view, an example of expressive activity that was "conduct," rather than "speech," was trespassing on private property during a sit-in demonstration at a restaurant to protest racial discrimination. In his dissenting opinion, Black voted to uphold the conviction on the ground that the state's interest in preventing violence outweighed the indirect effect the trespass law had on the expressive "conduct" of the protestors (see Black's dissenting opinion in *Bell v. Maryland*, 1964). This kind of "balancing" of the state's interests against the rights of individuals to express themselves, according to Black, was appropriate only in terms of expressive "conduct," not "speech," which in contrast received "absolute" protection.

On the other side of the debate were Justice John Marshall Harlan II and Justice Felix Frankfurter. Both of these jurists objected to Black's views that the scope of the First Amendment was limited to "speech" and that "speech" within the amendment had "absolute" protection. In his majority opinion in *Konigsberg v. State Bar of California* (1961), Harlan referred to both objections. "At the outset," he wrote, "we reject the view that freedom of speech and association . . . are 'absolutes,' not only in the undoubted sense that where the constitutional protection exists it must prevail, but also in the sense that the scope of that protection must be gathered solely from a literal reading of the First Amendment" (366 U.S. 36, 49–50 (1961)). In other words, courts were justified in holding that certain types of "speech" were outside the scope of the constitutional right and, for that reason, received no constitutional protection, while other types of "speech" or forms of "symbolic conduct" were within the amendment, but nonetheless might be subject to governmental control.

Regarding "speech" and "symbolic conduct" that were within the scope of free speech, Harlan argued in *Konigsberg* that judges must weigh the state's interest against the value of the asserted right of free speech. When "constitutional protections are asserted against the exercise of valid governmental power," Harlan wrote, "a reconciliation must be effected, and that perforce requires an appropriate weighing of the respective interests involved." Accordingly, Harlan advocated a two-step judicial process for the evaluation of free-speech claims: the judge first decides if the "speech" or "symbolic conduct" is within the scope of free speech: if it is not, then it is not protected; if it is, then the judge "balances" the value of the right against the importance of the governmental interest. The implication was that free-speech claims that were within the scope of freedom of speech should not always prevail, which conflicted with a central tenet of Black's "absolutist" approach.

Justice Frankfurter also defended a "balancing" approach to freedom of speech. He thought Black's literal reading of the First Amendment to be misguided. In his concurring opinion in *Dennis v. United States* (1951), a decision that upheld conspiracy convictions of the leaders of the American Communist Party, he referred to those "who find in the Constitution a wholly unfettered right of expression. Such literalness treats the words of the Constitution as though they were found on a piece of outworn parchment instead of being words that have called into being a nation with a past to be preserved for the future." The First Amendment was "to be read not as barren words found in a dictionary but as symbols of historic experience illumined by the presuppositions of those who employed them." A literal reading was also dangerous because absolute "rules would inevitably lead to absolute exceptions, and such exceptions would eventually corrode the rules" (341 U.S. 494, 521–523 (1951)). Accordingly, even though Frankfurter thought the laws under review in *Dennis* "no doubt restrict the exercise of free speech and assembly," they were justified based on the overwhelming importance of the governmental interest in protecting the American constitutional order from a Communist revolution.

Justice Black opposed this judicial "balancing" approach to freedom of speech because he thought it had a built-in bias in favor of upholding the legislature's assessment that the state's interest outweighed the value of free speech. In his dissent in *Konigsberg*, he rejected "the doctrine that permits constitutionally protected rights to be 'balanced' away whenever a majority of this Court thinks that a state might have interests sufficient to justify abridgment of those freedoms." Instead, Black believed "that the men who drafted our Bill of Rights did all the 'balancing' that was to be done in this field" (366 U.S. 36, 61 (1961)). If the founders "balanced" the relevant interests by inserting "absolutes" into the Constitution, so be it. In Black's opinion, there were "absolutes" in the Constitution, and "they were put there on purpose by men who knew what words meant, and meant their prohibitions to be 'absolutes'" (Black, p. 3). In short, according to Black, judges should respect the founders' constitutional "balances," not create new ones that in effect violate the Constitution.

Justice Black was never able to convince a majority of the Supreme Court of the validity of his "absolutist" interpretation of freedom of speech. One major obstacle was the number of Supreme Court precedents supporting the position that certain types of "speech" were categorically excluded from the First Amendment. Citing relevant precedents, the Court summed up this traditional view in *Chaplinsky v. New Hampshire* (1942):

> It is well understood that the right of free speech is not absolute at all times and under all circumstances. There are certain well-defined and narrowly limited classes of speech, the prevention and punishment of which have never been thought to raise any Constitutional problem. These include the lewd and obscene, the profane, the libelous, and the insulting or "fighting" words. (315 U.S. 568, 571–572 (1942))

The Court, in short, had decisively concluded in 1942 that certain categories of speech were not within the scope of freedom of speech (see Chapter 2). Black's "absolutist" interpretation of freedom of speech had to overcome the weight of this tradition, something it has never been able to do. As recently as 2010, the Supreme Court reconfirmed that there are "traditional categories" of speech "long familiar to the bar" that are not within the scope of freedom of speech, citing numerous cases in support of this position (*United States v. Stevens*, 2010). The Court's unwavering commitment to this understanding of free speech is a weighty objection to any claim it is an "absolute" right.

A second major obstacle to Black's "absolutist" interpretation of free speech is that the Supreme Court has repeatedly held that certain types of expression are within the scope of free speech, but government can nonetheless prohibit them in certain circumstances. Such *conditional* protection of speech or "symbolic conduct" is incompatible with an "absolutist" interpretation of the First Amendment. Judges must consider factors other than "speech" to determine whether the free-speech right should prevail in one set of circumstances but not in another. Relevant factors would include the importance of the government's interest, the proximity and imminence of harm, and the intent of the speaker. These factors require judges to engage in some sort of "balancing." Justice Black's fear that such "balancing" has a built-in bias against freedom of speech may seem a plausible one, but it is not necessarily true, at least not in all cases. For example, in *Cohen v. California* (1971), a case involving offensive words on a jacket, Justice Harlan wrote the majority opinion upholding the right of the speaker, while Justice Black dissented on the ground that the defendant's actions were "conduct," not "speech."

Whether a "balancing" approach to freedom of speech has a tendency to disfavor freedom of speech, such "balancing" is unavoidable so long as the Court continues to provide conditional protection to certain types of speech (see Chapter 3) and to regulate other forms of expression (see Chapter 4). In this regard, the Court stated in 2014 in reference to limits on campaign contributions that the "right to participate in democracy through political contributions is protected by the First Amendment," but then immediately added, "but that right is not absolute" (*McCutcheon v. FEC*, 134 S. Ct. 1434, 1441 (2014)). Even if the government cannot prohibit all campaign contributions, it can, the Court ruled, limit the aggregate total an individual can contribute for the "compelling" purpose of preventing political corruption. For the foreseeable future, there is little or no reason to believe that the Court will abandon this "balancing" approach to deciding whether expression within the scope of freedom of speech should be protected.

FURTHER READING

Black, Hugo. "The Bill of Rights." *New York University Law Review* 35 (1960): 3–36.

Frantz, Laurent B. "Is the First Amendment Law—A Reply to Professor Mendelson." *California Law Review* 51 (1961): 729–754.

Gunther, Gerald. "In Search of Judicial Quality on a Changing Court: The Case of Justice Powell." *Stanford Law Review* 24 (1972): 1001–1035.

Kalven, Harry. "Upon Rereading Mr. Justice Black on the First Amendment." *UCLA Law Review* 14 (1967): 428–453.

Kingkade, Tyler. "Americans Are Split Along Party Lines over Whether School Should Punish Racist Speech." *Huffington Post*, February 2, 2017, available at https://www.huffingtonpost.com/entry/poll-campus-racism_us_568342b9e4b0b958f65ac433.

Meikeljohn, Alexander. "The First Amendment Is an Absolute." *The Supreme Court Review* 1961 (1962): 245–266.

Mendelson, Wallace. *Justices Black and Frankfurter: Conflict in the Court.* Chicago, IL: University of Chicago Press, 1961.

Q4. DO CORPORATIONS HAVE MANY OF THE FREE-SPEECH RIGHTS THAT NATURAL-BORN U.S. CITIZENS HAVE?

Answer: Yes. Even though the Supreme Court has not yet granted "commercial speech" as much constitutional protection as other types of speech and corporations cannot, at this point in time, contribute money to political candidates, corporations have many of the free-speech rights that natural-born U.S. citizens have.

The Facts: The Supreme Court began to recognize the constitutional rights of corporations in the 19th century. For example, in 1819 the Supreme Court held that the Constitution's Contracts Clause, which bars states from enacting laws "impairing the Obligation of Contracts" (Art. I, § 10), prohibited New Hampshire from altering Dartmouth College's original charter. The state-granted charter was a "contract," in the Court's view, and the Contracts Clause was applicable even if Dartmouth College was a corporation (*Dartmouth College v. Woodward*, 17 U.S. 518 (1819)).

Later Supreme Court decisions granted corporations the right of "due process" and the right of "equal protection," the right against "unreasonable searches and seizures," the right to a jury trial in criminal cases, and the right to compensation if government exercises the power of eminent domain. (See *Minneapolis & St. Louis Railroad v. Beckwith*, 1889; *Hale v. Henkel*, 1906; *Armour Packing v. U.S.*, 1908; *Pennsylvania Coal Company v. Mahon*, 1922.) Freedom of speech, however, was not one of these early constitutional rights granted to corporations. The Tillman Act of 1907, for example, prohibited corporations from making contributions to federal political candidates. A 1939 plurality opinion of the Supreme Court denied an incorporated union any free-speech rights, claiming that only natural persons "are entitled to the privileges and immunities which §1 of the Fourteenth Amendment secures for 'citizens of the United States'" (*Hague v. Committee for Industrial Organization*, 307 U.S. 496, 512–513 (1939)). Consistent with this decision, Congress in 1947 prohibited unions and corporations from making any campaign "contributions or expenditures" in federal election campaigns.

One kind of speech that was especially important to business corporations was "commercial speech," that is, speech that advertises commodities or services, including prices. In *Valentine v. Chrestensen* (1942), the Court flatly refused to provide any constitutional protection to the distribution of handbill advertisements on public streets. However, the Court reversed itself in *Virginia Pharmacy Board v. Virginia Citizens Consumer Council* (1976), holding that a state could not punish pharmacists for "unprofessional conduct" if they advertised the prices of prescription drugs. In reaching this result, the Court found that commercial speech was within the scope of freedom of speech, but held that it was subject to more regulation than other types of protected speech. To find the right balance between "commercial speech" that could be regulated by the state and that which could not, the Court developed a four-part test in *Central Hudson Gas v. Public Service Commission* (1980): first, the advertising must "concern lawful activity"; second, it could not be "misleading"; third, the asserted government interest must be "substantial"; and, fourth, the regulation had to "directly advance" the asserted interest without being "more extensive" than was necessary to serve the asserted government interest (447 U.S. 557, 566 (1980)).

The *Central Hudson* test implied that a state could regulate truthful advertising if it was "necessary" to serve a "substantial" governmental interest. Nonetheless, in *44 Liquormart, Inc. v. Rhode Island* (1996), the Court invalidated a law that banned truthful advertisements of alcohol prices outside liquor stores on the ground that the ban was "more extensive" than it needed to be to achieve the law's purpose, which was to discourage alcohol use. The state could reduce the consumption of alcohol without intruding upon protected speech by enacting a sales tax on alcohol, by limiting per capita purchases, or by sponsoring an educational campaign about the dangers of alcohol consumption. The upshot is that the Supreme Court applied the *Central Hudson* test in a fairly rigorous manner. Of course, any Supreme Court decision that invalidates a state law regulating commercial speech on the ground that it does not "directly" advance the government's asserted interest or that it does so more "extensively" than what is necessary serves corporate interests by expanding the free-speech rights of corporations.

Parallel to the expansion of the right of corporations to engage in "commercial speech," the Supreme Court has also broadened the right of corporations to engage in political speech. One key precedent was *NAACP v. Button* (1963), which addressed the question whether NAACP lawyers who were recruiting plaintiffs for lawsuits attacking racial segregation of public schools could be found guilty of "improper solicitation." The Court held that the NAACP, a corporation, may assert the right of association "on its own behalf, because, though a corporation," it is directly engaged in "assisting persons who seek legal redress for infringements of their constitutionally guaranteed" rights. Accordingly, the Court concluded "that the activities of the NAACP, its affiliates, and legal staff . . . are modes of expression and association protected by the First and Fourteenth Amendments which Virginia may not prohibit" (371 U.S. 415, 428 (1963)). In short, a state cannot apply the rules regulating the legal profession in a way that violates the free-speech rights of a non-commercial corporation.

In *Buckley v. Valeo* (1976), the Court addressed the constitutionality of the Federal Election Campaign Act (FECA), a law passed by Congress in 1974 that limited campaign contributions and expenditures. In general, it held that federal law could limit campaign contributions to candidates for the purpose of preventing corruption, but that limits on independent campaign expenditures (those not coordinated with the candidate) violated freedom of speech. It did not matter if such expenditures financed speech that "expressly advocated" the election or the defeat of a candidate. In the Court's view, "Advocacy of the election or defeat of candidates for federal office is no less entitled to protection under the First Amendment than the discussion of political policy generally or advocacy of the passage or defeat of legislation" (424 U.S. 1, 22 (1976)). Accordingly, independent expenditures of money to expressly advocate the election or defeat of a federal candidate were protected by freedom of speech, but the Court did not explicitly affirm that this constitutional rule applied to corporate political expenditures.

Weeks after the decision, Congress responded to the ambiguity of the *Buckley* decision by amending FECA to prohibit corporations and unions from engaging in independent campaign expenditures that "expressly advocated" a candidate's election or defeat. However, the amendments permitted corporations and unions to sponsor "political action committees" (PACs) that solicited money from employees or members. The PACs could then use these "segregated funds" to make contributions to individual candidates up to the limits established by federal law or engage in independent expenditures that "implicitly" or "expressly" advocated the election or defeat of candidates. Many states enacted comparable laws for state elections.

Despite the congressional ban on corporate and union expenditures in federal elections, the Court in *First National Bank v. Bellotti* (1978) held that business corporations could use their corporate funds to pay for political speech in state referenda campaigns. The Court defended this position, in part, by claiming that the "proper question" was not "whether corporations 'have' First Amendment rights," but rather whether the law in question "abridges expression that the First Amendment was meant to protect." In the Court's opinion, speech in support or in opposition to a state referendum was a "type of speech indispensable to decision-making in a democracy" and the "inherent worth of the speech in terms of its capacity for informing the public does not depend upon the identity of its source, whether corporation, association, union, or individual" (435 U.S. 765, 776–777 (1978)). The Court, therefore, based a corporation's right to engage in political speech in a referendum not on the identity of the speaker, but rather on the capacity of corporate speech to inform the public.

In *McConnell v. Federal Election Commission* (2003), the issue before the Court was whether corporations had a free-speech right to use corporate funds to finance political ads that referred to specific candidates and were intended to influence the election, but did not expressly advocate their election or their defeat. A five-justice majority of the Court held that the federal government could ban such "issue ads" for 60 days prior to a general election and 30 days prior to a primary. However, seven years later, in *Citizens United v. Federal Election Commission* (2010), a different five-justice majority (Justice Samuel Alito had replaced Justice Sandra Day O'Connor) sharply expanded the free-speech right of corporations to engage in political speech during election campaigns. The case concerned a nonprofit corporation that produced a 90-minute documentary film on Hillary Clinton, a film the Court described as "a feature-length negative advertisement that urges viewers to vote against Senator Hillary Clinton for President." Despite the film's "express advocacy" of Clinton's defeat, the Court nonetheless held that it was protected by freedom of speech. In justifying this result, the Court relied on the central principle of *Bellotti*: "The First Amendment does not allow political speech restrictions based on a speaker's corporate identity" (558 U.S. 310, 325, 347 (2010)). The clear implication of the ruling was that wealthy commercial corporations had a free-speech right to make independent campaign expenditures that "expressly advocated" the election or defeat of specific candidates.

With four justices dissenting, the Court is, of course, sharply divided over whether corporations should have the right to "expressly advocate" the election of a candidate independently of the candidate's campaign organization. Public opposition to *Citizens United* has also been widespread (Eggen 2010). The decision, one commentator has argued, misguidedly supports the constitutional "myth" that corporations have the same rights of freedom of speech as natural-born individuals (Epps 2011). Although it is true that corporations cannot, as of yet, make direct contributions to political candidates, the free-speech rights of corporations are largely the same as those of individuals. After all, if a corporation has the right to engage in "express advocacy" on behalf of a particular candidate, the significance of its inability to contribute money to that candidate's campaign is significantly undermined. Also, the bar on contributions has no impact on a corporation's right to advocate the defeat of the preferred candidate's opponent. It is, therefore, not a myth to say that corporations have many of the rights natural-born citizens have to engage in political speech.

FURTHER READING

Eggen, Dan. "Poll: Large Majority Opposes Supreme Court's Decision on Campaign Financing." *Washington Post*, February 17, 2010, available at http://www.washingtonpost.com/wp-dyn/content/article/2010/02/17/AR2010021701151.html.

Epps, Garrett. "Constitutional Myth #5: Corporations Have the Same Free-Speech Rights as Individuals." *The Atlantic*, June 23, 2011, available at https://www.theatlantic.com/national/archive/2011/06/constitutional-myth-5-corporations-have-the-same-free-speech-rights-as-individuals/240874/.

La Raja, Raymond J. and Schaffner, Brian F. *Campaign Finance and Political Polarization: When Purists Prevail*. Ann Arbor: University of Michigan Press, 2015.

Mutch, Robert E. *Buying the Vote: A History of Campaign Finance Reform*. Oxford: Oxford University Press, 2016.

Piety, Tamara. *Brandishing the First Amendment: Commercial Expression in America*. Ann Arbor: University of Michigan Press, 2013.

Post, Robert C. and Karlan, Pamela S. *Citizens United: Campaign Finance Reform and the Constitution*. Cambridge, MA: Harvard University Press, 2016.

Q5. DOES THE FEDERAL CONSTITUTIONAL RIGHT TO FREEDOM OF SPEECH LIMIT HOW STATES CAN RESTRICT AN INDIVIDUAL'S RIGHT OF SELF-EXPRESSION?

Answer: Yes. Although the Bill of Rights of the U.S. Constitution did not initially apply to the states, the Supreme Court gradually "incorporated" most of these rights, including the right of free speech, into the due process clause of the Fourteenth Amendment, which explicitly limits how states can restrict an individual's rights to express his or her self.

The Facts: When the Bill of Rights was ratified in 1791, no reasonable person at the time thought that it was applicable to state governments. As a set of amendments to the U.S. Constitution, the Bill of Rights was understood to limit only the actions of the federal government (see *Barron v. Baltimore*, 1833). However, state constitutions of the founding era often included free speech and press provisions. For example, Article 13 of the 1776 Constitution of the Commonwealth of Pennsylvania proclaimed that "the people have a right to freedom of speech, and of writing, and publishing their sentiments." By the time the Bill of Rights was ratified, or soon thereafter, a large majority of the states had comparable provisions in their constitutions. There was, however, no national consensus on the meaning of these state provisions or how they should be applied to specific factual circumstances involving libel, obscenity, or other categories of unprotected speech. During the 19th century, Pennsylvania gradually adopted, for its time and place, a fairly expansive speech protective standard (Kreimer 2002, 19–22), but other states, especially those in the South, enacted laws that suppressed speech in response to the rising abolitionist movement. Such suppression was justified on the basis that abolitionist rhetoric might cause a slave revolt. For example, following John Brown's raid on Harper's Ferry, Virginia, in 1859, North Carolina convicted Reverend Daniel Worth of advocating the end of slavery and sentenced him to one year in prison (Curtis 1993, 1164–1167).

Following the Civil War, the Thirteenth, Fourteenth, and Fifteenth Amendments to the U.S. Constitution were quickly ratified. The Thirteenth abolished slavery (1865); the Fourteenth prohibited any state from abridging "the privileges or immunities of citizens of the United States," depriving any person of "life, liberty, or property, without due process of law," or denying any person within its jurisdiction "the equal protection of the law" (1868); and the Fifteenth gave the newly freed slaves the right to vote (1870). The Court provided its first interpretation of the "privileges or immunities" clause in the *Slaughterhouse Cases* (1873). Notwithstanding the broad language of the provision, the Court held that its scope included only a relatively narrow set of rights, including the right to travel to the seat of the federal government and transact business with it; a right of access to its seaports and offices, including the federal courts; and the right to peaceably assemble and petition Congress for the redress of grievances. Accordingly, the Fourteenth Amendment did not allow the federal government to enforce freedom of speech against the states. As the Court clarified two years later in *United States v. Cruikshank*, if the state, not the federal government, was violating freedom of speech, "the people must look to the States" to stop the violation. "The power for that purpose was originally placed there, and it has never been surrendered to the United States" (92 U.S. 542, 552 (1875)).

The federal guarantee of free speech, therefore, did not provide any protection against state action throughout the 19th century unless the state violated the "right of the people" to peaceably assemble for the purpose of petitioning Congress. Also, it is worth noting that the Court did not initially focus on freedom of speech when it expanded the set of national rights beyond those mentioned in the *Slaughterhouse Cases*. Rather, the Court began this expansion with the "freedom of contract," a right it injected into the "liberty" protected by the "due process clause" of the Fourteenth Amendment. For example, the Court held that a state law that limited the number of hours bakers could work per week (*New York v. Lochner*, 1905) violated the due process clause of the Fourteenth Amendment. In this fashion, the Court transformed the due process clause from a procedural constitutional guarantee into a substantive one. Even if a state legislature followed proper procedures in enacting a law that restricted the "liberty of contract," it could nonetheless violate the Fourteenth Amendment because it was "substantively unreasonable."

In cases such as *Nebbia v. New York* (1934), the Court retreated from its defense of the "right to contract" during the New Deal period, largely in response to the devastating effects of the Great Depression. However, the introduction of the concept of "substantive due process" into American constitutional law permitted the Court to gradually "incorporate" into the "due process clause" of the Fourteenth Amendment the "substantive" rights of the first eight amendments, including those of the First Amendment. For example, the Court took the important step of "incorporating" freedom of speech in *Gitlow v. New York* (1925). In this decision, the Court upheld convictions under the state's criminal anarchy law, but made it clear that the constitutional right of free speech was applicable to the states. We "may and do assume," the Court wrote, "that freedom of speech and of the press which are protected by the First Amendment from abridgment by Congress are among the fundamental personal rights and 'liberties' protected by the due process clause of the Fourteenth Amendment from impairment by the States" (268 U.S. 652, 666 (1925)). Six years later, the Court confirmed the preceding position by holding that it "is no longer open to doubt that the liberty of the press, and of speech, is within the liberty safeguarded by the due process clause of the Fourteenth Amendment from invasion by state action" (*Near v. Minnesota*, 283 U.S. 697, 707 (1931)).

Although the federal constitutional right of free speech applies against the states, thereby creating a truly national right of freedom of speech, that fact does not necessarily mean that one's free speech rights cannot vary to some extent from one state to another. First, the Court can include within the definition of an unprotected category of speech, such as obscenity, a criterion that requires the application of "community standards," which would allow a jury in a conservative state to find a film "obscene" that one in a liberal state could not (see Q12). Although the right of free speech is arguably the same across the country, it can, therefore, vary somewhat in its application because of how the Supreme Court has defined an unprotected category of free speech. This kind of variation, however, is rare because the Supreme Court does not typically define unprotected categories of speech in terms of local standards.

The more common form of variation of free speech rights from one state to another arises from the fact that the federal right of freedom of speech does not prohibit states from expanding free speech beyond the standards established by the Supreme Court. For example, in *Lloyd v. Tanner* (1972) the Supreme Court held that a privately owned shopping center could ban the distribution of handbills, including political leaflets opposing the Vietnam War, without any violation of freedom of speech. However, in *Robins v. Pruneyard Shopping Center* (1979), the California Supreme Court held that a private shopping center could not deny entry to a group seeking signatures for a foreign policy petition without violating the free speech clause of the state's constitution. The California Constitution, in other words, was an "adequate and independent state ground" for its decision (23 Cal. 3d 899 (1979)). The U.S. Supreme Court upheld California's decision in *Pruneyard*, conceding that the state has a "sovereign right to adopt in its own Constitution individual liberties more expansive than those conferred by the Federal Constitution" (*Pruneyard Shopping Center v. Robins*, 447 U.S. 74, 81 (1980)). Of course, not all state courts have followed the lead of the California Supreme Court. In fact, by 2000 the majority of the 21 state courts that considered the issue declined to enforce rights of free speech against private shopping centers (Coffin 2000, 625). The federal right of free speech, therefore, establishes a baseline for the protection of all types of speech across the country, one that states cannot violate by going below the line, but can, if it wishes, depart from it by going above the line, that is, by protecting more speech than the federal Constitution requires.

FURTHER READING

Alexander, Mark C. "Attention, Shoppers: The First Amendment in the Modern Shopping Mall." *Arizona Law Review* 41 (1999): 1–47.

Berger, Raoul. *The Fourteenth Amendment and the Bill of Rights*. Norman: University of Oklahoma Press, 1989.

Coffin, Jennifer Niles. "The United Mall of America: Free Speech, State Constitutions, and the Growing Fortress of Private Property." *University of Michigan Journal of Law Reform* 33 (2000): 615–648.

Curtis, Michael Kent. "The 1859 Crisis over Hinton Helper's Book, the Impending Crisis: Free Speech, Slavery, and Some Light on the Meaning of the First Section of the Fourteenth Amendment—Symposium on the Law of Slavery: Constitutional Law and Slavery." *Chicago-Kent Law Review* 68 (1993): 1113–1177.

Kreimer, Seth. "The Pennsylvania Constitution's Protection of Free Expression." *Journal of Constitutional Law* 5 (2002): 12–57.

Levy, Leonard W. and Fairman, Charles. *The Fourteenth Amendment and the Bill of Rights: The Incorporation Theory*. New York: Da Capo Press, 1970.

Q6. IF A LAW THAT PROHIBITS SPEECH CONTAINS LANGUAGE THAT IS "VAGUE" AND "OVERLY BROAD," CAN A SPEAKER WHO IS NOT PROTECTED BY FREEDOM OF SPEECH CHALLENGE IT AS A VIOLATION OF THE CONSTITUTIONAL RIGHT OF FREE SPEECH?

Answer: Yes. The Supreme Court has developed the "overbreadth" doctrine, which permits speakers who are *not* protected by freedom of speech to challenge laws that are so broad and vague that they encourage lawful speakers to engage in self-censorship by refraining from speech that is in fact protected by the constitutional right of free speech.

The Facts: The Supreme Court generally permits a litigant to challenge the constitutionality of a law only as it applies to him or her, not as it might apply to some other person. However, this rule is not followed in cases involving freedom of speech. If a law prohibits speech in an "overly broad" way, then it is possible that it could be applied not only to speakers who are not protected by the First Amendment but also to speakers who are protected, thus discouraging the latter from engaging in lawful expression. To address this problem of "self-censorship," the Supreme Court formulated the "overbreadth" doctrine in *NAACP v. Button* (1963):

> The objectionable quality of vagueness and overbreadth . . . depend[s] . . . upon the danger of tolerating, in the area of First Amendment freedoms, the existence of a penal statute susceptible of sweeping and improper application. These freedoms are delicate and vulnerable, as well as supremely precious in our society. The threat of sanctions may deter their exercise almost as potently as the actual application of sanctions. Because First Amendment freedoms need breathing space to survive, government may regulate in the area only with narrow specificity. (371 U.S. 415, 433 (1963))

According to the Court, "vague" and "overly broad" laws tend to deter speakers from engaging in protected speech. To prevent such self-censorship, the Constitution creates a "breathing space" for speech by requiring the government to regulate in the area of free speech "with narrow specificity." One way to achieve this goal was to permit speakers who were not protected by freedom of speech to challenge and invalidate "vague" and "overly broad" laws that could arguably be applied to others who were only exercising their legitimate free-speech rights.

Two years after *Button*, the Court elaborated on its justification for the "overbreadth doctrine" by stating that someone challenging an "overly broad" statute did not have to "demonstrate that his own conduct could not be regulated by a statute drawn with the requisite narrow specificity." The advantage of this approach, in the Court's view, was that it avoids delay. "By permitting determination of the invalidity of these statutes without regard to the permissibility of some regulation on the facts of particular cases, we have, in effect, avoided making vindication of freedom of expression await the outcome of protracted litigation." And it does not matter, in the particular case, whether it is unlikely that the litigation will end in a conviction. Even if the unprotected speaker is not likely to be convicted, he or she can challenge an "overly broad" law because the "chilling effect upon the exercise of First Amendment rights may derive from the fact of the prosecution, unaffected by the prospects of its success or failure" (*Dombrowski v. Pfister*, 380 U.S. 479, 486–487 (1965)). In short, prosecutions of speakers based on "overly broad" laws had such a "chilling effect" upon the exercise of First Amendment rights that the Court empowered defendants who were not protected by free speech to invalidate them.

In *Gooding v. Wilson* (1972), the Supreme Court struck down a Georgia statute that prohibited "opprobrious words or abusive language" on the grounds that it was vague and overbroad. Georgia claimed that its courts had limited the prohibition to "fighting words"—a category of speech excluded from the scope of freedom of speech (see Q10), but the Supreme Court rejected this claim, arguing that Georgia appellate court decisions had not restricted the statute to "words that 'naturally tend to provoke violent resentment,'" but rather adopted such a broad standard that it "effectively 'licenses the jury to create its own standard in each case'" (405 U.S. 518, 524–525, 528 (1972)). For that reason, the statute was deemed unconstitutionally overbroad.

A year later, in *Broadrick v. Oklahoma*, the Supreme Court imposed a significant limitation on the use of the "overbreadth doctrine." In this 5–4 decision, the Court, calling the doctrine "strong medicine" and a "last resort," held that it could be invoked only if the "overbreadth" of the challenged law was "real" and "substantial" in character. This was the right approach, the Court reasoned, because it was unknown to what degree any specific overly broad law actually deterred protected speech. "Although such laws, if too broadly worded, may deter protected speech to some unknown extent, there comes a point where that effect—at best a prediction—cannot, with confidence, justify invalidating a statute on its face, and so prohibiting a State from enforcing the statute against conduct that is admittedly within its power to proscribe." Such a result could be justified, the Court concluded, only in narrow circumstances: "The overbreadth of a statute must not only be real, but substantial as well, judged in relation to the statute's plainly legitimate sweep" (413 U.S. 601, 610–611, 613, 615 (1973)).

Relying on *Broadrick*'s requirement that "overbreadth" must be "real" and "substantial," the Court refused to facially invalidate New York's child pornography law in *New York v. Ferber* (1982) (see Q13). Even though certain photographs in medical textbooks and the *National Geographic* magazine might fall within the literal meaning of the statute, the Court thought it was doubtful whether the "arguably impermissible applications of the statute amount to more than a tiny fraction of the materials within the statute's reach." The statute was therefore "not substantially overbroad and whatever overbreadth exists should be cured through case-by-case analysis of the fact situations to which its sanctions, assertedly, may not be applied" (458 U.S. 747, 773–774 (1982)).

The Court imposed another limitation on the use of the "overbreadth doctrine" in *Brockett v. Spokane Arcades, Inc.* (1985). This case dealt with Washington's obscenity law that defined "prurient interest," one of the requirements for an obscenity conviction (see Q12), as "that which incites lasciviousness or lust." In the Court's view, this language was "overbroad" because it could be applied, not just to material appealing to a "shameful or morbid interest" in sex but also to material "that is constitutionally protected by the First Amendment: material that, taken as a whole, does no more than arouse 'good, old fashioned, healthy' interest in sex." However, despite the "overbreadth" of the statute, the Court refused to invalidate the law in its entirety because the law's challenger was not engaged in unprotected speech. Ironically, the Court insisted that only challengers engaged in unprotected speech could invoke the "overbreadth doctrine." The Court's reasoning was as follows:

> An individual whose own speech or expressive conduct may validly be prohibited or sanctioned is permitted to challenge a statute on its face because it also threatens others not before the court—those who desire to engage in legally protected expression but who may refrain from doing so rather than risk prosecution. . . . It is otherwise where the parties challenging the statute are those who desire to engage in protected speech that the overbroad statute purports to punish. . . . There is then no want of a proper party to challenge the statute, no concern that an attack on the statute will be unduly delayed or protected speech discouraged. The statute may forthwith

be declared invalid to the extent that it reaches too far, but otherwise left intact. (472 U.S. 491, 499, 503–504 (1985))

In this decision, the Court makes an important distinction between
speakers engaged in protected speech and those engaged in unprotected
speech. Only the latter are permitted to bring "overbreadth" challenges
that invalidate the entire statute in question, while the former are confined to "as applied" challenges that invalidate only that part of a statute
that is being unconstitutionally applied to him or her. Accordingly, the
Court did not invalidate Washington's obscenity law, but rather ruled that
the state's definition of "prurient interest" must be adjusted to coincide
with federal constitutional norms. The Court did not address whether
such an "as applied" challenge, if successful, left open the distinct possibility that provisions of the same law not implicated by the facts of the
challenger's case may also be "overbroad," yet survive the "as applied"
challenge and, therefore, continue to have a "chilling effect" on freedom
of speech. Nor did the Court fully explain why speakers unprotected by
the First Amendment should be granted more power to reduce the "chilling effect" of overbroad laws than speakers who are protected.
    Although the Court has limited "overbreadth" invalidation of stat-
utes to cases involving speakers unprotected by freedom of speech if the
"overbreadth" is "real" and "substantial," it yet remains an important and
valid basis for invalidating statutes that suppress speech. For example, in
Ashcroft v. Free Speech Coalition (2002), the Court invalidated the federal Child Pornography Prevention Act of 1996 on the grounds that its
"overbreadth" was "real" and "substantial." Noting that the law banned
"virtual child pornography" composed of computer-generated images as
a means to ban "real child pornography," the Court argued that it "turns
the First Amendment upside down." "The Government may not suppress lawful speech as the means to suppress unlawful speech." Any such
law violates the "overbreadth doctrine" because "a substantial amount of
protected speech is prohibited or chilled in the process" (535 U.S. 234,
255 (2002)).
    More recently, the Court in *United States v. Stevens* (2010) invalidated
as "overbroad" a federal law that criminalized the "commercial creation,
sale, or possession" of depictions of "animal cruelty." The law defined
"animal cruelty" as depictions "in which a living animal is intentionally
maimed, mutilated, tortured, wounded, or killed," even though the law
exempted depictions "that have serious religious, political, scientific, educational, journalistic, historical, or artistic value." Relying on this statute, the government indicted Stevens for the possession of three videos

of dogfighting, which is unlawful in all 50 states. Invoking the "overbreadth doctrine," the Court found the prohibition to be "of alarming breadth." First, the statute could be applied to a depiction of intentional "wounding" or "killing" of any animal even if it did not involve "cruelty." Second, the requirement that the depicted conduct must be illegal did little to limit the statute's scope. Apart from cruel treatment, many laws prohibit what humans can do to animals, such as laws that protect endangered species or laws that criminalize theft of animals. A depiction of a "humane slaughter of a stolen cow," according to the Court, could, therefore, fall within the prohibition. Third, the depicted conduct needed to be illegal only in the jurisdiction where the "creation, sale, or possession" of the depiction takes place. Accordingly, since hunting is unlawful in Washington, D.C., the sale or possession of any photo, video, or magazine depicting "kills" in a state or jurisdiction where hunting is lawful would be illegal in D.C. Finally, in the Court's view, exempting depictions of "animal cruelty" that had "serious value" from the prohibition did not save the law because "the presumptively impermissible applications" of the law, including depictions that have less than "serious value," such as depictions contained in hunting magazines and videos, "far outnumber any permissible ones." The law is therefore "substantially overbroad, and therefore invalid under the First Amendment" (559 U.S. 460, 464, 474–476, 478–480 (2010)). The "overbreadth doctrine" may be "strong medicine," but clearly the Court thinks that such "medicine" is at times what is needed.

FURTHER READING

Buck, Stuart and Rienzi, Mark L. "Federal Courts, Overbreadth, and Vagueness: Guiding Principles for Constitution Challenges to Uninterpreted State Statutes." *Utah Law Review* (2002): 381–471.

Buell, Samuel W. "The Upside of Overbreadth." *New York University Law Review* 83 (2008): 1491–1564.

Dorf, Michael C. "Facial Challenges to State and Federal Statutes." *Stanford Law Review* 46 (1994): 235–304.

Fallon, Richard H. "Making Sense of Overbreadth." *The Yale Law Journal* 100 (1991): 853–908.

Hill, Alfred. "The Puzzling First Amendment Overbreadth Doctrine." *Hofstra Law Review* 25 (1997): 1063–1089.

Holland, Keith H. "The Doctrine of Substantial Overbreadth: A Better Prescription for 'Strong Medicine' in Missouri." *Missouri Law Review* 79 (2014): 185–204.

Q7. IS FREEDOM OF SPEECH ONLY A LIMITED INDIVIDUAL RIGHT TO ENGAGE IN CONSTITUTIONALLY PROTECTED SPEECH?

Answer: No. Freedom of speech also imposes on the government a general constitutional duty not to "take sides" in political debate by regulating or punishing speech based on its "content" or "viewpoint," regardless of whether the speech in question is protected by the individual right of free speech.

The Facts: The idea that freedom of speech imposes on government a constitutional duty not to "take sides" in political debate evolved from Justice Robert Jackson's majority opinion in *West Virginia State Board of Education v. Barnette* (1943). In this decision, as noted in Q2, the Court invalidated a state law compelling schoolchildren to pledge allegiance to the flag. The Court held that the law violated freedom of speech for two reasons: because it "compelled" speech and because the government violated its general duty not to "take sides" in political debates. In the words of Jackson, "If there is any fixed star in our constitutional constellation, it is that no official, high or petty, can prescribe what shall be orthodox in politics, nationalism, religion, or other matters of opinion or force citizens to confess by word or act their faith therein." It was unconstitutional for a state to compel its citizens to say they believed in X, but it was also unconstitutional for government officials to "prescribe what shall be orthodox" and thereby punish or regulate speech based on its "content" (319 U.S. 624, 642 (1943)).

Justice Hugo Black elaborated on what constitutes "content-based" discrimination in his concurring opinion in *Cox v. Louisiana* (1965), a decision that invalidated the conviction of a defendant who participated in a civil-rights street demonstration. This concurrence is noteworthy because Justice Black's view was that "picketing," even though "it may be utilized to communicate ideas, is not speech, and, therefore, is not of itself protected by the First Amendment." But even if "picketing" was outside the scope of the individual right of free speech, Black argued that the conviction was nonetheless unconstitutional because Louisiana law "expressly provides" that labor unions can picket to protest "unfair treatment of union members" (379 U.S. 536, 578, 581 (1965)). According to Black, a state is engaged in unconstitutional censorship in violation of freedom of speech if it favored the content of some ideas over others, even in regard to conduct that was not protected by the individual right of free speech.

A majority of the Court applied the distinction between "content-based" and "content-neutral" laws in *Police Department of the City of Chicago v. Mosley* (1972), a decision that invalidated a municipal ordinance that prohibited picketing within 150 feet of a school in session except "peaceful picketing of any school involved in a labor dispute." Citing Justice Black's concurrence in *Cox*, the Court wrote:

> The central problem with Chicago's ordinance is that it describes the permissible picketing in terms of its subject matter. Peaceful picketing on the subject of a school's labor-management dispute is permitted, but all other peaceful picketing is prohibited. The operative distinction is the message on a picket sign. But, above all else, the First Amendment means that government has no power to restrict expression because of its message, its ideas, its subject matter, or its content. (408 U.S. 92, 95 (1972))

Of course, the government could enforce reasonable "time, place and manner" regulations regarding picketing on public streets (see Q26), but such regulations could not prohibit speech "in terms of its subject matter," which, the Court insisted, "is never permitted" (*Id.* at 98–99).

Even if the wording of a law is "facially" (literally) neutral, the Court has held that the government can yet violate its duty of neutrality if the *purpose* of the law is to favor certain ideas or ideals over others. For example, in *United States v. Eichman* (1990), the Court invalidated the Flag Protection Act, a federal law that prohibited all flag burning (other than disposal) "without regard to the actor's motive, his intended message, or the likely effects of his conduct on onlookers" (see Q21). Even though the law banned flag burning without reference to the "content" of ideas, the Court held that the government's asserted interest— "protect[ing] the physical integrity of the flag under all circumstances"— was derived from "a perceived need to preserve the flag's status as a symbol of our Nation and certain national ideals." However, the flag's status is threatened only if it is burned to communicate a "message . . . that is inconsistent with those ideals" (496 U.S. 310, 315–316 (1990)). By protecting the flag's physical integrity in this way, the Court reasoned, the government is using its power to favor national ideals over contrary ones. The government, therefore, violated its obligation to be "neutral" even if the statute's language was neutral. The Court has recently reaffirmed the position that government cannot enforce a literally neutral statute with hostility to a certain viewpoint in *Masterpiece Cakeshop, Ltd. v. Colorado Civil Rights Commission* (2018). According to the Court, Colorado had applied a neutral nondiscrimination law against a baker who refused to bake a wedding cake for a gay couple on religious grounds, but it had done so with a degree of hostility against the baker's religion, which violated its First Amendment obligation to remain neutral.

Despite the earlier statement in *Mosley* that "content-based" laws were "never permissible," the Court in *Burson v. Freeman* (1992) concluded that such laws could be constitutional if they passed the "strict scrutiny" test, that is, if they were a "necessary" (or "narrowly tailored") means to a "compelling" governmental interest. The law reviewed in *Burson* prohibited the solicitation of votes, the display of political posters or signs, and the distribution of candidates' brochures within 100 feet of a polling place. The law contained a "content-based" distinction because it banned only "political" forms of expression within the 100-foot radius, but a four-justice plurality nonetheless held that the law was constitutional since it passed the test of strict scrutiny:

> In conclusion, we affirm that it is the rare case in which we have held that a law survives strict scrutiny. This, however, is such a rare case. Here, the State . . . has asserted the exercise of free speech rights conflicts with another fundamental right, the right to cast a ballot in an election free from the taint of intimidation and fraud. A long history, a substantial consensus, and simple common sense show that some restricted zone around polling places is necessary to protect that fundamental right. (504 U.S. 191, 211 (1992))

The protection of a fundamental constitutional right was a "compelling" interest that justified an infringement of the government's duty of neutrality since it was a "necessary" means to that end. Two other justices joined the Court's judgment that the law was constitutional despite the "content-based" distinction, implying that a majority of the Court believed that such distinctions, in a narrow set of circumstances, were constitutional.

Of course, when the Court applies the "strict scrutiny" test to protected speech, especially "core" political speech, the typical result is that the law is invalidated because it fails to meet this high standard. This was the result in *Republican Party of Minnesota v. White* (2002), a decision that invalidated a provision of a state's code of judicial conduct. The provision in question prohibited judicial candidates from "announcing" their "views on disputed legal or political issues." The "content-based" distinction of this prohibition resided in the separate treatment of "disputed" legal and political issues from comparable issues of a "non-disputed" character. The Court applied strict scrutiny and concluded that the "announce" clause failed strict scrutiny because it did not significantly advance the government's interest of preserving "the impartiality or the appearance of impartiality of the state judiciary" (536 U.S. 765, 775–778 (2002)). However, in *Williams v. Florida Bar* (2015), the Court upheld a state law prohibiting judicial candidates from personally soliciting funds for their campaigns, concluding that the "content-based" distinction between "solicitations of funds" and other types of expression was a "narrowly tailored" means of advancing the government's "compelling" purpose of preserving the public's confidence in "the integrity of the judiciary" (135 S. Ct. 1656 (2015)). Accordingly, if a "content-based" distinction satisfies the "strict-scrutiny" test, it is consistent with freedom of speech (see also *Holder v. Humanitarian Law Project*, 2010).

But what about laws that utilized "content distinctions" to regulate expression that was outside the scope of freedom of speech? As noted earlier, Justice Black addressed this issue in his concurring opinion in *Cox v. Louisiana*, but the full Court did not explicitly consider this question until it reviewed *R.A.V. v. City of St. Paul* (1992), a case involving the burning of a cross in front of the home of an African American family. An ordinance of St. Paul, Minnesota, banned "fighting words" (insults likely to provoke violence—see Q10 and Q16) that were based on "race, color, creed, religion or gender." Even though "fighting words" were not within the scope of freedom of speech, the ordinance, nonetheless, violated the First Amendment, the Court reasoned, because it made a "content distinction" between certain types of "fighting words" that were prohibited, such as racial or ethnic epithets, and other types that were not, such as those directed at "political affiliation, union membership or homosexuality." Moreover, the ordinance appeared to prohibit the use of certain "fighting words," such as "aspersions upon a person's mother" (calling someone an SOB) against those who favored racial, ethnic, religious, and sexual equality, but not against those who supported these forms of inequality. If this ordinance was constitutional, Justice Scalia wrote in the majority opinion

> One could hold up a sign saying, for example, that all "anti-Catholics bigots" are misbegotten; but not that all "papists" are, for that would insult and provoke violence "on the basis of religion." St Paul has no such authority to license one side of a debate to fight freestyle, while requiring the other to follow Marquis of Queensbury Rules." (505 U.S. 377, 391–392 (1992))

The ordinance, therefore, constituted "viewpoint discrimination," in Scalia's opinion, because it not only prohibited certain "fighting words" based on the content of the language (e.g., the use of racial epithets), but also disfavored the "viewpoints" of those opposed to racial, religious, or gender equality, even if their "fighting words" were not explicitly based on race, ethnicity, religion, or gender. Such "viewpoint" discrimination was, in the Court's view, the most constitutionally suspect form of "content" discrimination.

Although the Court invalidated the ordinance in R.A.V., it clearly indicated that laws with "content" or "viewpoint" distinctions that prohibit "proscribable" speech outside the scope of the First Amendment need not pass the high test of "strict scrutiny" for them to be consistent with freedom of speech. For example, Justice Scalia indicated that such laws could be constitutional if there was "no realistic possibility that official suppression of ideas is afoot"—a fairly low standard. In contrast, "content-based" laws addressing speech within the constitutional guarantee must pass strict scrutiny, regardless of whether any "official oppression" is taking place. The Court came to this conclusion in *Reed v. Town of Gilbert* (2015), a decision that invalidated a town's code regulating how outdoor signs could be displayed. The code classified signs into different categories and imposed different rules on each category. For example, "ideological" signs that communicated a message or idea could be up to 20 square feet, while "political" signs designed to influence an election could be no more than 16 square feet, and "directional signs" that directed the public to an event could be no more than 6 square feet.

The Court ruled that Gilbert's code was "content-based" on its face and was therefore "subject to strict scrutiny regardless of the government's benign motive, content-neutral justification, or lack of 'animus toward the ideas contained' in the regulated speech" (135 S. Ct. 2218, 2228 (2015)). While an illicit governmental motive can, as in *Eichman*, render a "facially" neutral law into one that is unconstitutional, a benign motive cannot save a "content-based" law prohibiting or regulating protected speech unless it can pass the "strict scrutiny" test. The town of Gilbert had, therefore, violated its free-speech duty to be "neutral" to all ideas and opinions.

The government's duty to be "neutral" is one reason why government cannot solve today's problem of "fake" news. Any attempt by the government to separate news that is "true" from what is "fake" is "content-based" and doomed to be unconstitutional for that reason. The underlying theory of freedom of speech is that the "marketplace of ideas," rather than government, must sift the truth from the misleading and false statements circulating in the press and on the Internet, including social media sites such as Facebook, Twitter, and YouTube. One might be skeptical whether the typical consumer of ideas has the wherewithal to perform this function, especially since people often consume "news" that reinforces their preexisting beliefs and convictions (Waldrop 2017) and foreign governments have deliberately used social media to spread "disinformation" to targeted audiences inside the United States, such as Russia's attempt to influence the 2016 presidential election (Fandos et al. 2017). The problem of "fake" news is therefore serious, but the premise of freedom of speech is that the potential ineffectiveness of the "marketplace of ideas" is far less of a danger to American liberties than a governmental censor with the power to decide, in the words of Justice Jackson, "what shall be orthodox in politics, nationalism, religion, or other matters of opinion."

FURTHER READING

Fandos, Nicholas, Kang, Cecelia, and Isaac, Mike. "House Intelligence Committee Releases Incendiary Russian Social Media Ads." *The New York Times*, November 1, 2017, available at https://www.nytimes.com/2017/11/01/us/politics/russia-technology-facebook.html.

Kendrick, Leslie. "Content Discrimination Revisited." *Virginia Law Review* 98 (2012): 231–300.

Kreimer, Seth F. "Good Enough for Government Work: Two Cheers for Content Neutrality." *University of Pennsylvania Journal of Constitutional Law* 16 (2014): 1261–1351.

McDonald, Barry. "Speech and Distrust: Rethinking the Content Approach to Protecting the Freedom of Expression." *Notre Dame Law Review* 81 (2006): 101–181.

Waldrop, Mitchell M. "The Genuine Problem of Fake News." *Proceeding of the National Academy of Sciences of the United States of America* 114 (November 28, 2017): 12631–12634.

Wright, George R. "Content-Neutral and Content-Based Regulations of Speech: A Distinction That Is No Longer Worth the Fuss." *Florida Law Review* 67 (2016): 2081–2102.

Q8. IF FREEDOM OF SPEECH PROHIBITS GOVERNMENT FROM EITHER ENGAGING IN "CONTENT" OR "VIEWPOINT" DISCRIMINATION OR VIOLATING THE FREE-SPEECH RIGHTS OF AN INDIVIDUAL, IS IT ALSO AN AMERICAN CULTURAL AND SOCIETAL IDEAL?

Answer: Yes. Although a rising tide of "political correctness" may be undermining free speech's status as a societal and cultural ideal, a significant number of Americans still believe they should be tolerant of speech they dislike, even though in particular situations they may not be able to live up to this ideal.

The Facts: A 2017 survey by the Cato Institute reports that 59 percent of Americans believe that people should be allowed to express opinions that are "deeply offensive to other people" (Ekins 2017, 11). A different 2017 survey by Rasmussen Reports claims that a whopping 73 percent of Americans agree with Voltaire's famous statement: "I disapprove of what you say, but will defend to the death your right to say it" (Rasmussen Reports). Despite these results, the CATO survey also concludes that certain groups of Americans think it is acceptable to react to offensive speakers in distinctively punitive ways. For example, 51 percent of strong liberals think it is "morally acceptable" to punch Nazis, while 53 percent of Republicans support stripping flag burners of their citizenship and nearly two-thirds of African Americans and Latinos believe that supporting the free-speech rights of racists is as bad as being a racist (Cato Survey 20, 23, 31). Moreover, although 59 percent of Americans favor protection for "offensive speech," the CATO survey finds that an even larger majority (79 percent) believe it is "morally unacceptable" to engage in speech that "might be offensive to racial or religious groups," which suggests that a large majority of Americans believe that such speakers can be morally criticized for what they say. Obviously, such expressions of moral disapproval discourage speakers from expressing their beliefs, thereby producing a form of self-censorship that in today's world is known as "political correctness." There is evidence that such self-censorship is occurring in the United States. The CATO survey finds that 58 percent of Americans claim they do not say what they believe because of the "political climate" and that 70 percent think that "political correctness" is a "big problem" (Ibid., 13, 35, 34). The Rasmussen survey reports that only 28 percent of today's Americans think they have "true freedom of speech" and most think the country is too "politically correct" (see Rasmussen Reports).

While the preceding data presents a confusing picture of whether and to what extent freedom of speech is an American societal and cultural ideal, they do cast serious doubt on the claim that the vast majority of Americans, in their diverse social interactions, enthusiastically support freedom of speech as an ideal. Any such claim is often based on evidence that conflates how Americans perceive governmental censorship with how ordinary Americans perceive speakers or publishers who engage in offensive speech. For example, a 2016 report of the Pew Research Center asserts that "Americans are much more tolerant of *offensive* speech than people in other nations," claiming that 77 percent of Americans "support the right of others to make statements that are offensive to their own religious belief." But the survey question that was the basis for this judgment asked whether "*government* should be able to prevent people from saying . . . things . . . that are offensive to your religion or beliefs" (Wike 2016, emphasis added). The question was, therefore, directed at governmental censorship, not at social or cultural censorship. Therefore, there is no basis for using the results of this survey to conclude that Americans are "tolerant of offensive religious-based speech," much less that they are "much more tolerant" than "people in other nations."

One reason for the confusion is that freedom of speech as a societal and cultural ideal is a complex and nuanced subject. Some clarification of what this ideal means is necessary before one can decide whether and to what extent it is an American cultural ideal. One political philosopher who explicitly addressed the meaning of freedom of speech as such an ideal is John Stuart Mill. He addressed this topic because he thought that the greatest threat to freedom in the modern world was not government, but the penetrating and pervasive influence of public opinion:

> Society can and does execute its own mandates: and if it issues wrong mandates instead of right, or any mandates at all in things with which it ought not to meddle, it practices a *social* tyranny more formidable than many kinds of political oppression, since, though not usually upheld by such extreme penalties, it leaves fewer means of escape, penetrating much more deeply into the details of life, and *enslaving the soul itself*. Protection, therefore, against the tyranny of the magistrate is not enough: there needs protection also against the *tyranny of the prevailing opinion and feeling*; against the tendency of society to impose, by other means than civil penalties, its own ideas and practices as rules of conduct on those who dissent from them. (Mill, 4, emphasis added)

This claim that the "tyranny of public opinion" is the most serious threat to liberty in today's society is the fundamental premise of Mill's argument. His argument is more convincing to the degree this premise is accepted.

Regarding limits to freedom, Mill generally adopted the same principle for government, public opinion, speech, and conduct: the harm principle.

According to this standard, neither government nor public opinion could punish speech or conduct that did not "harm" others. Applying the "harm" principle, Mill concluded that "there ought to exist the fullest liberty of professing and discussing, as a matter of ethical conviction, any doctrine, however immoral it may be considered." One of his examples was tyrannicide. People should be free to advocate it as a general doctrine without incurring any legal punishment or society's moral disapproval. In his view, advocacy of the doctrine became "a proper subject of punishment," whether by the government or public opinion, only if one "instigated" the killing of a tyrant and "only if an overt act has followed, and at least a probable connection can be established between the act and the instigation" (Ibid. 15n). In the same vein, he argued:

> An opinion that corn-dealers are starvers of the poor, or that private property is robbery, ought to be unmolested when simply circulated through the press, but may justly incur punishment when delivered orally to an excited mob assembled before the house of a corn-dealer, or when handed about among the same mob in the form of a placard. (Ibid. 53)

Although the speaker here does not explicitly advocate that the mob should attack the corn-dealer's house, the expression of opinion "that corn-dealers are starvers of the poor" in such circumstances may constitute an indirect form of unlawful incitement, a type of speech that can be subject to punishment, whether by government (see Q14) or public opinion.

Although members of the public have no right to "morally disapprove" of speakers or publishers who advocate immoral doctrines, they were, according to Mill, permitted to have a negative reaction to them. "Though doing no wrong to any one, a person," Mill argues, "may so act [by speaking or publishing] as to compel us to judge him, and feel to him, as a fool, or as a being of an inferior order." In that case, one is permitted to "warn" someone about to advocate an immoral doctrine that such speech will force others to think less of him or her. Moreover, if such immoral advocacy takes place, one has the "right" to avoid the speaker's society, but "not to parade the avoidance"; "to caution others against him," but only if "we think his example or conversation likely to have a pernicious effect on those with whom he associates"; and to give others "preference over him in optional good offices [jobs]," but not those offices that would "tend to his improvement." Mill called these responses to the advocacy of immoral doctrines "natural penalties" that are "the spontaneous consequences" of the advocacy itself, not reactions that "are purposely inflicted on him for the sake of punishment" (Ibid. 75–76).

Mill believed that the distinction between "natural penalties" and "punishment," including punishment consisting of society's moral disapproval, was an important one. It makes a "vast difference," he argued, "both in our feelings and in our conduct towards him," whether a speaker "displeases us in things in which we think we have a right to control him, or in things in which we know that we have not." We may "express our distaste" and we may "stand aloof" from such a speaker, but "we shall not therefore feel called on to make his life uncomfortable" or "treat him like an enemy of society." We might look upon him or her as "an object of pity, perhaps of dislike, but not of anger or resentment" (Ibid. 77). The implication is that Mill limits the free-speech rights of those who wish to express their moral disapproval of "immoral" speech to avoid the self-censorship that is an inevitable by-product of the "tyranny of public opinion" or, in today's parlance, the "tyranny of political correctness." He favors this trade-off because those who object to offensive speech, in his opinion, generally have no right to morally punish the speaker. According to Mill, the general advocacy of immoral doctrines does not "harm" those who happen to hear the speech or read the publication, while the expressions of moral disapproval directed at offensive speakers or publishers do in fact cause "harm" because they are a form of "punishment."

Mill's approach to freedom of speech, of course, does not have any authoritative status, but it is a coherent theory that provides a perspective on whether freedom of speech is a societal and cultural ideal of the United States. In his view, it cannot be said that the United States truly respects freedom of speech as such an ideal unless Americans refrain from expressing "anger" and "resentment" at those who generally advocate doctrines that are thought by society to be immoral, such as racism, ethnic hatred, religious intolerance, sexual inequality, or homophobia. Of course, to the degree that these speakers or publishers go beyond the expression of their general views and engage in "fighting words" or "unlawful advocacy," they cross a line that would justify members of society in voicing their moral disapproval and perhaps government in punishing them. However, the surveys cited at the beginning of this essay strongly suggest that a significant number of Americans will not wait until speakers or publishers cross the above line before they morally condemn them for what they say or write. A Nazi can be punched, a flag burner can be stripped of citizenship, and someone who defends the free-speech rights of racists can presumably be called "a racist."

But these same surveys also provide evidence that a comparable number of Americans have a more tolerant attitude toward offensive speech, even speech they intensely dislike. It is noteworthy, for instance, that the aforementioned 2017 Rasmussen poll found that 73 percent of Americans agree with Voltaire's statement and that 59 percent believe that "offensive" speech should be "allowed." It is a mixed picture, but the survey results suggest that freedom of speech is yet an American societal and cultural ideal, but it may not be one supported by an overwhelming consensus. And even those who accept freedom of speech as a societal and cultural ideal, who believe that they should socially tolerate "offensive" speech, may not be able to live up to what the ideal requires in particular circumstances. It is not all that uncommon for human beings to act in ways that are inconsistent with their own ideals. But even so, even if a significant number of Americans believe that their actions do not live up to their ideal of freedom of speech, that in itself is evidence that it remains a significant American societal and cultural ideal.

FURTHER READING

Bollinger, Lee C. *The Tolerant Society: Free Speech and Extremist Speech in America*. New York: Oxford University Press, 1986.

Ekins, Emily. *The State of Free Speech and Tolerance in America: Attitudes about Free Speech, Campus Speech, Religious Liberty, and Tolerance of Political Expression: Findings from the Cato Institute 2017 Free Speech and Tolerance Survey*. Washington, DC: Cato Institute, 2017, available at https://object.cato.org/sites/cato.org/files/survey-reports/pdf/the-state-of-free-speech-and-tolerance.pdf.

Hare, Ivan and Weinstein, James. *Extreme Speech and Democracy*. New York: Oxford University Press, 2011.

Inazu, John D. *Confident Pluralism: Surviving and Thriving through Deep Difference*. Chicago, IL: University of Chicago Press, 2016.

Mill, John Stuart. *On Liberty*. Edited by H. B. Acton. *Utilitarianism, On Liberty, and Considerations on Representative Government*. London: J. M. Dent & Sons Ltd, 1972.

Rasmussen Reports. "73% Say Freedom of Speech Worth Dying For." August 23, 2017, available at http://www.rasmussenreports.com/public_content/lifestyle/general_lifestyle/august_2017/73_say_freedom_of_speech_worth_dying_for.

"Symposium: Hate Speech and Political Legitimacy," *Constitutional Commentary* 32 (2017): 527–617.

Voegeli, William. "2017 Editors' Symposium: Liberalism and Tolerance." *San Diego Law Review* 54 (2017): 319–338.

Wike, Richard. "Americans More Tolerant of Offensive Speech Than Others in the World." Pew Research Center, October 12, 2016, available at http://www.pewresearch.org/fact-tank/2016/10/12/americans-more-tolerant-of-offensive-speech-than-others-in-the-world/. The questions used in the Pew survey are available at http://www.pewglobal.org/files/2015/11/Pew-Research-Center-Democracy-Report-FINAL-TOPLINE-FOR-RELEASE-November-18-2015-.pdf.

2

❖

Unprotected Speech

As noted in Q3, the Supreme Court in *Chaplinsky v. New Hampshire* (1942) excluded certain categories of speech, such as "the lewd and obscene, the profane, the libelous, and the insulting or 'fighting' words," from any protection under the First Amendment. These types of speech were excluded, the Court explained, because "such utterances are no essential part of any exposition of ideas, and are of such slight social value as a step to truth that any benefit that may be derived from them is clearly outweighed by the social interest in order and morality" (315 U.S. 568, 572 (1942)). Other categories of excluded speech include threats, solicitations of unlawful conduct, conspiracy, and perjury. Following *Chaplinsky*, the Court has dropped "profanity" and "lewd" speech (outside of public schools—see Q28) from the list of unprotected categories of speech and added "child pornography," while at the same time it has significantly narrowed the legal definitions of "libel," "obscenity," and "fighting words." The clear inference is that the types of unprotected speech are not set in stone and their boundaries can evolve over time.

The fact that certain categories of speech are excluded from the First Amendment affects how judges decide cases dealing with them. In such cases, the issue is not one of "balancing" the importance of the government's interest versus the value of the kind of speech under consideration, but rather whether the speech activity in question fits the definition of the excluded category—a form of judicial decision making referred to as "categorization." If it fits the definition, then it is not protected by free speech;

if it does not fit, then it is protected. Accordingly, the determination is made without any apparent judicial balancing of values or interests. A purported value of "categorization" is that it gives citizens a "bright line"; they do not have to wait for a judge to engage in "balancing" to decide after the fact whether the government's interest is more important than speech. However, it is not entirely clear that the two approaches are fundamentally different if judges engage in "balancing" as they define the excluded category or if the definition requires a judicial assessment of the context of the speech activity. In these two ways, some sort of "balancing" may creep into the "categorization" approach. Chapter 3 will consider cases involving judicial "balancing," which will allow consideration of the differences between the two approaches and what form of judicial decision making is preferable in terms of deciding cases dealing with freedom of speech.

Q9. IS IT CONSISTENT WITH THE CONSTITUTIONAL RIGHT OF FREE SPEECH TO CONVICT SOMEONE OF A "THREAT" EVEN IF HE OR SHE HAS NO INTENTION OF CARRYING IT OUT?

Answer: Yes, but only if the speaker "intends" to express a threat or "knows" that the expression is a threat.

The Facts: If a speaker has no intent to carry it out, a threat to kill or assault someone may seem harmless, but threats of this type have generally been subject to criminal liability in the United States. Typically such prosecutions occurred at the local level since states have the primary responsibility for enforcing criminal law. However, early in the history of the United States the federal government did prosecute a person for making a "threat" under the Alien and Sedition Acts of 1798. When a cannon salute was used to greet President John Adams, a bystander commented, "There goes the President and they are firing at his ass." Not to be outdone, Luther Baldwin responded that he would not be concerned "if they fired through his ass." He was convicted of speaking "sedicious words tending to defame the President and Government of the United States," fined, and jailed until his fine and fees were paid (Smith 1966, 270–274). It is noteworthy that, in the late 18th century, despite the constitutional right of free speech, the mere expression of unconcern about the president's death was enough to incur criminal liability, even if the context strongly suggested that the expression was a joke.

During World War I, Congress enacted a law, Threats against the President and Successors to the Presidency, that prohibited anyone from "knowingly and willfully" conveying "any threat to take the life or to inflict bodily harm" upon the president and the vice president. Affirming a conviction under this provision, the 7th Circuit Court of Appeals in *Ragansky v. United States* (1918) concluded that a threat (1) "is knowingly made, if the maker of it comprehends the meaning of the words uttered by him" and (2) "is willfully made," that is, "if in addition to comprehending the meaning of the words uttered by him, the maker voluntarily and intentionally utters them as the declaration of an *apparent* determination to carry them into execution" (253 F. 643, 644 (1918), emphasis added). In a similar vein, the government during World War II prosecuted a person who "knowingly" and "publicly" posted and displayed posters, circulars, and caricatures that urged bystanders to "hang [President] Roosevelt" and other public officials. The federal district judge, citing *Ragansky*, refused to quash the indictment, holding that the expression could still be a "threat," even if it was not communicated to the president, at least if the statement indicated "disloyalty" bordering on treason, "menaced" the peace and safety of the country, "tended" to encourage the lawless element, and aroused "resentment" and "concern" on the part of patriotic citizens (*United States v. Apel*, 44 F. Supp. 592, 593 (1942)).

In 1969 the Supreme Court interpreted the 1917 statute in *Watts v. United States*. This case concerned a drafted 18-year-old who said the following to a crowd gathered near the Washington Monument grounds during the Vietnam War:

> They always holler at us to get an education. And now I have already received my draft classification as 1-A and I have got to report for my physical this Monday morning. I am not going. If they ever make me carry a rifle the first man I want to get in my sights is L.B.J. They are not going to make me kill my black brothers.

The Court held that the statute was constitutional on its face but overturned the conviction on the ground that the government had to prove that the defendant engaged in a "true" threat rather than overheated rhetoric. Since the statute "makes criminal a form of pure speech," the Court reasoned, "it must be interpreted with the commands of the First Amendment clearly in mind." The constitutional basis for the Court's holding meant that all federal and state laws that prohibited "threats," not just the one that prohibited "threats" against the president, must limit criminal liability to "true" threats. *Watts*, therefore, was a sharp departure from earlier lower federal court decisions.

The Court did not believe that Watt's "political hyperbole" constituted a "true" threat because the opposite conclusion would undermine our "profound national commitment to the principle that debate on public issues should be uninhibited, robust, and wide-open." The defendant's diatribe merely reflected the fact that the language of American political life is "often vehement, abusive, and inexact." Accordingly, Watts's statement was not a "true" threat, but a "very crude offensive method of stating a political opposition to the President." As an aside, the Court added that the *Ragansky* interpretation of the "willfulness" requirement of the 1917 statute: may be "correct, although we have grave doubts about it." In expressing such doubts, the Court was hinting that, even if the crowd took Watts's statement as a serious threat, which it did not, that fact may not be enough evidence of the speaker's "determination" to carry out the threat. After all, an "*apparent* determination" to carry out a threat need not be an "actual" one. However, beyond expressing "grave doubts" about the *Ragansky* formulation, the Court declined in *Watts* to elaborate on what mental element would satisfy the "willfulness" requirement of the 1917 law (*Watts v. United States*, 394 U.S. 705–709 (1969), emphasis added).

The Supreme Court returned to the issue of what constituted a "threat" in *Virginia v. Black* (2003), a decision that addressed the constitutionality of a state statute that prohibited cross-burning as a form of "intimidation." "Intimidation in the constitutionally proscribable sense of the word," the Court explained, "is a type of true threat, where a speaker directs a threat to a person or group of persons with the intent of placing the victim in fear of bodily harm or death." In such a case, the speaker must "communicate a serious expression of an intent to commit an act of unlawful violence to a particular individual or group of individuals," but the speaker "need not actually intend to carry out the threat."

The Court came to this conclusion by endorsing the view that the purpose of statutes prohibiting "threats" was not just to deter assaults and homicides, but also to prevent fear and disruption in the community. A "prohibition on true threats protects individuals from the fear of violence and the disruption that fear engenders, as well as the possibility that the threatened violence will occur." What the Court is underlining is that threats that are "apparent," but not "real," still cause general harms. For this reason, the Court refused to limit "true threats" to threats the speaker intended to carry out, but the government still had to prove that the speaker's "intent" was to place the victim "in fear of bodily harm or death" (538 U.S. 343, 344 (2003)).

The rise of social media, such as Facebook, YouTube, and Twitter, has raised the question of whether Internet-based "threats" are subject to the same criteria as "threats" in the physical world. The Court addressed this question in *Elonis v. United States* (2015). After his wife left him in 2010, Anthony Elonis posted violent song lyrics and imagery under a new Facebook user name ("Tone Dougie"), along with disclaimers that the lyrics were "fictitious," that the lyrics did not refer to "real persons," and that he was writing them for "therapeutic" reasons. (It "helps me deal with the pain.") The lyrics contained threatening language regarding Elonis's coworkers, his estranged wife, police officers, and an FBI agent. His posting was inspired by a comic's sketch regarding threats to kill the president, but substituting "wife" for the "president." At the bottom of the post, Elonis wrote: "Art is about pushing limits. I'm willing to go to jail for my Constitutional rights."

Based on these lyrics and comparable Facebook postings, Elonis was convicted under a federal law that prohibited "any communication containing any threat . . . to injure the person of another." However, the Supreme Court overturned the conviction on the ground that the trial judge had not required the government to prove that the defendant "intended" or "knew" that the posts contained "threats." In fact, in its closing argument at trial, the government claimed that it was irrelevant whether Elonis intended the postings to be "threats"—"it doesn't matter what he thinks." The conviction was, therefore, based solely on how "his posts would be understood by a reasonable person," which, according to the Court, "is inconsistent with 'the conventional requirement for criminal conduct—*awareness* of some wrongdoing.'" Basing criminal liability on how a reasonable person would understand the expression, without any examination of the mental state of the defendant, is to adopt a negligence standard, which is typically not used in federal criminal law. "Under these principles," the Court concluded, "'what [Elonis] thinks' does matter." Elonis does not need to know that what he is doing is illegal to incur criminal liability, but he must either "intend" his expression as a "threat" or "know" that it is one (*Elonis v. United States*, 135 S. Ct. 2001, 2005–2007, 2011 (2015)).

Elonis is largely consistent with the Court's ruling in *Virginia v. Black*. While the earlier ruling had required an "intent of placing the victim in fear of bodily harm or death" and the latter one required an "intentional" or "knowing" threat, the two formulations are close in substance, and both cases imply that an "intent" to carry out a "threat" is not necessary for an expression to constitute a "true threat." If the speaker "knows" or "intends" his or her expression to be a "threat," it is outside the protection of freedom of speech, even if there is no intent to carry the threat out.

It is also important to realize that the Court in *Elonis* justifies the inclusion of a mental element within its definition of a "threat" on fundamental principles of criminal liability, rather than on the principles of free speech. However, *Elonis* should be understood in light of *Virginia v. Black*, which explicitly justified a mental element for a conviction of a "true threat" on the ground of freedom of speech. So, even if the Court does not explicitly discuss the constitutional limits of freedom of speech in *Elonis*, the decision bolsters the view that "intentional" or "knowing" threats are totally excluded from the First Amendment. However, if only by implication, the decision suggests that both "negligent" threats (speakers who should have known that their expressions were threats but did not in fact know) and threats that do not qualify as "true threats" because they are political hyperbole or jokes are likely protected by freedom of speech.

The Court declined in *Elonis* to rule on whether "reckless" threats were inside or outside the scope of freedom of speech. A "reckless threat" is one in which the speaker knows that the expression "might be" a threat, but not that it "is" one, knows that the "line" of wrongdoing is quite close, but not that he or she has crossed it. A good example of such "reckless threats" may well be Elonis's song lyrics. Accordingly, it is not clear whether Elonis's conviction would have been upheld if the trial judge had imposed on the government the burden of proving beyond a reasonable doubt that Elonis knew that what he posted on the Internet might reasonably be considered a threat. Consequently, the Court's definition of a "true" threat—a category of speech totally excluded from the constitutional guarantee—still has a degree of "fuzziness," but, all in all, the definition is fairly precise.

FURTHER READING

Elrod, Jennifer. "Expressive Activity: True Threats, and the First Amendment." *Connecticut Law Review* 36 (2004): 541–608.

Karst, Kenneth L. "Threats and Meanings: How the Facts Govern First Amendment." *Stanford Law Review* 58 (2006): 1337–1412.

Pierce, Michael. "Prosecuting Online Threats after *Elonis*." *Northwestern University Law Review* 110 (2016): 995–1005.

Redish, Martin H. and Fisher, Matthew. "Terrorizing Advocacy and the First Amendment: Free Expression and the Fallacy of Mutual Exclusivity." *Fordham Law Review* 86 (2017): 566–590.

Segall, Eric J. "The Internet as a Game Changer: Reevaluating the True Threats Doctrine." *Texas Tech Law Review* 44 (2011): 183–196.

Smith, James Morton. *Freedom's Fetter's: The Alien and Sedition Laws and American Civil Liberties*. Ithaca, NY: Cornell University Press, 1966, pp. 270–274.

Q10. ARE ANY FACE-TO-FACE INSULTS OF ANOTHER PERSON EXCLUDED FROM FREE SPEECH?

Answer: Yes. Some personal insults are excluded from free speech on the ground that it is common knowledge that they are "fighting words" likely to cause violence and that they are uttered in circumstances "inherently likely" to provoke a violent reaction.

The Facts: The Supreme Court provided its initial definition of "fighting words" in *Chaplinsky v. New Hampshire* (1942), a case dealing with a defendant who called a city marshal a "God damned racketeer" and "a damned Fascist." According to the Court, "fighting words" were "those which, by their very utterance, inflict injury or tend to incite an immediate breach of the peace." The Court's rationale for excluding such expressions from the First Amendment was that they had "no essential part of any exposition of ideas, and are of such slight social value as a step to truth that any benefit that may be derived from them is clearly outweighed by the social interest in order and morality." Applying the aforementioned definition, the Court upheld Chaplinsky's conviction, finding that "argument" was "unnecessary to demonstrate that the [above] appellations . . . are epithets likely to provoke the average person to retaliation, and thereby cause a breach of peace" (315 U.S. 568, 572, 574 (1942); see also *Cantwell v. Connecticut*, 1940). The fact that the city marshal did not respond violently (but arrested Chaplinsky instead) was irrelevant.

At first the Supreme Court interpreted the Chaplinsky definition of "fighting words" somewhat broadly. The Court overturned the breach-of-peace conviction of a speaker who condemned an unruly crowd as "slimy scum" and "snakes" in *Terminiello v. Chicago* (1949), but sustained the disorderly conduct conviction of a speaker who called President Truman and the mayor of Syracuse, New York, "bums" and the American Legion "a Nazi Gestapo" in *Feiner v. New York* (1951). The Court did not begin to take a more restrictive approach to the "fighting words" doctrine until the civil rights demonstrations of the 1960s (see, for example, *Cox v. Louisiana* (1965) and the anti–Vietnam War demonstrations of the late 1960s and early 1970s). In these latter cases, the Court began to overturn breach-of-peace convictions on the ground that the statutes in question were too vague and broad. A pivotal decision was *Cohen v. California* (1971), a case that dealt with both "fighting words" and "offensive speech" (See Q22). The Court conceded that expression on the back of Cohen's jacket ("F*** the Draft") contained a four-letter word that was "not uncommonly employed in a personally provocative fashion" and it may, for that reason constitute a "fighting word" in certain circumstances. However, the Court continued, in Cohen's context, no individual "actually or likely to be present could reasonably have regarded the words . . . as a direct personal insult." Accordingly, he or she could not be convicted of breach of peace. Any statute prohibiting speech "likely to disturb the peace" had to be narrowly drawn, not reaching beyond "direct personal insults" that had a real "likelihood" of provoking violence in the situation in which they were spoken.

The Court's opinion in *Cohen* also arguably eliminated the first prong of the *Chaplinsky* definition of "fighting words": those "which, by their very utterance, *inflict injury*" (emphasis added). This prong of the definition seemed to permit the punishment of abusive speech that made people feel "ashamed," "less worthy," "resentful," "depressed," or "dehumanized" independently of whether they were likely to provoke a violent reaction. Although not denying that abusive speech can cause such harms, the Court in *Cohen* held that California could not constitutionally "protect the sensitive from otherwise unavoidable exposure to appellant's crude form of protest." Any broader governmental authority, the Court reasoned, would "effectively empower a majority to silence dissidents simply as a matter of personal predilections." This is so because there is no principled way to distinguish between Cohen's "offensive" speech and "any other offensive word" that might cause mental or emotional harm. "Surely the State has no right to cleanse public debate to the point where it is grammatically palatable to the most squeamish among us," the Court argued, yet "no readily ascertainable general principle exists for stopping short of that result" if Cohen's expression was punishable as "fighting words." As the Court succinctly put it, "one man's vulgarity is another's lyric" (*Cohen v. California*, 403 U.S. 15, 20–21, 25 (1971)).

A year after *Cohen*, the Court underlined its position that "fighting words" were confined to those "that 'have a *direct* tendency to cause *acts of violence by the person to whom, individually, the remark is addressed*'" (*Gooding v. Wilson*, 405 U.S. 518, 525 (1972), emphasis added). "Fighting words" were limited to personal insults that (1) were "addressed" or "directed" at a specific individual(s), (2) had a "direct tendency" to cause violence, and (3) only the reactions of the "addressed individuals" were relevant to determining whether there was a likelihood of a violent reaction. Applying these criteria later that year, the Court overturned the convictions of three defendants: one who, at a school board meeting with children present, described teachers and members of the board as "m*****f*****s" four times; another who called the police "g*****n m*****f***** police"; and a third who employed the same vulgar terminology in describing "fascist pig" cops (*Rosenfeld v. New Jersey*, 408 U.S. 901, 913, 914 (1972)). None of these expressions qualified as "fighting words," in the Court's judgment, because, in their contexts, the addressees were not likely to respond violently because of police training (see *Houston v. Hill*, 1987) or the expression was not directed at a specific person or group of persons.

The early 1970s, therefore, marked a turning point in the Supreme Court's "fighting words" doctrine by apparently dropping the "psychic injury" prong of the *Chaplinsky* definition. Later decisions support this conclusion. In *Texas v. Johnson* (1989) the Court explicitly defined "fighting words" as those "that are 'likely to provoke the average person to retaliation, and thereby cause a breach of the peace'" (491 U.S. 397, 409 (1989)), confirming implicitly that causing "psychic injuries" was no longer a sufficient basis for criminal liability. The Court made the same point in *Virginia v. Black* (2003) by limiting fighting words to "those personally abusive epithets which, when addressed to the ordinary citizen, are, as a matter of common knowledge, inherently likely to provoke violence" (538 U.S. 343, 358 (2003)). A personal insult can qualify as a "fighting word" only if it satisfies this relatively high standard. In part because of its restrictive definition, the Court has not upheld a "fighting words" conviction since *Chaplinsky*, even though it has recently reaffirmed that this type of expression remains "one of the categorical exclusions from First Amendment protection" (*Snyder v. Phelps*, 562 U.S. 443, 451, 131 fn.3 (2011)).

An important implication of the Supreme Court's present definition of "fighting words" is that much of the "hate speech" that occurs in today's society is protected by freedom of speech. No matter how racist, sexist, bigoted, or homophobic an expression happens to be, it is within the scope of the First Amendment if it is not a "personal insult" directed at a particular "ordinary" person or persons. In the same vein, even if insulting "hate speech" is directed at a particular "ordinary" person(s), it is protected unless it is "common knowledge" that the expression is likely to cause violence and that, in the circumstances of its utterance, it is "inherently likely" to do so. Of course, certain well-known racial epithets would meet this standard if used in the context of a one-on-one confrontation.

Accordingly, despite the widespread character of this misconception, the "fighting words" doctrine does not provide a legal foundation for the eradication of all forms of "hate speech" from American society (see Carroll 2015; Volokh 2015). Only "hate speech" that satisfies the criteria of one of the unprotected categories of speech, such as "true threats" (see Q9) or "fighting words," is totally excluded from the protection of the First Amendment.

FURTHER READING

Caine, Burton. "The Trouble with 'Fighting Words': Chaplinsky v. New Hampshire Is a Threat to First Amendment Values and Should Be Overruled." *Marquette Law Review* 88 (2004): 441–562.

Carroll, Lauren. "CNN's Chris Cuomo: First Amendment Doesn't Cover Hate Speech." *Politifact*, May 7, 2015, available at http://www.politifact.com/punditfact/statements/2015/may/07/chris-cuomo/cnns-chris-cuomo-first-amendment-doesnt-cover-hate/.

Gard, Stephen W. "Fighting Words as Free Speech." *Washington University Law Quarterly* 58 (1980): 531–581.

Greenawalt, Kent. *Fighting Words.* Princeton: NJ: Princeton University Press, 1996.

Nevin, George C. "'Fighting Slurs': Contemporary Fighting Words and the Question of Criminally Punishable Racial Epithets." *First Amendment Review* 14 (2015): 127–158.

O'Neil, Robert M. "Hate Speech, Fighting Words, and Beyond—Why American Law Is Unique." *Albany Law Review* 76 (2012/2013): 467–498.

Volokh, Eugene. "No, There's No 'Hate Speech' Exception to the First Amendment." *The Washington Post*, May 7, 2015, available at https://www.washingtonpost.com/news/volokh-conspiracy/wp/2015/05/07/no-theres-no-hate-speech-exception-to-the-first-amendment/.

Q11. IF "LIBEL" IS EXCLUDED FROM THE SCOPE OF FREEDOM OF SPEECH, DOES THIS CATEGORY INCLUDE ALL "FALSEHOODS" THAT "HARM" ANOTHER PERSON'S "REPUTATION"?

Answer: No. "Falsehoods" that "harm" the reputation of "public officials" or "public figures," as opposed to "private individuals," are not libel "unless" the publisher "knew" the statement was false or was "reckless" in regard to its truth or falsity.

The Facts: "Defamatory" statements are those that harm the reputation of a "public official," a "public figure," or a "private individual." Such statements can be of two kinds: "libel," which consists of a defamatory written statement; or "slander," which consists of comparable verbal statements. Either type of statement is a potential basis for criminal liability (punishment by the state) or civil liability (the state requires the "libeler" to pay compensation for the harm done to the reputation of the "libeled"). Both forms of liability were commonplace during the 19th century. The Supreme Court did not begin to consider whether freedom of speech placed limits on how states could define "libel" until after it applied the First Amendment to the states by incorporating it into the due process clause of the Fourteenth Amendment in *Gitlow v. New York* (1925) (see Q5). At first, the Court was quite deferential. For example, in *Beauharnais v. Illinois* (1952), the Court upheld a criminal conviction of "group libel," which is a defamatory statement about a particular race or ethnic group. According to the Court, a speaker who uttered defamatory falsehoods of this sort libeled every member of that particular race or ethnic group.

The Court in *New York Times v. Sullivan* (1964) undermined the significance of *Beauharnais* without explicitly overruling it. Sullivan was the police commissioner of Montgomery, Alabama, who sued the *Times* on the basis of a paid political advertisement it published that had been signed by the "Committee to Defend Martin Luther King and the Struggle for Freedom in the South." Even though the ad did not mention him by name, Sullivan claimed it referred to him because it said that the "police" had "ringed the Alabama State College Campus," "padlocked" the "dining hall . . . in an attempt to starve" the student body, arrested King seven times, and responded to King's protests by "bombing his home, assaulting his person, and charging him with perjury." None of these claims were factually accurate. The Alabama trial judge ruled that the ad was "libelous per se," and therefore "falsity and malice" were "presumed," which meant that Sullivan did not have to prove that his reputation was actually damaged or that the *Times* or the "Committee" knew or should have known that the statements were false. Unless the defendants could prove that the statements "were true in all their particulars," the only issue left to the jury was whether the false statements were "of and concerning" Sullivan. The jury concluded that the statements were about Sullivan and awarded him $500,000.

The Supreme Court insisted that the constitutionality of this libel award had to be considered "against the background of a profound national commitment to the principle that debate on public issues should be uninhibited, robust, and wide-open, and that it may well include vehement, caustic, and sometimes unpleasantly sharp attacks on government and public officials." With that premise in mind, the Court argued in *New York Times v. Sullivan* that some erroneous statements are "inevitable in free debate" and that they "must be protected if the freedoms of expression are to have the 'breathing space' that they 'need . . . to survive.'" Moreover, the Court continued, injury to the reputation of a public official "affords no more warrant for repressing speech that would otherwise be free than does factual error" and the "combination of the two elements [falsity and defamation] is no less inadequate." Lastly, in the Court's view, the allowance of a defense of truth did not save the Alabama law. "A rule compelling the critic of official conduct to guarantee the truth of all his factual assertions—and to do so on pain of libel judgments virtually unlimited in amount—leads to . . . 'self-censorship,'" which "dampens the vigor and limits the variety of public debate." The Court concluded that Alabama libel law was therefore "inconsistent" with freedom of speech.

The Court's ruling in *Sullivan* did not abolish "libel" as an unprotected category of speech, but it did narrow the category significantly by adopting what has become known as the "malice rule." This rule prohibited "a public official from recovering damages for a defamatory falsehood relating to his official conduct unless he proves that the statement was made with 'actual malice'—that is, with knowledge that it was false or with reckless disregard of whether it was false or not." Mere proof of "negligence" would not suffice for liability. If a publisher "should have known" that the statement was false, but did not, then the false defamatory statement was outside the unprotected category of "libel" and within the scope of freedom of speech (*New York Times v. Sullivan*, 376 U.S. 254, 257–259, 262, 267, 270–73, 279, 283–84 (1964)).

The Court extended the "malice rule" to cases involving *criminal* libel in *Garrison v. Louisiana* (1964) and to "public figures" in *Curtis Publishing Company v. Butts* (1967). The latter was a libel case based on a *Saturday Evening Post* story that included the claim that the University of Georgia athletic director had "fixed" a football game. The Court held that the "malice rule" was appropriate since Butts, although not a "public official," was a "public figure." The Court's rationale for this extension of the "malice rule" was that "the distinctions between governmental and private sectors" in the United States have "increasingly" become "blurred," that "public figures" often play "an influential role in ordering society," and that they "have as ready access as 'public officials' to mass media of communication, both to influence policy and to counter criticism of their views and activities."

The major question left outstanding by *Curtis Publishing Company* was whether the "malice rule" should also apply to defamation suits by private individuals, thereby creating a more or less uniform rule for libel lawsuits and prosecutions. In *Rosenbloom v. Metromedia, Inc.* (1971), a plurality of the Court favored extending the rule to private individuals if the false defamatory statement "concerned matters of general or public interest," but the Court reversed itself three years later in *Gertz v. Robert Welch, Inc.* (1974). Gertz, a prominent Chicago lawyer, sued on the basis of a magazine article that claimed he had "framed" a police officer for murder and that he was a "Communist-fronter." The Court held that the "malice rule" was not applicable to libel actions by private individuals because (1) private individuals are more "vulnerable to injury" from negligent false defamatory statements since they typically do not have a "realistic opportunity to counteract" them through the media; (2) "public officials and public figures have voluntarily exposed themselves to increased risk of injury from defamatory falsehood concerning them"; and lastly, (3) it would not be wise to have judges "decide on an ad hoc basis which publications address issues of 'general or public interest' and which do not." Only by confining the "malice rule" to "public officials and figures," the Court concluded, can due weight be given to the harms caused by negligent defamatory falsehoods, which were harms that were at the core of "our concept of the essential dignity and worth of every human being" (*Gertz v. Robert Welch, Inc.*, 418 U.S. 323, 344–346 (1974)).

Although the Court in *Gertz* refused to apply the "malice rule" to private individuals, it did impose additional requirements. First, states were not permitted to "impose liability without fault," which meant that publishers of defamatory falsehoods could incur liability only if they "should have known" that they were false. Second, private individuals are only entitled to compensation for the "actual injury" of defamatory statements; no presumed or punitive damages are permitted unless the plaintiff can establish "malice," that is, that the publisher "knew" what it published was false or published it with "reckless" disregard for the truth. Lastly, the Court made it clear that a state could not avoid the "malice rule" by simply classifying persons like Gertz as "public figures," a term that was composed of two types: (1) in some instances, "an individual may achieve such pervasive fame or notoriety that he becomes a public figure for all purposes and in all contexts" and (2) but more commonly, "an individual injects himself or is drawn into a particular public controversy and thereby becomes a public figure for a limited range of issues"—a "limited public figure." A plaintiff of the second type became a "public figure" only if the allegedly false and defamatory statement concerned an issue within the "limited range" (*Id.* at 347, 349–350, 351–352). In the Court's view, Gertz did not meet either test, and therefore freedom of speech did not require that the "malice rule" be applied to his libel lawsuit.

The Supreme Court has struggled with the distinction between a "public figure" and a "private individual." While the Court classified a university's athletic director as a "public figure" in *Curtis Publishing Company* (1967), it held in *Time, Inc. v. Firestone* (1976) that Mary Alice Firestone, the former wife of Russell Firestone, "the scion of one of America's wealthiest industrial families," was not a "public figure" for purposes of her libel lawsuit against *Time* magazine, which she claimed had mischaracterized her divorce. By way of explanation, the Court noted that Ms. Firestone had not assumed "any role of especial prominence in the affairs of society, other than perhaps Palm Beach society" (424 U.S. 448, 449 (1976)). The Court made the same finding in *Wolston v. Reader's Digest Association, Inc.* (1979), a case in which the *Reader's Digest* in 1974 called Wolston, who had been convicted in 1958 of criminal contempt for refusing to appear before a grand jury investigating Soviet espionage, a "Soviet agent." Wolston, therefore, only had to prove that the *Reader's Digest* was "at fault," not that it had "intentionally" or "recklessly" published a defamatory falsehood. If anything, these cases suggest that the Court has tightened the criteria of who qualifies as a "public figure," thereby confining the "malice rule" to a more narrow set of libel cases.

Later Supreme Court decisions sharpened the definition of libel and elaborated on the procedures required by the *Sullivan/Gertz* framework. In *Philadelphia Newspapers, Inc. v. Hepps* (1986), the Court endorsed a "constitutional requirement that the plaintiff bear the burden of showing falsity, as well as fault, before recovering damages" (475 U.S. 767, 776 (1986)). This decision insulated from liability defamatory false statements if the plaintiff could not "prove" them false, presumably by the same "clear and convincing" standard that the plaintiff had to meet in terms of "fault," that is, in terms of whether the publisher was "negligent" or acted with "malice." In *Masson v. New Yorker Magazine, Inc.* (1991), the Court held that "minor inaccuracies" do not establish "falsity so long as 'the substance, the gist, the sting'" of the statement is basically true (501 U.S. 496, 517 (1991)). In *Milkovich v. Lorain Journal Company* (1990), the Court endorsed the *Gertz* principle that "there is no such thing as a false idea," but also held that no publisher could escape liability by simply adding "in my opinion" to a culpable defamatory false statement. A statement of opinion could constitute libel if it contained a "provable false factual connotation," such as the expressions "I think Jones is a liar" or "In my opinion, Jones is a liar." The context of the statement would largely determine whether such an expression is a "factual assertion" masquerading as an opinion (497 U.S. 1, 18–19 (1990)).

This latter holding deserves attention because of the widespread misconception that you "can say anything you want on the internet," especially if you say it anonymously in a comment section of a blog (Grossman 2003, 4). The truth is that the same legal rules regarding "libel" that apply to hardcopy publications in the physical world also apply to electronic publications in the cyber world, whether they appear on websites, social media platforms, comment sections, or chat rooms. It is true that context matters and that certain websites or chat rooms may be well known as forums for humor, ribaldry, and hyperbole, but even here liability could be incurred if one maliciously, recklessly, or negligently publishes a falsehood that harms someone's reputation, even if the falsehood is "dressed up" as an "opinion."

Another myth that must be deflated is the one Donald Trump propagated when he was running for president during the 2016 election. During a rally in Fort Worth, Texas, he said that one "of the things I'm going to do if I win, and I hope we do and we're certainly leading. I'm going to open up our libel laws so when they [newspapers such as *The New York Times* and *The Washington Post*] write purposely negative and horrible and false articles, we can sue them and win lots of money" (Gold 2016). Trump's statement contains two fundamental "untruths." First, the president cannot "open up" the libel laws because rules and procedures defining libel are required by the free-speech clause of the First Amendment. No president can change these rules and procedures. Second, if newspapers publish "false articles" that are "purposely negative," there is no need to "open up our libel laws" because "public officials and figures" can already win such libel cases under the *Sullivan* "malice rule." Trump's statement, therefore, propagates myths, in terms of both what he can lawfully do as president and why he wants to do it.

FURTHER READING

Gold, Hadas. "Donald Trump: We're Going to 'Open Up' Libel Laws." Politico.com, February 26, 2016, available at https://www.politico.com/blogs/on-media/2016/02/donald-trump-libel-laws-219866.

Grossman, Mark. *Technology Law: What Every Business (And Business-Minded Person) Needs to Know.* New York: Scarecrow Press, a Division of Rowman & Littlefield, 2003.

Hall, Kermit L. and Urofsky, Melvin I. *New York Times v. Sullivan: Civil Rights, Libel Law, and the Free Press.* Lawrence: University of Kansas Press, 2011.

Jones, RonNell Andersen and West, Sonja R. "The Fragility of the Free American Press." *Northwestern University Law Review* (2017): 567–595.

Smolla, Rodney A. "Let the Author Beware: The Rejuvenation of the American Law of Libel." *University of Pennsylvania Law Review* 132 (1983): 1–94.

Waldron, Jeremy. "Dignity and Defamation." *Harvard Law Review* 123 (2010): 1596–1657.

Q12. IF EXPRESSIVE MATERIAL IS EXCLUDED FROM FIRST AMENDMENT PROTECTION ON THE GROUND THAT IT IS "OBSCENE," DOES THIS JUDGMENT IMPLY THAT THE MATERIAL IN QUESTION IS "UTTERLY WITHOUT REDEEMING SOCIAL VALUE"?

Answer: No. If material lacks "serious literary, artistic, political, or scientific value," it can be "obscene" and outside constitutional protection even if it is not "utterly without redeeming social value."

The Facts: During the 19th century, states routinely punished the publishing and selling of "obscene" materials, whether books, magazines, or pictures. In 1873, the federal government enacted the Comstock Act, which authorized fines and imprisonment for anyone using the federal mail service to send or receive publications that were "obscene," "lewd," "lascivious," or "filthy." To determine if a publication was "obscene" during this time period, courts typically used the definition adopted by a British court in *Hicklin v. Regina* (1868): "Whether the tendency of the matter . . . is to deprave and corrupt those whose minds are open to such influences." On the basis of this definition, works by Theodore Dreiser, James Joyce, D. H. Lawrence, and Henry Miller were banned in the first half of the 20th century.

The Supreme Court rejected the *Hicklin* definition in *Roth v. United States* (1957), relying on the assumption that "the standards for judging obscenity [must] safeguard the protection of freedom of speech." In place of the *Hicklin* definition, the Court endorsed the following: "Whether, to the average person, applying contemporary community standards, the dominant theme of the material, taken as a whole, appeals to prurient interest" because it has "a tendency to excite lustful thoughts" (354 U.S.

476, 488–489 (1957)). Unfortunately, later cases showed there was little consensus on the Court as to how this definition should be applied. Frustrated by the Court's inability to come up with a clear definition of the term, Justice Potter Stewart famously remarked, "perhaps I could never succeed in intelligibly" defining obscenity, but "I know it when I see it" (*Jacobellis v. Ohio*, 378 U.S. 184, 197 (1964)). Two years after Stewart's observation, a three-justice plurality defined the category in *Memoirs v. Massachusetts* as follows:

> (a) the dominant theme of the material taken as a whole appeals to a prurient interest in sex; (b) the material is patently offensive because it affronts contemporary community standards relating to the description or representation of sexual matters, and (c) the material is utterly without redeeming social value. (383 U.S. 413, 418 (1966))

The fact that this definition did not win the endorsement of a majority of the justices shows that the Court had yet to achieve consensus on the issue.

Despite this controversy concerning the definition of "obscenity," the Court in *Stanley v. Georgia* (1969) reversed a conviction for "knowingly possessing" obscene material "in the privacy of a person's own home." In the Court's view, if freedom of speech "means anything, it means that a State has no business telling a man, sitting alone in his own house, what books he may read or what films he may watch" (394 U.S. 557, 564–565 (1969)). The state could prohibit the sale, distribution, and purchase of "obscene" materials, but once they were within the home, the state could not punish mere possession. It deserves to be emphasized that the Court came to this conclusion despite a lack of agreement on the definition of "obscenity."

Finally, in *Miller v. California* (1973), a five-justice majority rejected the plurality's view in *Memoirs* that the unprotected category of "obscenity" only included works that were "utterly without redeeming social value." Instead, the *Miller* majority held that works depicting or describing "sexual conduct" were "obscene" if they met the following three conditions: (1) "the average person, applying contemporary community standards[,] would find that the work, taken as a whole, appeals to the prurient interest," (2) "the work depicts or describes, in a patently offensive way, sexual conduct specifically defined by the applicable state law"; and finally, (3) "the work, taken as a whole, lacks serious literary, artistic, political, or scientific value" (413 U.S. 15, 24 (1973)). The Court conceded that its new definition, with its reference to community standards, abandoned "fixed, uniform national standards of precisely what appeals to the 'prurient interest' or is 'patently offensive.'" It justified its position by observing that "our Nation is simply too big and too diverse" for a "single formulation, even assuming the prerequisite consensus exists" (*Id.* at 30). The implication was that a jury in rural Georgia could find a film "obscene," while one in New York City could come to the opposite conclusion.

The *Miller* Court's inclusion of "lacks serious value" in the third criterion of its definition obviously broadened the unprotected category of "obscenity." Accordingly, although this new definition clearly granted constitutional protection to medical texts, photographs of Michelangelo's *David*, or works by Dreiser, Lawrence, Joyce or Miller, it was not clear how it applied to films shown at "adult" theaters. In *Paris Adult Theatre I v. Slaton* (1973), a case decided with *Miller*, the Court made it clear that such films were subject to the new definition, even if the theater restricted admission to consenting adults over 21 years of age. The Court justified its expanded definition of "obscenity" in the following way:

> We hold that there are legitimate state interests at stake in stemming commercialized obscenity, even assuming it is feasible to enforce effective safeguards against exposure to juveniles and to passersby. Right and interests "other than those of the advocates are involved." These include the interest of the public in the quality of life and the total community environment, the tone of commerce in the great city centers, and, possibly, the public safety itself. . . . As Chief Justice Warren stated, there is a "right of the Nation and of the States to maintain a decent society." (413 U.S. 49, 57–59 (1973))

According to the Court, "decency," the "quality of life," and the "tone of commerce," along with a possible link between "obscenity" and criminal activity near "adult" theaters, justified excluding from the First Amendment speech that had "value," but not the "serious" value required by the *Miller* definition.

The following year, in *Jenkins v. Georgia*, the Court addressed what role, if any, appellate courts have in overturning how local juries assessed whether a work was "patently offensive" according to "community standards." The work in question was the film *Carnal Knowledge*, starring Jack Nicholson, Art Garfunkel, Ann-Margaret, and Candice Bergen. Notwithstanding its view that determinations of whether a work is "patently offensive" were "essentially questions of fact," the Court wrote, "it would be a serious misreading of *Miller* to conclude that juries have unbridled discretion in determining what is 'patently offensive.'" While *Carnal Knowledge* at times implied that "ultimate sexual acts" were occurring, there was "no exhibition whatever of the actors' genitals, lewd or otherwise, during these scenes." There were "occasional scenes of nudity, but nudity alone is not enough to make material legally obscene under the *Miller* standards." Accordingly, the Court in *Jenkins* held that local juries had discretion to make determinations of whether a work appealed to "prurient interests" or was "patently offensive" only if it was a "public portrayal of hard core sexual conduct for its own sake." If a work was not of this character, appellate courts were not obliged to defer to local juries regarding whether the film appealed to "prurient interests" or was "patently offensive." They could reverse such convictions because the films could not legally be "obscene" consistent with the First Amendment (418 U.S. 153, 160–161, 157 (1974)).

A decade after *Jenkins*, the Court in *Pope v. Illinois* (1987) made it clear that "community standards" were not relevant to the assessment of whether a work satisfied the third prong of the *Miller* standard, that is, whether the work, "taken as a whole, lacks serious literary, artistic, political, or scientific value." In the language of the Court,

> Just as the ideas a work represents need not obtain majority approval to merit protection, neither, insofar as the First Amendment is concerned, does the value of the work vary from community to community based on the degree of local acceptance it has won. The proper inquiry is not whether an ordinary member of any given community would find serious literary, artistic, political, or scientific value in allegedly obscene material, but whether a reasonable person would find such value in the material, taken as a whole. (481 U.S. 497, 500–501 (1987))

Accordingly, even if a jury finds that a "public portrayal of hard core sexual conduct for its own sake" does appeal to "prurient interest" and is "patently offensive" according to "contemporary standards," it would be a violation of freedom of speech to find the work "obscene" if a "reasonable person" would judge the work to have "serious value." If a local jury's verdict is inconsistent with this assessment by a "reasonable person," then federal judges must protect freedom of speech by overturning the conviction.

Pope's "reasonable person" approach to the question whether a work has "serious value" increased the significance of expert witnesses at obscenity trials. An example is the 1990 obscenity prosecution of the Cincinnati Contemporary Arts Center and its director, Dennis Barrie, for the display of seven photos by Robert Mapplethorpe. The prosecution claimed that five of these photos were "obscene" on the basis of their homoerotic and sadomasochistic nature. One photograph, for example, showed a man urinating into the mouth of another man. Janet Kardon, director of the Institute of Contemporary Art in Philadelphia, who had originally assembled the retrospective of Mapplethorpe's work, testified for the defense that what qualifies as "art" depends on "the intent and the qualification of the person that made [the work] and the judgment of professionals that work with these matters." Based on these criteria, her opinion was that the Mapplethorpe photos had "serious artistic value." Also appearing on behalf of the defense, Jacquelynn Bass, director of the University Art Museum in Berkeley, California, testified that Mapplethorpe's work had "serious artistic value because of its technical quality and because 'there is content and subject matter that are effectively conveyed.'" Regarding one of the photos, she testified that "the tension between the physical beauty of the photograph and the brutal nature of what's going on in it" gives the photo "the particular quality that this work of art has" (Masters 1990). With such testimony in the record, the jury had to decide whether these two "expert" witnesses were "reasonable" or "unreasonable." Not surprisingly, the jury acquitted both Berrie and the museum.

A similar result occurred when the sheriff of Broward County, Florida, tried to prosecute a record store for selling "As Nasty as They Wanna Be," a rap album produced by 2 Live Crew. Although the prosecution was unsuccessful, a federal district court in a related civil suit found that the album's lyrics were "obscene." However, the 11th Circuit reversed, noting that a number of experts on pop music had testified that the lyrics had "serious artistic value" and that the district judge did not have the "literary knowledge or skills" to decide if the lyrics lacked "serious artistic value" (*Luke Records Inc. v. Navarro*, 960 F. 2d 134, 138 (11th Cir. 1992)).

The practice of relying on expert testimony to help juries assess whether an allegedly "obscene" work has "serious value" has led to a sharp decrease in the number of obscenity prosecutions since the 1990s. However, despite this falloff, it is premature, if not incorrect, to argue that obscenity has "disappeared because the Court realized that it could not protect art unless it protected pornography as well" (Frye 2012, 276). First, federal law still prohibits the interstate shipment of obscene materials, and many states still have obscenity criminal statutes on the books, waiting for the right case to come along. Moreover, in 2005, the George W. Bush administration established the Obscenity Prosecution Task Force in the Department of Justice, which initiated a significant number of prosecutions. Although the Obama administration disbanded this task force, Jeff Sessions, President Trump's nominee to be attorney general, testified at his confirmation hearing in January 2017 that federal obscenity laws "should be continued to be effectively and vigorously prosecuted" (Stahl 2017). As one commentator has recently observed, despite the availability of obscene or quasi-obscene material (especially on the Internet), it is a "myth" that the legal definition of obscenity is "obsolete" (see Kinsley 2015). The legal framework permitting the prosecution of such expression remains intact. "Obscenity" continues to be a category of speech unprotected by the constitutional right of free speech.

FURTHER READING

Cole, David. "Playing by Pornography's Rules: The Regulation of Sexual Expression." *University of Pennsylvania Law Review* 143 (1994): 111–177.

Frye, Brian L. "The Dialectic of Obscenity." *Hamline Law Review* 35 (Winter, 2012): 229–278.

Kinsley, Jennifer M. "The Myth of Obsolete Obscenity." *Cardozo Arts and Entertainment Law Journal* 33 (2015): 607–671.

Masters, Kim. "Obscenity Trial Asks." *The Washington Post*, October 2, 1990, available at https://www.washingtonpost.com/archive/lifestyle/1990/10/02/obscenity-trial-asks/359c3893-a59a-43ab-bf21-228cca304937/.

Nagle, John Copeland. "Pornography as Pollution." *Maryland Law Review* 70 (2011): 939–984.

Schauer, Frederick. "Speech and 'Speech'—Obscenity and 'Obscenity': An Exercise in the Interpretation of Constitutional Language." *The Georgetown Law Journal* 67 (1979): 899–933.

Stahl, Jeremy. "Jeff Sessions Just Said He'd Prosecute Porn." *Slate*, January 10, 2017, available at https://slate.com/news-and-politics/2017/01/jeff-sessions-says-hed-prosecute-porn-trump-appeared-in-multiple-porns.html.

Wilkerson, Isabel. "Cincinnati Jury Acquits Museum in Mapplethorpe Obscenity Case." *New York Times*, October 6, 1990, available at https://www.nytimes.com/1990/10/06/us/cincinnati-jury-acquits-museum-in-mapplethorpe-obscenity-case.html.

Q13. IF A WORK OF "CHILD PORNOGRAPHY" HAS "SERIOUS ARTISTIC VALUE" AND IS THEREFORE NOT "OBSCENE," IS IT STILL EXCLUDED FROM THE SCOPE OF THE CONSTITUTIONAL RIGHT OF FREE SPEECH?

Answer: Yes. Even if "child pornography" has "serious artistic value" and is therefore not "obscene," it is excluded from free-speech protection to prevent harm to minors, such as the harm suffered by teenagers who engage in "sexting."

The Facts: As a matter of legal terminology, "pornography" is a broader concept than "obscenity." All works that are "obscene" are necessarily "pornographic," but not vice versa. Accordingly, "pornography" is within the scope of freedom of speech unless the work in question is "obscene" or unless it constitutes "child pornography." At the federal level, Congress prohibited "obscene" child pornography in the Protection of Children Against Sexual Exploitation Act of 1977. In the same year, New York prohibited "child pornography," dropping the federal requirement that the pornographic image of a juvenile must also be "obscene." The New York law prohibited "the use of a child" under 16 years of age "in a sexual performance," which was defined as "any performance" that includes "actual or simulated sexual intercourse, deviate sexual intercourse, sexual bestiality, masturbation, sado-masochistic abuse, or lewd exhibition of the genitals." In *New York v. Ferber* (1982), the Supreme Court reviewed the constitutionality of a conviction under this law based on two films that were "devoted almost exclusively to depicting young boys masturbating." Despite the fact that the two films were not "obscene," the Supreme Court upheld the conviction by creating a new category of unprotected speech: "Recognizing and classifying child pornography as a category of material outside the protection of the First Amendment is not incompatible with our earlier decisions" (458 U.S. 747, 751–752, 763 (1982)).

The Court's justification for the exclusion of "child pornography" from the First Amendment relied heavily on the state's "compelling" interest in "safeguarding the physical and psychological wellbeing" of children in light of the large "multimillion dollar child pornography market" that the press had exposed in the late 1970s (Adler 2001, 230). Not only the production but also the sale and distribution of "child pornography" were excluded from free speech because the circulation of pornographic images "harms" the child a second time and because "the distribution network for child pornography must be closed if the production of material which requires the sexual exploitation of children is to be effectively controlled." Lastly, the Court noted in *New York v. Ferber* that the "value of permitting live performances and photographic reproduction of children engaged in lewd sexual conduct is exceedingly modest, if not *de minimis*" and, therefore, it was "unlikely" that such depictions "would often constitute an important and necessary part of a literary performance or scientific or educational work" (*Id.* at 756–763).

In defining the new term of "child pornography," the Court "adjusted" the *Miller* definition of obscenity. In a prosecution of "child pornography," (1) a trier of fact "need not find that the material appeals to the prurient interest of the average person," (2) it is also "not required that sexual conduct portrayed be done so in a patently offensive manner," and lastly, (3) "the material at issue need not be considered as a whole." Conversely, the prohibited conduct "must be adequately defined by the applicable state law" and it must be "limited to works that visually depict sexual conduct by children below a specified age." The New York law met these two criteria: it only prohibited depictions of children under 16 years of age, and the images had to be of the types listed in the statute mentioned earlier. The Court declined to decide whether such a narrowly drawn statute might be applied to "child pornography" that had "serious literary, scientific or educational value," such as medical textbooks, because it doubted whether "a substantial number of [such] impermissible applications" would occur (*Id.* 764–765, 771).

In response to *Ferber*, Congress enacted the Child Protection Act of 1984, which dropped the requirement of "obscenity" from the federal child pornography law. The new federal law generally tracked the language of the New York statute, but raised the age limit of minors to 18 and replaced "lewd" with "lascivious" exhibition of the genitals. Six years later, in *Osborne v. Ohio*, the Court expanded the scope of liability under child pornography laws by holding that the mere possession of four photos of nude minors in a desk drawer of one's bedroom was punishable. In coming to this conclusion, the Court distinguished its 1969 ruling in *Stanley*, which held that possession of "obscene" materials in the home was protected by the right of privacy and the First Amendment (see Q12), arguing that "the interests underlying child pornography prohibitions far exceed the interests justifying the Georgia law at issue in *Stanley*." While the state's interest in *Stanley* was that "obscenity would poison the minds of its viewers," the purpose of child pornography laws is to "protect the victims" and to "destroy a market for the exploitative use of children" (495 U.S. 103, 108–109, 111 (1990)).

The 3rd Circuit Court of Appeals in *United States v. Knox* (1994) held that photos of clothed or partially clothed minors could qualify as "lewd exhibitions of nudity." Since the case involved a conviction under the federal child pornography law, the issue was what constituted a "lascivious exhibition of the genitals or pubic area." The 3rd Circuit Court argued that such a "lascivious" exhibition did not require a depiction of actual nudity, whether of "the genitals" or the "pubic area." The only requirement was that a photo "depicts some 'sexually explicit conduct' by the minor subject which appeals to the lascivious interest of the intended audience." Accordingly, the 3rd Circuit Court concluded, "Non-nude visual depictions . . . can qualify as lascivious exhibitions" and "this construction does not render the statute unconstitutionally overbroad" (32 F.3d 733, 747, 736 (3rd Cir. 1994)). Knox appealed his conviction to the Supreme Court, but the justices declined to review it (*Knox v. United States*, 1995). It is arguable that *Knox* broadened the definition of "child pornography" significantly.

Technological developments since *Knox* have complicated issues involving "child pornography," especially the development of sophisticated computer software, digital imaging tools, and the rapid expansion of the Internet. For example, in *Ashcroft v. Free Speech Coalition* (2002), the Supreme Court addressed whether Congress's Child Pornography Prevention Act of 1996 could expand the category of "child pornography" to include "sexually explicit images that appear to depict minors but were produced without using any real children," whether by "using adults who look like minors or by using computer imaging." The Court's answer was consistent with the basic rationale of *Ferber*: the prevention of child abuse was the purpose of child pornography laws, not the suppression of the content of child pornography. If adults are used in a film containing scenes that suggest but do not actually contain sexually explicit images of minors, or if a computer generates such images, then no abuse of children has occurred and there are no victims created by the film's production. The government contended that such "virtual child pornography" was indistinguishable from "real child pornography." It therefore "whets the appetites of pedophiles and encourages them to engage in illegal conduct." But in the Court's view, the "mere tendency of speech to encourage unlawful acts is not a sufficient reason for banning it." Free speech is "most in danger when the government seeks to control thought or to justify its laws for that impermissible end" (*Ashcroft v. Free Speech Coalition*, 535 U.S. 234, 239–240, 249, 253–254 (2002)).

Congress responded to *Ashcroft* in 2003 by enacting the PROTECT Act, which included a new "pandering provision" that criminalized "solicitations" and "advertisements" of child pornography by mail, on the Internet, or by any other means, regardless of whether the material in question was "actual" or "virtual" child pornography. In *United States v. Williams* (2008), the Supreme Court upheld the constitutionality of the new provision but insisted that it could be applied to purveyors of "virtual" child pornography only if the purveyors "intended to cause another to believe" that the material is "actual" child pornography and to recipients of child pornography only if they "solicit" it "in a manner that reflects" a subjective and "reasonable" belief that the material is of the same character. If these criteria are satisfied, the Court concluded, "offers to provide or requests to obtain child pornography are categorically excluded from the First Amendment," just as child pornography itself was excluded. However, the Court noted that the statute did not cover "offers" or "requests" of "virtual" child pornography. "Simulated child pornography will be as available as ever, so long as it is offered as *such*, and not as real child pornography" (553 U.S. 285, 295–296, 299, 303 (2008)). Marketing "virtual child pornography" is constitutionally protected if it is not marketed as "actual child pornography."

The rise of social media sites, smartphones, and text messaging has led many teenagers to engage in "sexting"—the voluntary transfer of sexually related photos. Of course, any adult who engages in "sexting" with a teenager (the infamous Anthony Weiner case) is committing a crime, but what about one teenager "sexting" with another, perhaps a romantic partner? Many teenagers are blithely unaware that such activity might be the basis for liability, whether they are criminally prosecuted as an adult or adjudicated as a juvenile delinquent. A 2014 Drexel University study found that 28 percent of the undergraduate students surveyed at a northeastern university had sent photographic "sexts" as minors and that 61 percent were not aware that such conduct might be illegal (Strohmaier et al. 2014; Lorang et al. 2016).

Contrast these statistics with the realities of law enforcement and prosecution. A 2012 study found that in 2009 there were 4,901 arrests for possession of child pornography and that 7 percent of those arrested "were age 17 or younger" (Wolak et al. 2012). A 2013 survey of 378 state prosecutors of crimes against children found that 62 percent had worked on "sexting" cases involving juveniles, that 36 percent had filed charges in these cases, and that 16 percent of the cases resulted in convictions that required mandatory sex offender registration (Walsh et al. 2013). Mandatory sex offender registration laws require persons convicted of sex offenses to register with local police, and most states allow public access to these registries via the Internet, which means that the public has access to the names and addresses of juveniles convicted of child pornography, thereby exposing them to threats, harassment, and social ostracism.

Several states have enacted "sexting" statutes, with less severe penalties than "child pornography" laws (Ibtesam 2017), but many states have not. Moreover, some state appellate courts have not hesitated to uphold child pornography convictions of teenagers who engage in "sexting." For example, in 2007, a Florida appellate court upheld a juvenile delinquency adjudication of a 16-year-old female who e-mailed photos of her and her 17-year-old boyfriend engaged in sexual behavior to another computer. Despite the fact that the two did not send the photos to a third party, the appellate court held that the state had a "reasonable expectation that the material will ultimately be disseminated" and that possibility was sufficient to constitute "a compelling state interest for preventing the production of this material." On the basis of this rationale, the juvenile adjudication of the 16-year-old female was upheld (*A.H. v. State*, 2007) and the Florida Supreme Court declined to review the case. The takeaway point is that teenage sexting of "lascivious" images is not protected by the constitutional right of free speech and is often subject to criminal liability.

FURTHER READING

Adler, Amy. "The Perverse Law of Child Pornography." *Columbia Law Review* 101 (2001): 209–273.

Department of Justice. *National Strategy for Child Exploitation Prevention and Interdiction: A Report to Congress.* (April 2016): 1–156, available at https://www.justice.gov/psc/file/842411/download.

Ibtesam, Rayeed. "On Teenage 'Sexting' and the Law." *Hamline Journal of Public Law and Policy* 37 (2017): 246–277.

Lorang, Milissa R., McNeil, Dale E., and Binder, Renee L. "Minors and Sexting: Legal Implications." *Journal of the American Academy of Psychiatry and the Law Online* 44 (2016): 73–81.

Minor, Angela D. "Sexting Prosecutions: Teenagers and Child Pornography Laws." *Howard Law Journal* 60 (2016): 309–324.

Strohmaier, Heidi, Murphy, Megan, and Matteo, David. "Youth Sexting: Prevalence Rates, Driving Motivations, and the Deterrent Effect of Legal Consequences." *Sexuality Research and Social Policy* 11 (2014): 245–255.

Walsh, W., Wolack, J., and Finkelhor, D. "Sexting: When Are State Prosecutors Deciding to Prosecute?" *The Third National Juvenile Online Victimization Study.* (University of New Hampshire: Crimes Against

Children Research Center, 2013): 1–4, available at http://www.unh
.edu/ccrc/pdf/CV294_Walsh_Sexting%20&%20prosecution_2-6-13
.pdf.

Wolak, Janis, Finklhofer, David, and Mitchell, Kimberly F. "Trends in
Arrests for Child Pornography Possession: The Third National Juvenile Online Victimization Study" (Durham, NH: Crimes Against
Research Center, 2012): 1–6, available at https://scholars.unh.edu/cgi/
viewcontent.cgi?article=1045&context=ccrc.

3

Conditionally Protected Speech

Unlike unprotected speech that receives no constitutional protection (see Chapter 2), the Supreme Court places conditionally protected speech within the First Amendment, but yet grants the government the authority to prohibit it depending on the nature and circumstances of the expression. The Supreme Court has developed criteria for the different types of conditionally protected speech by "balancing" the value of free speech against the importance of relevant state interests that support prohibition. Justice Hugo Black criticized the "balancing" approach to resolving issues regarding freedom of speech because, in his view, it implicitly favors the government's efforts to prohibit untoward or controversial speech (see Q3). In support of Black's point of view, Ken White, a First Amendment litigator, argued that "American courts don't decide whether to protect speech by balancing its harm against its benefit." To justify his claim, White quotes the following from a 2010 Supreme Court opinion:

> Free speech does not extend only to categories of speech that survive an ad hoc balancing of relative social costs and benefits. The First Amendment itself reflects a judgment by the American people that the benefits of its restrictions on the Government outweigh the costs. (White 2017)

But this quote was taken from a passage in which the Court declined to create a new category of "unprotected" speech by balancing the value of depictions of animal cruelty against the free speech rights of those who create such depictions, whether they are photographs or videos (*United States v. Stevens*, 2010). The Court denied that "ad hoc" balancing could justify the creation of such an "unprotected" category of speech, but it never hinted that "balancing" was not inherently a factor in deciding when the government can prohibit conditionally protected speech. It is, therefore, a fundamental misconception to believe that the Court does not use "balancing" in making its judgments concerning whether government can or cannot prohibit conditionally protected speech.

It is also a myth that a "balancing" approach to freedom of speech is inherently hostile to the First Amendment. Throughout the 20th century, the Supreme Court used such an approach to decide when conditionally protected speech should be protected. During that time frame, the Court expanded the right of free speech significantly, and the trend has continued into the 21st century. For example, Geoffrey Stone, a prominent proponent of free speech at the University of Chicago, claims that the Roberts Court "has given more protection to free speech across a larger range of areas than any of its predecessors have—although sometimes unwisely" (Chapman 2017). In other words, despite the Court's use of a "balancing" approach, it has nonetheless, according to Stone, expanded freedom of speech to an "unwise" degree. Accordingly, a "balancing" approach to freedom of speech is not incompatible with a robust understanding of the scope and importance of conditionally protected speech.

FURTHER READING

Chapman, Steve. "The Roberts Court: Champion of Free Speech." *Chicago Tribune*, July 26, 2017, available at https://www.chicagotribune .com/news/opinion/chapman/ct-john-roberts-court-free-speech-20170726-column.html.

White, Ken. "Actually, Hate Speech Is Protected Speech." *Los Angeles Times*, June 8, 2017, available at https://www.latimes.com/opinion/op-ed/ la-oe-white-first-amendment-slogans-20170608-story.html.

Q14. CAN THE GOVERNMENT PUNISH UNLAWFUL ADVOCACY IF THE ILLEGAL ACT DOES NOT OCCUR?

Answer: Yes. A speaker who advocates an illegal act can be punished if it does not occur if the speaker "intended" it and the unlawful harm was "imminent" and "likely."

The Facts: Individuals alone or in groups can engage in speech that advocates unlawful action. Of course, all such advocacy is relatively harmless unless third parties act upon it, so it is not obvious whether the government, consistent with freedom of speech, should be permitted to punish unlawful advocacy that does not result in any criminal conduct. In 1919, the Supreme Court confronted this question in three cases involving obstructing the draft and causing insubordination in the military during World War I. In each of these cases, the Court upheld convictions for unlawful advocacy that did not result in criminal conduct based on the "clear and present danger" doctrine, a test of unlawful advocacy formulated by Justice Oliver Wendell Holmes, who wrote the majority opinions in all three cases. "The question in every case," he wrote, "is whether the words used are used in such circumstances and are of such a nature as to create a clear and present danger that they will bring about the substantive evils that Congress has a right to prevent" (*Schenk v. United States*, 249 U.S. 47, 52 (1919)). The advocacy, therefore, did not have to actually obstruct the draft or cause insubordination in the military to incur criminal liability. All that was necessary was that a speaker "intended" that others should violate the law and that the relevant expression created a "clear and present danger" of this eventuality. If these two facts were established, then the government could punish the speaker. It was, Holmes conceded, a "question of degree": judges must "balance" the proximity of the expression to the illegal act against the value of the right of free speech.

In *Schenk*, the first of the three cases, the Court upheld the conviction of a group of individuals who sent leaflets to men already drafted advocating the obstruction of conscription and insubordination in the military. The Court did the same in *Frohwerk v. United States* (1919), a case involving an employee of a newspaper, along with its owner, who circulated 12 newspaper articles highly critical of conscription, possibly in neighborhoods "where a little breath would be enough to kindle a flame, and that the fact was known and relied upon by those who sent the paper out" (249 U.S. 204, 207–209 (1919)).

Lastly, in *Debs v. United States* (1919) the Court refused to overturn the conviction of Eugene Debs, the leader of the American Socialist Party who had won over 900,000 votes (nearly 6 percent of the total) in the 1912 presidential election, even though he did not literally advocate illegal action, but only praised comrades who had resisted the draft. Holmes specifically noted that the jury was "carefully instructed that they could not find the defendant guilty for advocacy of any of his opinions unless the words used had as their natural tendency and reasonably probable effect to obstruct the recruiting service, &c., and unless the defendant had the specific intent to do so in his mind" (249 U.S. 211, 213, 215–216 (1919)). The words of a speaker were, therefore, relevant to assess both whether there was a likelihood of unlawful action and whether the speaker had the "specific intent" to bring about that result, but it was not necessary for the speaker to literally advocate illegal action.

Later that same year, in *Abrams v. United States* (1919), the Court considered a case not involving the obstruction of the draft or insubordination in the military, but rather advocating "resistance" to the U.S. war effort or "curtailment" of the production of war materials in the conflict with Germany. A crucial fact of the case was that the defendants, who were recent Russian immigrants, did not intend to obstruct the U.S. war effort against Germany, but rather its 1918 intervention into the Communist revolution in Russia, an intervention intended to restore the czarist government and revoke the peace treaty that the new Soviet Union had recently signed with Germany. The majority of the Court, departing from the standards of the "clear and present danger doctrine," endorsed what became known as the "bad tendency" test, which required for a conviction neither an "intent" to obstruct the war against Germany nor a likelihood of that result.

> It will not do to say . . . that the only intent of these defendants was to prevent injury to the Russian cause. Men must be held to have intended, and to be accountable for, the effects which their acts were likely to produce. Even if their primary purpose and intent was to aid the cause of the Russian Revolution, the plan of action which they adopted necessarily involved, before it could be realized, defeat of the war program of the United States, for the obvious effect of this appeal, if it should become effective, as they hoped it might, would be to persuade persons . . . not . . . to work in ammunition factories where their work would produce "bullets, bayonets, cannon" and other munitions of war the use of which would cause the "murder" of Germans and Russians. (250 U.S. 616, 621 (1919))

Accordingly, if any expression had a "reasonably foreseeable" tendency to cause the unlawful result, the government could punish it, even if there was no "intent" to oppose the war against Germany and even if the harm was neither "likely" nor "imminent." Unwilling to accept the implications of the "bad tendency" test, Holmes dissented in *Gitlow*.

During the 1920s and later in the 1950s, the Supreme Court considered free-speech issues that were similar to those discussed earlier, but also distinguishable because the primary issue was not unlawful advocacy of immediate action, but rather whether the government could impose criminal liability on members of a group that was advocating violent unlawful actions—a Communist revolution—at some point in the indefinite future (see Q15). The Court did not return to the issue of advocacy of immediate unlawful action until *Brandenburg v. Ohio* (1969), at which point the Court had the option of reaffirming the "bad tendency" test of *Abrams* or Holmes's "clear and present danger" doctrine. The case concerned a leader of the Ku Klux Klan whose speech at a rally included the following: "We're not a revengent organization, but if our President, our Congress, our Supreme Court, continue to suppress the white, Caucasian race, it's possible that there might have to be some revengeance taken." The Court reversed the conviction and firmly endorsed the essentials of Holmes's "clear and present danger" doctrine, holding that "the constitutional guarantees of free speech and free press do not permit a State to forbid or proscribe advocacy of the use of force or of law violation except where such advocacy is directed to inciting or producing imminent lawless action and is likely to incite or produce such action" (395 U.S. 444, 446–447 (1969)). Individual advocacy of unlawful action is, therefore, protected by freedom of speech unless the speaker's "intent" is to produce an unlawful act and the act is both "imminent" and "likely."

In *Hess v. Indiana* (1973), the Court applied the *Brandenburg* test to reverse a disorderly conduct conviction of a bystander at an antiwar demonstration who allegedly said, "We'll take the f*****g street later." The Court reasoned that Hess's statement, at best, "could be taken as counsel for present moderation" or, at worst, "it amounted to nothing more than advocacy of illegal action at some indefinite future time" (414 U.S. 105, 108 (1973)).

The Court reached a comparable result in *NAACP v. Clairborne Hardware Company* (1982), which overturned a civil damages award against civil rights leaders who had initiated and enforced an economic boycott against white-owned commercial establishments in Mississippi. A leader of the boycott warned members of his audience "that the Sheriff could not sleep with boycott violators at night" and that if "we catch any of you going in any of them racist stores, we're gonna break your damn neck." The Court conceded that these expressions "might have been understood as inviting an unlawful form of discipline," but also noted that the remarks were part of "lengthy addresses" that generally called for the realization of political and economic power through black unity, mutual support, and respect for each other. In this type of context, the Court concluded, an "advocate must be free to stimulate his audience with spontaneous and emotional appeals for unity and action in a common cause" and that when "such appeals do not incite lawless action, they must be regarded as protected speech" or else the Court would be ignoring "the 'profound national commitment' that 'debate on public issues should be uninhibited, robust, and wide-open'" (458 U.S. 886, 902, 927–928 (1982)).

It is not clear whether the Court in *Clairborne* is adding an additional requirement to *Brandenburg's* criteria: that unlawful action must not only be "intended," "imminent," and "likely," but it must also actually occur before liability could be imposed on a speaker. To this day, the Court has not yet explicitly clarified its positions. However, during the interim, the spread of domestic and international terrorism has raised the question whether the liability for unlawful advocacy should be relaxed, rather than tightened, as the Court arguably did in *Clairborne*. For example, four years after the 1995 Oklahoma City bombing, Congress made it a crime to teach or demonstrate how to make or use explosives or weapons of mass destruction if done with the "knowledge" or "intent" that the instruction will be used in furtherance of "an activity that constitutes a Federal crime of violence." The statute did not require that the crime of violence be "imminent," but it is arguable that the law did not punish simply "unlawful advocacy," but rather a more culpable form of conduct, informing others *how* to commit a crime, which arguably makes the defendant less of a speaker and more of a participant in the crime itself.

The more difficult issue, following the tragic 9/11 attacks, is the use of the Internet by al-Qaeda and other extremist groups not only to recruit members but also to inspire sympathizers to commit acts of violence in their home countries. Confronting this trend of violence, prosecutors in the United States have relied heavily on a federal statute that bans "knowingly" providing "material support" to designated terrorist groups. The ban defines "material support" to include "intangible property," "service," "training," and "expert advice or assistance." In *Holder v. Humanitarian Law Project* (2010), the Court considered whether this federal law could be applied to those who sought to support the "lawful, nonviolent purposes" of two designated terrorist groups by "monetary contributions, other tangible aid, legal training, and political advocacy." The Court conceded that some of this support was clearly "in the form of speech," yet ruled in favor of the government's authority to prohibit such speech because "the Government's interest in combating terrorism is an urgent objective of the highest order" and because "'foreign terrorist organizations do not maintain legitimate *financial* firewalls between those funds raised for civil, nonviolent activities, and those ultimately used to support violent, terrorist operations.'" If a terrorist organization receives free training, expert advice, and expert assistance as to how it should conduct its civil, nonviolent activities, the organization can easily reallocate any money saved by such speech-based assistance to terrorist purposes. The Court made it clear in *Holder*, however, that the ban on providing "speech-based" support to terrorist groups covered speech only if it was "coordinated with or under the direction of a designated foreign terrorist organization. Independent advocacy that might be viewed as promoting the [terrorist] group's legitimacy was not covered" by the federal ban (561 U.S. 1, 8, 9, 28, 31–32 (2010)).

The Court in *Holder* never attempted to reconcile its reasoning regarding "providing material support" with its approach to unlawful advocacy. Accordingly, what if sympathizers of a designated terrorist group operate a website in the United States without any coordination with the group and not under its direction, one that fosters recruitment for the group, glorifies its martyrs, and advocates the use of its violent methods? Would such speech activity be unprotected only if the sympathizers "intended" unlawful acts that were "imminent" and "likely?" The Court will eventually have to address the question whether *Brandenburg's* criteria of unlawful advocacy are consistent with the Court's ruling regarding "providing material support" in *Holder*.

FURTHER READING

Cole, David. "The First Amendment's Borders." *Harvard Law & Policy Review* 6 (2012): 147–177.

Crocker, Thomas P. "Free Speech and Terrorist Speech: An Essay on Dangerous Ideas." *Vanderbilt Law Review En Banc* 70 (2017): 49–67.

Donahue, Laura. "Terrorist Speech and the Future of Free Expression." *Cardozo Law Review* 27 (2005): 233–341.

Pohlman, H. L. *Justice Oliver Wendell Holmes: Free Speech and the Constitution.* New York: New York University Press, 1993.

Rohr, Marc. "'Threatening' Speech: The Thin Line between Implicit Threats, Solicitation, and Advocacy of Crime." *Rutgers Journal of Law and Public Policy* 13 (2015): 150–173.

Stone, Geoffrey. "The Origins of the 'Bad Tendency' Test: Free Speech in Wartime." *Supreme Court Review* (2002): 411–453.

"Symposium: Terrorist Incitement on the Internet." *Fordham Law Review* 86 (2017): 367–631.

Q15. DOES FREEDOM OF SPEECH AND ASSOCIATION PROTECT SOMEONE FROM CRIMINAL LIABILITY IF HE OR SHE ORGANIZES OR JOINS A GROUP ADVOCATING THE VIOLENT OVERTHROW OF GOVERNMENT?

Answer: No, not if the speaker is an "active member" with "knowledge" of the group's unlawful methods and goals and "intends" a violent overthrow of the government, and the group "advocates" such a violent overthrow.

The Facts: The Supreme Court first considered the liability of individuals who organize in a group that advocates the violent overthrow of organized government in *Gitlow v. New York* (1925), a case involving the publication of the Left Wing Manifesto of the Left Wing Section of the Socialist Party. Gitlow arranged for the printing and circulation of the manifesto, which called for "the necessity of accomplishing the 'Communist Revolution' by a militant and 'revolutionary Socialism', based on 'the class struggle' and mobilizing the 'power of the proletariat in action,' through mass industrial revolts . . . and 'revolutionary mass action'" (268 U.S. 652, 654–656 (1925)). The Court upheld Gitlow's conviction under New York's criminal anarchy statute, which imposed liability on anyone who "advocates, advises, or teaches the duty, necessity, and propriety of overthrowing and overturning organized government by force, violence and unlawful means," even though there was no evidence that the publication and circulation of the manifesto had any deleterious effect. The Court underlined the fact that the statute did "not penalize the utterance or publication of abstract 'doctrine' or academic discussion having no quality of incitement to any concrete action," but rather only prohibited "language advocating advising, or teaching the overthrow of government by unlawful means."

In the Court's view, the government can punish such speech, even if there is no "likelihood" of "imminent" harm, because

> the immediate danger is none the less real and substantial because the effect of a given utterance cannot be accurately foreseen. . . . A single revolutionary spark may kindle a fire that, smouldering for a time, may burst into a sweeping and destructive conflagration. (*Id.* at 669)

Accordingly, the state need not wait until there is an "imminent and immediate danger," but can rather "suppress the threatened danger in its incipiency." After all, the Court reasoned, if "the State were compelled to wait until the apprehended danger became certain, then its right to protect itself would come into being simultaneously with the overthrow of the government" (*Id.*).

In his dissent, Justice Holmes cast doubt on the intelligibility of the Court's distinction between "advocacy of abstract doctrine" and "advocacy of unlawful action," remarking that "every idea is an incitement" because it "offers itself for belief, and if believed, it is acted on." Holmes thought the better approach was to require some degree of a real and present danger before unlawful advocacy by a group could be suppressed. The Court's majority, however, argued that Holmes's "clear and present danger" doctrine "was manifestly intended" to apply only to cases "where the statute merely prohibits certain acts involving the danger of substantive evil, without any reference to language itself," such as obstruction of the draft or causing insubordination in the military. It did not apply, in the majority's view, to statutes "where the legislative body itself has previously determined the danger of substantive evil arising from utterances of a specified class." Since New York's criminal anarchy statute prohibited a certain type of dangerous utterance—advocacy of violent overthrow of organized government—the Court concluded that it "was not necessary . . . that the defendant should have advocated 'some definite or immediate act or acts' of force, violence, or unlawfulness," or "that the language should have been 'reasonably and ordinarily calculated to incite certain persons' to acts of force, violence or unlawfulness." Any member of a group advocating the violent overthrow of government was punishable even if there was no likelihood that the advocacy would result in any violent conduct (*Id.* at 669–73).

The Court revisited the issue of whether freedom of speech protected group-based advocacy of violent revolutionary action in *Whitney v. California* (1927), upholding the conviction of a member of the Communist Labor Party (CLP). Even though there was evidence that Whitney personally favored peaceful, rather than violent, political change, the Court reasoned that the jury had determined that Whitney was a "member" of the CLP and "knew" about CLP's advocacy of violent revolution. Therefore, her offense, the Court suggested, "partakes of the nature of a criminal conspiracy" and it was clear that "such united and joint action involves even greater danger to the public peace and security than the isolated utterances and acts of individuals" (274 U.S. 357, 359–360, 367, 371–372 (1927)). Joining a conspiracy that relied on unlawful advocacy to achieve its aim of violent revolution was such a dangerous act—one far more dangerous, in the Court's opinion, than individual acts of unlawful advocacy—that government could punish membership in such an organization without violating freedom of speech or association. Membership in such a "conspiracy" was punishable even if the defendant did not "intend" violent revolutionary action and if such action was neither "likely" nor "imminent."

During the late 1940s and early 1950s, Senator Joseph McCarthy conducted a number of congressional hearings investigating the degree to which Communists had infiltrated the American government, labor unions, educational institutions, and the entertainment industry. The public's fear of a Communist "fifth column" set the stage for the federal government's prosecution of the national leaders of the American Communist Party. The prosecution proceeded under the conspiracy provisions of the Smith Act of 1940, which made it illegal "to organize or help to organize" any group advocating the violent overthrow of the U.S. government.

In *Dennis v. United States* (1951), the Supreme Court upheld the constitutionality of the convictions, arguing that the Smith Act did not prohibit the forming of a group for the purpose of an "academic discussion of the merits of Marxism-Leninism," but only forming a group for the purpose of "advocating" a violent overthrow of the U.S. government "as speedily as circumstances would permit."

In *Dennis*, the Court argued that Holmes did not formulate his clear-and-present-danger test for unlawful advocacy to confront "the development of an apparatus [the Communist Party] designed and dedicated to the overthrow of the Government, in the context of world crisis after crisis." Accordingly, the Court applied the doctrine but at the same time endorsed a revision of it: in each case, the Court said, judges "must ask whether the gravity of the 'evil,' discounted by its improbability, justifies such invasion of free speech as is necessary to avoid the danger." This new formulation clearly envisioned the possibility that an "evil," such as the overthrow of the U.S. government, could be so "grave" that, even when its "improbability" is "discounted," there was a large enough remainder to justify the government's punishment of expressive conduct that was within the scope of freedom of speech (341 U.S. 494, 494–496, 501–502, 505, 510 (1951)).

Six years after *Dennis*, in *Yates v. United States* (1957), the Supreme Court overturned 14 additional convictions of members of the American Communist Party (ACP), claiming that the government had only proven that the defendants had advocated the "abstract doctrine of forcible overthrow" of the government, while the Smith Act only prohibited advocacy "of a kind calculated to 'incite' persons to action." Even if such "abstract advocacy" is engaged in with evil intent, even if, in other words, the speaker's ultimate goal is the violent overthrow of the government, the federal law only prohibited advocacy that had the "capacity to stir listeners to forcible action." The "essential" distinction, the Court wrote, "is that those to whom the advocacy is addressed must be urged to *do* something, now or in the future, rather than merely to *believe* in something" (354 U.S. 298, 312–315, 324–325 (1957)), such as the desirability or inevitability of a violent revolution. Speakers who conspire with others to inspire such "beliefs," rather than "violent actions," are protected by the constitutional right of free speech.

The Smith Act also prohibited anyone from being a "member" of a group that advocated violent overthrow of the government, but only if the member "knew" of the group's illegal advocacy and had "a specific intent to accomplish overthrow 'as speedily as circumstances would permit.'" Based on this understanding, the Court in *Scales v. United States* (1961) upheld a conviction of an "active member" of the ACP because the defendant "knew" that the ACP was engaged in "unlawful advocacy" of violent action and had a "specific intent" to bring about a violent overthrow of the government "as soon as circumstances would permit" (367 U.S. 203, 206, 228–230 (1961)). However, in *Noto v. United States* (1961), the Court overturned a conviction based on the membership provision of the Smith Act because the government's evidence only showed that the leadership of the ACP was "preparing the way for a situation in which future acts of sabotage might be facilitated." But that kind of evidence was insufficient to sustain a conviction. There must be evidence of "*present* advocacy," not merely evidence of "an intent to advocate in the future or a conspiracy to advocate in the future once a groundwork has been laid" (367 U.S. 290, 298 (1961)). So, even if Noto presently "intended" to advocate violent action to overthrow the government at some point in the future, the First Amendment protected his unlawful advocacy because the ACP was not yet advocating the violent overthrow of the government, but only the "abstract doctrine of forcible overthrow." Membership in such a group is protected by freedom of speech and association.

These cases dealing with the ACP's advocacy of the violent overthrow of the federal government are the backdrop for any consideration of how free speech relates to radical Islamic groups inciting terrorist acts of violence on the Internet by posting radical lectures, such as those by Anwar al-Awlaki; or photos that glorify violence against the West, such as pictures of the 9/11 attacks, the shootings at Fort Hood, Texas, the Boston Marathon bombing, and the San Bernardino massacre. Of course, many of these websites operate outside the United States and are generally beyond the reach of American law, but what about individuals inside the United States who advocate violent acts of terrorism? One might argue that the "gravity" of the advocated "evil"—acts of terrorism—may not match the "gravity" of the "evil" of the violent overthrow of the federal government, but the murder of innocent Americans is presumably a greater "evil" than that of obstructing the draft or causing military insubordination, the types of harms to which Holmes applied his "clear and present danger" doctrine in 1919 (see Q14). Accordingly, if a single individual, not a member of any terrorist group, is operating a website advocating violent terrorist actions, can the government punish him or her only if a terrorist act is "likely" and "imminent" or, applying the standard of *Dennis*, is the "evil" so great that, after discounting the "improbability" of the terrorist act, it yet justifies the imposition of criminal liability on the website operator? The Supreme Court has yet to address this specific question.

Based on the Communist cases discussed earlier, the answer is somewhat easier if the website operator is a member of a terrorist group who "knew" the advocacy was "unlawful" and "intended" to produce violent terrorist acts. *Dennis* and *Scales* strongly support the view that criminal liability would be justified on the theory that conspiracies are more dangerous than individual acts of unlawful advocacy. However, the federal government has not relied on any "conspiracy" theory to prosecute those who advocate terrorist violence. Instead, it has relied on a federal statute that prohibits providing "material support" to "known" designated terrorist groups or "known" groups that engage in terrorism. This provision prohibits anyone from providing, attempting to provide, or conspiring with others to provide "anything of value" to such a terrorist group (so long as it is done under the "direction or control" of the group), regardless of whether the "thing of value" is speech protected by the First Amendment (*Holder v. Humanitarian Law Project*, 2010). If membership in such a group could be punished, consistent with freedom of speech, then presumably any speaker advocating violent terrorist acts on the Internet who is a "member" of a terrorist group, acting under its "direction and control," could also be punishable, consistent with freedom of speech. In fact, membership alone, apart from advocacy of terrorist violence, would probably be enough to justify liability, at least if the "member" in question "knows" that the group is currently advocating "violent action" and "intends" that result.

FURTHER READING

Cole, David. "The First Amendment's Borders." *Harvard Law & Policy Review* 6 (2012): 147–177.

Donahue, Laura. "Terrorist Speech and the Future of Free Expression." *Cardozo Law Review* 27 (2005): 233–341.

Feltner, Kasey. "Swipe Right for ISIS: Social Media and Material Support to Foreign Terrorist Organizations." *Buffalo University Public Interest Law Journal* 26 (2017): 95–114.

Greenawalt, Kent. *Speech, Crime, and the Uses of Language.* Oxford: Oxford University Press, 1992.

Healy, Thomas. "Brandenburg in a Time of Terror." *Notre Dame Law Review* 84 (2009): 655–731.

Linde, Hans. "'Clear and Present Danger' Reexamined: Dissonance in the Brandenberg Concerto." *Stanford Law Review* 22 (1970): 1163–1186.

VanLandingham, Rachel E. "Jailing the Twitter Bird: Social Media, Material Support to Terrorism, and Muzzling the Modern Press." *Cardozo Law Review* 39 (2017): 1–57.

Volokh, Eugene. "Crime-Facilitating Speech." *Stanford Law Review* 57 (2005): 1095–1222.

Q16. DOES FREEDOM OF SPEECH PROTECT "HATE SPEECH" THAT DENIGRATES PEOPLE ON THE BASIS OF THEIR RACE, ETHNICITY, RELIGION, SEX, OR SEXUAL ORIENTATION?

Answer: Yes. Freedom of speech generally protects "hate speech," especially if the prohibition violates the overbreadth doctrine of freedom of speech (see Q6) or qualifies as "content" or "viewpoint" discrimination (see Q7), but "hate speech" can be punished if it constitutes a "true threat," constitutes a "fighting word," or is a virulent type of intimidation.

The Facts: A 2017 study found that 44 percent of college students do not believe that the First Amendment protects "hate speech" (Villasenor 2017), which is troubling because such speech is actually constitutionally protected unless it qualifies as a type of unprotected speech. For this reason, "true threats" and "fighting words" masquerading as "hate speech" have no constitutional protection, assuming, of course, that the prohibition under which such speakers are prosecuted is "neutral" and not "overly broad." "Intimidating" or "coercive" speech is trickier since not all forms of "intimidating" or "coercive" speech are outside the scope of freedom of speech. The Court addressed the constitutionality of "coercive" speech in *NAACP v. Clairborne Hardware Company* (1982), a case dealing with how black leaders enforced an economic boycott against white merchants in Mississippi by "naming" boycott violators in a newspaper and "ostracizing" them from the black community. The Court conceded that the black leaders sought "to persuade others to join the boycott through social pressure and the 'threat' of social ostracism," but speech of this kind, in the Court's view, did "not lose its protected character . . . simply because it may embarrass others or coerce them into action." Even if speech had a "coercive" influence over others, the Court concluded, it was nevertheless protected by the First Amendment (458 U.S. 886, 910–911 (1982)), at least if the means used to enforce the boycott were lawful and the "coercive speech" was part of an effort to effect political change.

Of course, once "coercive" or "intimidating" speech rises to the level of a "true threat" of violence, then it loses its constitutional protection and the government can punish it. The Court made this clear in *Virginia v. Black* (2003), a decision interpreting a Virginia statute that prohibited anyone from burning a cross "on the property of another, a highway or other public place" if done "with the intent of intimidating any person or group." The Court held that the statute was constitutional because intimidation "in the constitutionally proscribable sense of the word" is a type of "true threat."

> First Amendment permits Virginia to outlaw cross burning done with the intent to intimidate because burning a cross is a particularly virulent form of intimidation. Instead of prohibiting all intimidating messages, Virginia may choose to regulate this subset of intimidating messages in light of cross burning's long and pernicious history as a signal of impending violence. (538 U.S. 363 (2003))

In the end, the Court upheld Virginia's statute for two reasons: first, it did not prohibit "all intimidating messages," which would have rendered the statute "overbroad," but only a subset of them; second, the subset it chose to prohibit, cross burning with the intent to intimidate, was constitutional because history showed that it was "a particularly virulent form of intimidation," one indistinguishable, in the Court's view, from a "true threat."

Although the government can punish "hate speech" if it is a "true threat" or a "fighting word," these categories of unprotected speech are narrow in scope, implying that a large amount of "hate speech" is fully protected by the First Amendment. The Court has, therefore, implicitly endorsed the view of Justice Oliver Wendell Holmes, who in 1929 wrote that "if there is any principle of the Constitution that more imperatively calls for attachment than any other, it is the principle of free thought—not free thought for those who agree with us, but freedom for the thought that we hate" (*United States v. Schwimmer*, 279 U.S. 644, 654–655 (1929)). Holmes meant that free speech, as a constitutional principle, would have little to no significance if it only protected speech we agreed with and not speech that we hated. Of course, in today's world, a type of speech that is very much hated is "hate speech," but that does not change the principle. "Hate speech" is within the scope of freedom of speech and is protected if it does not qualify as a "true threat" or a "fighting word."

However, even if the government prohibits "hate speech" only that fits one of these two categories of unprotected speech, it must do so with a "narrowly drawn" statute that is "neutral" in character. The statute cannot, in other words, contain "overly broad" words or engage in "content" or "viewpoint" discrimination. The problem of "overbreadth" was the primary reason a federal district court in 1989 overturned a public university's speech code that prohibited any verbal behavior "that stigmatizes or victimizes" someone on the basis of his or her race, ethnicity, religion, sex, sexual orientation, and so on. The court found that "stigmatizes" and "victimizes" were too "vague" and "overbroad," sweeping into the prohibition expressive conduct that would not qualify either as "true threats" or as "fighting words" (*Doe v. University of Michigan*, 1989; also see *UWM Post v. University of Wisconsin*, 1991 and *Collin v. Smith*, 1978). The code was therefore "facially" invalid and, for that reason, could not be applied to any expressive conduct, including speech activities that were "true threats" or "fighting words."

The Supreme Court considered the constitutionality of prohibitions of "hate speech" in *R.A.V. v. City of St. Paul* (1992), a decision clearly upholding the principle that any such prohibition could be constitutional only if it was not "overbroad" and if it did not contain "content" or "viewpoint" distinctions. The decision concerned six teenagers who taped together broken chair legs in the form of a cross and burnt it on the yard of a black family. This conduct allegedly violated a municipal ordinance prohibiting anyone from placing

> on public or private property a symbol, object, appellation, characterization or graffiti, including, but not limited to, a burning cross or Nazi swastika, which one knows or has reasonable grounds to know

arouses anger, alarm or resentment in others on the basis of race, color, creed, religion or gender commits disorderly conduct and shall be guilty of a misdemeanor. (505 U.S. 377, 379 (1992))

The Minnesota Supreme Court tried to solve the "overbreadth" problem with the ordinance (the fact that it prohibited the use of symbols that aroused "anger, alarm, or resentment") by limiting this language to "fighting words." A four-justice minority of the Supreme Court concluded that this solution was inadequate and that the ordinance should be invalidated on the ground that it would "chill" protected speech and was "overbroad" for that reason.

The majority of the Court, however, opted to accept the Minnesota Supreme Court's interpretation of the ordinance, but nonetheless invalidated it because St. Paul was illicitly using both "content" and "viewpoint" distinctions to limit liability under the provision to "fighting words" that focused on "race, color, creed, religion, or gender" (see Q7). In effect, the city was "taking sides" in an ideological debate by favoring certain "fighting words" over others:

> The ordinance goes even beyond mere content discrimination, to actual viewpoint discrimination. Displays containing some words— odious racial epithets, for example—would be prohibited to proponents of all views. But "fighting words" that do not themselves invoke race, color, creed, religion, or gender—aspersions upon a person's mother, for example—would seemingly be usable *ad libitum* ["at one's pleasure"] in the placards of those arguing *in favor* of racial, color, etc., tolerance and equality, but could not be used by those speakers opponents. (*Id.* at 391)

According to the majority, St. Paul's ordinance was "facially" invalid on the ground of these "content" and "viewpoint" distinctions, and, therefore, it could not constitutionally be applied, not even to racial epithets that qualified as true "fighting words."

The majority, however, recognized that its rule prohibiting the use of "content" distinctions in regard to speech outside the First Amendment was "not absolute." First, the state could, for example, choose to prohibit only the most egregious forms of a type of unprotected speech, such as not all "true threats," but only "true threats" against the president's life, or not all obscenity, but only the obscenity "which is the most patently offensive *in its prurience*—i. e., that which involves the most lascivious displays of sexual activity." Second, a state could treat a "content-defined subclass of proscribable speech" differently because it "happens to be associated with particular 'secondary effects' of the speech," so that the prohibition is justified, not on the basis of its content, but rather on the basis of such harmful "secondary effects." For example, the government could subject adult-movie theaters to more regulations than other entertainment sites because they are often associated with crime and prostitution (see Q23). Third, the Court announced that it would permit the use of "content" or "viewpoint" distinctions in prohibitions of speech outside the First Amendment if "there is no realistic possibility that official suppression of ideas is afoot" (*Id.* at 387–388, 390). Of course, in the Court's view, none of these three exceptions applied to St. Paul's ordinance, and therefore, it violated freedom of speech.

Events following the Court's decision in June 1992 showed that what the teenagers did in *R.A.V.* was not protected by freedom of speech, but only from conviction based on an improperly worded prohibition. In October 1992, the U.S. attorney for the District of Minnesota charged the teenagers with three federal crimes, including conspiring to infringe upon the civil rights of the African American family, and a federal district court soon thereafter convicted them on all counts. Based largely on *R.A.V.*, the teenagers appealed their convictions, but the 8th Circuit Court of Appeals held that the federal law was very different from the St. Paul ordinance invalidated by the Supreme Court. For example, the federal law is "directed only at intentional threats, intimidation, and interference with federally guaranteed rights" and the relevant federal statutes "punish *any* threat or intimidation, or conspiracy to threaten or to intimidate . . . regardless of the viewpoint guiding the action" (*United States v. J.H.H.* 22 F.3d 821, 825 (1994)). Accordingly, the 8th Circuit Court concluded that the federal statutes were neither "overbroad" nor "content-based." Consistent with freedom of speech, the government can apply "narrowly drawn" and "neutral" statutes to punish anyone who burns a cross intending to "threaten" or "intimidate" someone with physical violence or who conspires with others to do so.

A question related to the constitutionality of punishing "hate speech" is the issue of whether the government can enhance penalties for those convicted of "hate crimes," that is, crimes in which the victim is selected on the basis of his or her "race, religion, color, disability, sexual orientation, national origin or ancestry." The Supreme Court addressed this question in *Wisconsin v. Mitchell* (1993), a case dealing with a young African American who, following a discussion of the film *Mississippi Burning*, yelled, "You all want to f*** somebody up? There goes a white boy;

go get him." Relying on Wisconsin's penalty-enhancement statute, the trial judge increased Mitchell's sentence from two to seven years' imprisonment, but on appeal the Wisconsin Supreme Court overturned the conviction, arguing that the government was engaged in "content" discrimination in violation of *R.A.V.* because it was enhancing punishment based on "the *reason* the defendant selected the victim, the *motive* behind the selection."

The Supreme Court reversed Wisconsin's high court, claiming that the government can enhance penalties for illegal "conduct" based on "motive" without running afoul of *R.A.V.* First, the "defendant's motive for committing the offense is one important factor" that "sentencing judges have [traditionally] considered . . . in determining what sentence to impose on a convicted defendant," so long as the judge does not take into consideration "a defendant's abstract beliefs." Second, increasing a defendant's sentence because of a "discriminatory" motive or reason is not qualitatively different from the role motive plays in state and federal antidiscrimination laws. For example, Title VII of the federal Civil Rights Act prohibits employers from discriminating against an employee because of his or her "race, color, religion, sex, or national origin." St. Paul's ordinance was "explicitly directed at expression (i.e., 'speech' or 'messages')", the Court concluded, while "the statute in this case is aimed at conduct unprotected by the First Amendment" (508 U.S. 476, 480, 482, 485, 487 (1993)).

In *Matal v. Tam* (2017), the Supreme Court addressed whether the federal government could refuse to register a trademark on the ground that it would "disparage . . . or bring . . . into contemp[t] or disrepute" any "persons, living or dead"—arguably a form of "hate speech." A trademark, in general, is a government-issued monopoly over the use of a "word name, symbol or design" to identify and distinguish one's goods and services from competitors. The applicants for a trademark in *Matal* were members of an Asian American dance-rock band who wanted to call themselves "The Slants" as a way "to 'reclaim' the term" (historically used as a slur against people of Asian descent) and "drain its denigrating force." Although trademarks are arguably a type of "commercial speech," and therefore, subject to a lower standard of constitutional review (see Q4), the Court, nonetheless, held that the federal law prohibiting "disparaging" trademarks violated freedom of speech.

The Court issued three opinions in *Matal*, with the result that its rationale for the decision is somewhat fragmented. However, a plurality of four justices echoed Holmes's 1929 understanding of the principle of free speech by remarking that the "proudest boast of our free speech jurisprudence is that we protect the freedom to express 'the thought that we hate.'" Four other justices came to the same result but opted to characterize their constitutional objection to the law, not in terms of the First Amendment's protection of "hate speech," but rather in terms of the First Amendment's command to the government not to engage in "content" or "viewpoint" discrimination. According to this plurality the fatal flaw of the law was that it permitted the government to register "a positive or benign" trademark, "but not a derogatory one." The law therefore "reflects the Government's disapproval of a subset of messages it finds offensive. This," in the plurality's view, "is the essence of viewpoint discrimination" (137 S. Ct. 1744, 1764, 1766 (2017)).

Despite the fragmented nature of the opinions it issued in *Matal*, the Court's unanimous decision was welcome to those, like The Slants, who wished to trademark a "derogatory" slur as a way to drain it of "its denigrating force," but perhaps less so for members of minority groups who simply object to the use of such names and symbols, such as those who object to the names and logos of the Cleveland "Indians" or the Washington "Redskins" (Conrad 2018). Nevertheless, the central holding of Matal was that such "disparaging" trademarks—arguably a form of "hate speech"—were nonetheless protected by the First Amendment even though commercial speech has less constitutional protection than other types of speech.

FURTHER READING

Citron, Danielle Keats. *Hate Crimes in Cyberspace.* Cambridge, MA: Harvard University Press, 2016.

Conrad, Mark. "*Matal v. Tam*—A Victory for the Slants, a Touchdown for the Redskins, But an Ambiguous Journey for the First Amendment and Trademark Law." *Cardozo Arts & Entertainment Law Journal* 36 (2018): 83–147.

Delgado, Richard. *Understanding Words That Wound.* New York: Routledge, 2004.

Gellman, Susan. "Sticks and Stones Can Put You in Jail, But Can Words Increase Your Sentence?" *UCLA Law Review* 39 (1991): 333–396.

Lewis, Anthony. *Freedom for the Thought That We Hate.* New York: Basic Books, 2007.

Neier, Aryeh. *Defending My Enemy: American Nazis, the Skokie Case, and the Risks to Freedom.* New York: E. P. Dutton, 1979.

Strossen, Nadine. "Regulating Speech on Campus: A Modest Proposal." *Duke Law Journal* (1990): 484–573.

Villasenor, John. "Views among College Students Regarding the First Amendment: Results from a New Survey." Brookings: Fisgov, September 18, 2017, available at https://www.brookings.edu/blog/fixgov/2017/09/18/views-among-college-students-regarding-the-first-amendment-results-from-a-new-survey/.

Waldron, Jeremy. *The Harm in Hate Speech*. Cambridge, MA: Harvard University Press, 2014.

Q17. IF "HARASSMENT" IS NEITHER A "TRUE THREAT" NOR A "FIGHTING WORD," CAN THE STATE NONETHELESS PUNISH SUCH EXPRESSIVE BEHAVIOR?

Answer: Yes. An intimidating type of "harassment," even if it is not literally a "true threat" or "fighting words," can be prohibited consistent with free speech if it unreasonably intrudes upon a person's privacy, such as the privacy of one's home, or if it is part of a "pattern" of abuse "directed" at a single individual or a small group of individuals.

The Facts: "Harassment" is distinguishable from "hate speech" on the ground that the latter can be targeted at a specific individual or group of individuals but need not be. For example, a racist could express a virulent form of racism, which would certainly qualify as "hate speech," but the audience's racial makeup and beliefs may be the same as the speaker's. In that case, hate speech is an expression of general ideology, but it is not directed at individuals of the hated class. In contrast, "harassment" is generally limited to expressions that target individuals or small groups of individuals. Accordingly, if a speaker denigrates an individual or group of individuals on the basis of race, sex, religion, or sexual orientation, then that expression may constitute both "hate speech" and "harassment." Of course, if a speaker engages in such expression for the purpose of placing the target in fear of life or limb, or for the purpose of provoking a fight, then it can, whether it is called "hate speech" or "harassment," qualify as a "true threat" or "fighting words," both of which are not protected by freedom of speech (see Q9 and Q10).

However, criminal harassment of an individual or a small group of individuals need not be based on race, sex, religion, or sexual orientation, the characteristics typically associated with "hate speech." A speaker can criminally "harass" someone for all sorts of reasons: from simple hatred to jealousy or sexual infatuation. The key is whether the speaker intentionally engages in expression (or other forms of symbolic conduct) that creates in the targeted individual a reasonable fear for personal safety or the safety of his or her family. Typically, but not always, a "pattern of conduct" is required before expressive conduct rises to the level of criminal harassment, at least if the conduct in question is not a literal "true threat" or the equivalent of such a threat, such as brandishing a firearm or a knife.

The requirement of a "pattern of conduct" is in part derived from what the Supreme Court has ruled regarding the power of government to protect "unwilling listeners" from "unwanted" speech. For example, in *Rowan v. U.S. Post Office Department* (1970), the Supreme Court upheld the right of an addressee to refuse to receive any further mail from a particular sender. The Court began its analysis with the observation that "the right of every person 'to be let alone' must be placed in the scales with the right of others to communicate." Since the Court traditionally has "respected the right of a householder to bar, by order or notice, solicitors, hawkers, and peddlers from his property," so also an addressee can give notice "that he wishes no further mailing from the mailer." The Court therefore "categorically rejected[ed] the argument that a vendor has a right, under the Constitution or otherwise, to send unwanted material into the home of another." Even if the "prohibition operates too impede the flow of even valid ideas," the vendor has no such right because "no one has a right to press even 'good' ideas on an unwilling recipient" (397 U.S. 728, 736–738 (1970)).

In *Hill v. Colorado* (2000), the Court extended the rights of the "unwilling recipient" by upholding a law that banned protestors, if within 100 feet of a healthcare facility, from approaching within 8 feet of an individual to hand out leaflets without the consent of the recipient. The purpose of the law was to prevent anti-abortion protestors from handing out their literature to patients entering abortion clinics. It was an attempt to balance a person's free speech right to protest and persuade others not to have an abortion against another patient's right to obtain medical counseling and treatment in an "unobstructed manner." The Court conceded that the protestors' "leafleting, sign displays, and oral communications are protected by the First Amendment" and that free speech "includes the right to persuade others to change their views." But the Court nonetheless upheld the aforementioned prohibition (a class 3 misdemeanor) on the ground that the "unwilling" recipient had no way to avoid offensive speech. Even if offensive speech is generally protected by freedom of speech, it "does not always embrace offensive speech that is so intrusive that the unwilling audience cannot avoid it" (530 U.S. 703, 715–716 (2000)).

This principle of the "unwilling recipient" explains why a "pattern of harassment" is not protected by freedom of speech even if there is no evidence of a literal "true threat" or its equivalent. If the "pattern" is so "intrusive" that the victim has no way to avoid it, then the speaker can be punished, especially if the "pattern" of expression causes the target to "reasonably" fear for his or her physical safety or the safety of loved ones. However, the Court has made it clear that offensive utterances that cause simple irritation or annoyance will not suffice for criminal harassment, especially if the expressive conduct in question is a single event that the recipient can avoid if he or she chooses to do so.

A borderline type of expressive conduct is "catcalling," which consists of sexually suggestive street comments, typically directed at women by men. A 2014 national study by the advocacy organization Stop Street Harassment finds that 51 percent of the female respondents reported experiencing "verbal street harassment" in their lifetimes, while only 6 percent of the men reported comparable experiences. In addition, 68 percent of the female respondents reported that, at the time of the incident, they were concerned that the incident would escalate, with an alarming number reporting that they were touched or brushed up against (20 percent), followed (20 percent), flashed (14 percent), or forced to do something of a sexual nature (9 percent) (Kearl 2014, 16). Even though the sponsor of this study is an advocacy organization, these statistics clearly establish a factual foundation for why women have valid apprehensions and concerns when they are verbally abused on the streets. At a minimum, these statistics expose the "mythical" nature of the claim that "catcalling" is a way to compliment a woman. It is particularly unsettling that, while 72 percent of Americans believe it is never appropriate to catcall, a 2014 study found that 45 percent of those under 30 years of age think that catcalls are complimentary in nature (Moore 2014).

Obviously, if such verbal abuse leads to physical touching or grabbing or if the expression constitutes a "threat" or "fighting words" or if the expression becomes unduly "intrusive" (e.g., if it is accompanied by following), then it could, depending on the totality of circumstances, constitute criminal harassment. However, the typical case of "catcalling" does not rise to the level of criminal harassment because the speaker does not engage in a "pattern of conduct." A female victim may subjectively feel that she is experiencing such a pattern, but that is usually the result of a series of different men at different times and locations directing remarks at her that have, in varying degrees, a sexual connotation or innuendo. All of the remarks may be "unwanted," but it is less clear whether they are "offensive" ("Have a nice day!" "What's up beautiful?" "Nice!" "Yeah

Baby!") or whether they "intrude" upon a woman's right "to be let alone" if the incident occurs on a public street and the speaker makes only a single comment. However, certain men repeatedly make such comments to any number of women they daily encounter on the street, while certain women endure such comments on a daily or hourly basis, making them feel uncomfortable and, in certain cases, unsafe. For this reason, there are efforts in various states to make egregious forms of "catcalling" (those that resemble "threats," "fighting words," or unduly "intrusive" behavior) a type of criminal harassment (Arndt 2018), but at this point in time much of what falls under the term "catcalling" is presumably protected by freedom of speech. Because the Supreme Court has yet to address the issue, a precise line cannot be drawn between "catcalling" that is protected by freedom of speech and criminal harassment.

An example of a type of "harassment" not protected by freedom of speech is "stalking," a term that refers to someone who repeatedly follows another person, shows up at their doorstep or across the street from their home, calls them by phone, or writes them obscure letters or messages. Obviously, "catcalling" could evolve into "stalking" and, at that point, it would not be protected by freedom of speech. The key would be whether the "catcalling" was part of a "pattern of conduct" from which a jury could reasonably infer that the stalker's intent was to cause the victim fear and distress and that the target had a reasonable concern for his or her welfare. Such cases of "stalking" often involve people who know each other intimately, whether they are married, separated, divorced, or living together. However, an intimate connection between the "stalker" and the "stalked" is not necessary. "Stalkers" can target people they have "catcalled" on the street, fellow employees, distant relatives, even complete strangers (including celebrities).

In many cases of harassment, the victim is able, before a criminal prosecution is brought, to get a restraining order from a judge compelling the stalker to maintain a reasonable distance, usually somewhere between 100 and 150 yards. The specific criteria for such restraining orders vary from state to state, but generally the victim must show, as in a criminal prosecution, how the stalker's "pattern of conduct" establishes a reasonable basis for the victim's fear or apprehension, whether the evidence relates to the stalker's proneness to violence or his or her mental illness or instability. However, since the "pattern of conduct" targets an "unwilling recipient," it is reasonable for judges to apply these criteria with some degree of flexibility, depending on the unique facts of each case. After all, if an "unwilling recipient" can refuse a "good" communication in the privacy of the home, as the Supreme Court said in *Rowan*, and an "offensive" communication on the street if it is "intrusive," as the Court said in *Hill*, then *a fortiori* an "unwilling recipient" should be able to stop a targeted "pattern of communications" by a violent-prone or mentally disturbed individual if it raises the victim's "apprehension" or "distress," even if the pattern does not literally contain a "true threat" or a "fighting word."

A relatively new form of criminal harassment is "cyber-stalking" or "cyberbullying" on the Internet. The federal government enacted an interstate stalking law in 1996, but it limited criminal liability to those who transmit a threat to kidnap or injure a person through interstate or foreign commerce (which would include Internet communications). States have either enacted separate cyber-stalking statutes or have applied general criminal harassment provisions to cyber-communications. While a "threat" directed at a specific individual, such as in an e-mail, is outside constitutional protection if the threat is real and credible, it is more doubtful whether a targeted insult communicated by e-mail could ever qualify as a "fighting word" given the fact that there is no face-to-face encounter. Moreover, given the anonymity of the Internet, it may be difficult, and perhaps too expensive, to investigate and prosecute cases of this type, unless they are especially egregious.

The more general problem, however, is what to do with "cyber-stalking" consisting of communications that are not sent "to" the victim, but are instead "about" the victim and posted on social media sites for the world to see. Such postings can reveal true but private information about a person, including home addresses, e-mail addresses, phone numbers, social security numbers, employment information, pregnancy status, infidelity, sexual orientation, and photos of all types, including ones of a sexual nature. It is not clear how such communications "target" the victim, which is typically required in cases of criminal harassment, or how it constitutes (if the information "about" the victim is contained in a single posting) a "pattern" or "course" of conduct, which is typically required in cases of "stalking." Moreover, the Supreme Court has never exempted private information about other persons from First Amendment protection (see Q11). It is, therefore, unclear whether the nature of Internet communications, especially on social media sites, requires that "cyber-stalking" should be interpreted more broadly than "stalking" in the physical world. Does the First Amendment permit the imposition of criminal liability on speakers who post on the Internet private information that has little or no social or political value, such as nude photos or tapes of intimate conversations, if their purpose is to "annoy" or "torment" someone? The law is uncertain because the Supreme Court has so far been silent on the issue, but it is fairly clear that the posting of such private information would be constitutionally protected from criminal liability if it was related to an issue of public concern, for example, private information relevant to an assessment of the character of a public official or figure.

FURTHER READING

Arndt, Donja. "Street Harassment: The Need for Criminal Remedies." *Hastings Women's Law Journal* 81 (2018): 81–100.

Citron, Danielle Keats. *Hate Crimes in Cyberspace*. Cambridge, MA: Harvard University Press, Reprint edition, 2016.

Kearl, Holly. "Unsafe and Harassed in Public Spaces: A National Street Harassment Report." Reston, Virginia: Stop Street Harassment, 2014, available at http://www.stopstreetharassment.org/wp-content/uploads/2012/08/2014-National-SSH-Street-Harassment-Report.pdf.

Moore, Peter. "Catcalling: Never OK and Not a Compliment." *YouGov*, August, 15, 2014, available at https://today.yougov.com/topics/lifestyle/articles-reports/2014/08/15/catcalling.

Nguyen, Andy. "Man Who Stalked Sandra Bullock Receives Probation and 10-Year Restraining Order." *Los Angeles Times*, May 24, 2017, available at http://www.latimes.com/socal/glendale-news-press/news/tn-gnp-me-corbett-pleads-20170524-story.html.

Singh, Anita. "Justin Timberlake Wins Restraining Order against Female Stalker." *The Telegraph*, November 10, 2009, available at https://www.telegraph.co.uk/news/celebritynews/6537128/Justin-Timberlake-wins-restraining-order-against-female-stalker.html.

Volokh, Eugene. "One-to-One Speech vs. One-to-Many Speech, Criminal Harassment Laws, and 'Cyberstalking.'" *Northwestern University Law Review* 107 (2013): 731–794.

Q18. CAN AN EMPLOYER BE SUBJECT TO CIVIL LIABILITY OR AN EMPLOYEE SANCTIONED FOR EXPRESSIVE CONDUCT THAT DOES NOT CONSTITUTE CRIMINAL HARASSMENT, BUT CREATES A "HOSTILE" OR "OFFENSIVE" WORK ENVIRONMENT?

Answer: Yes. An employer can be subject to civil liability, and an employee can be sanctioned with measures including termination of employment, for expressive conduct that creates a "hostile" or "offensive" work environment.

The Facts: Civil liability for harassment in the workplace is based on Title VII of the Civil Rights Act of 1964, which prohibits employers from discriminating against employees on the basis of race, color, religion, sex (including sexual orientation), or national origin. In 1967, Congress added "age" to the list of prohibited categories followed by individuals with disabilities in 1990. The Supreme Court established a link between workplace "harassment" and "discrimination" in *Meritor Savings Bank v. Vinson* (1986). In this decision, the Court distinguished between discrimination based on unequal treatment in terms of "tangible benefits," such as amounts of compensation, and discrimination based on "harassment," which involved either the exchange of tangible benefits for sexual favors (quid pro quo harassment) or the creation of an "intimidating, hostile, or offensive working environment" (hostile-work-environment harassment). A clear implication of the decision was that employee speech in the workplace could be conditionally prohibited consistent with freedom of speech, depending on whether it constituted "discrimination," that is, whether the expression created an "intimidating, hostile, or offensive working environment" based on one of Title VII's prohibited categories.

While only an employer's "supervisors" can engage in quid pro quo harassment because only they have control over "tangible job benefits," a "hostile work environment" can result from the expressive conduct of "supervisors," "managers," or "coworkers." In trying to draw a line between freedom of speech and "harassment" involving a "hostile" or "offensive" workplace environment, the Court in *Meritor* insisted that "not all workplace conduct that may be described as harassment" is a sufficient basis to impose civil liability on the employer. The "harassment" must be "sufficiently severe or pervasive" to "alter the conditions of [the victim's] employment and create an abusive working environment." And even if the "harassment" was "severe" or "pervasive," the Court argued in *Meritor* that it was wrong to "impose absolute liability on employers for the acts of their supervisors, regardless of the circumstances of a particular case." The employer also had to be found "at fault" (or negligent) before civil liability could be properly imposed. This rule applied equally to all types of harassment based on the categories of discrimination prohibited by Title VII (477 U.S. 57, 63–67, 73 (1986)).

In 1998, the Court decided two companion cases that significantly revised the legal framework for deciding the civil liability of employers for "work environment" harassment. One of the cases, *Faragher v. City of Boca Raton*, involved an ocean lifeguard who claimed that her two immediate "supervisors" created a "sexual hostile atmosphere" at the beach by repeatedly subjecting her "and other female lifeguards to 'uninvited and offensive touching,' by making lewd remarks, by speaking of women in offensive terms," and by telling her, "Date me or clean the toilets for a year" (524 U.S. 775, 780 (1998)). The other case, *Burlington Industries Inc. v. Ellerth*, involved a female employee in Chicago who claimed that a male manager in New York who was not her immediate supervisor told her, "you know, Kim, I could make your life very hard or very easy at Burlington." At another time, after she received a promotion, the same manager said, "you're gonna be out there with men who work in factories, and they certainly like women with pretty butts/legs." Lastly, after he denied her the use of a logo, he observed, "are you wearing shorter skirts yet, Kim, because it would make your job a whole heck of a lot easier" (524 U.S. 742, 747–748 (1998)).

In *Faragher*, the Court held that expressions of this sort were unlawful harassment only if they were "both objectively and subjectively offensive, one that a reasonable person would find hostile or abusive, and one that the victim in fact did perceive to be so." In making such a determination, courts must take into account "all the circumstances," including "the frequency of the discriminatory conduct; its severity; whether physically threatening or humiliating, or a mere offensive utterance; and whether it unreasonably interferes with an employee's work performance." For this reason, a supervisor's utterance of an offensive ethnic or racial epithet "would not sufficiently alter terms and conditions of employment to violate Title VII." In the same vein, the Court indicated that "simple teasing," "offhand comments," and "isolated incidents (unless extremely serious)" do not constitute "harassment." The expressive conduct "must be *extreme* to amount to a change in the terms and conditions of employment" (*Id.* at 787–788, emphasis added). Applying these criteria, the Court upheld the findings in both cases that the expressive conduct altered the conditions of employment and, for that reason, created an illegal "hostile" or "offensive" work environment.

To decide whether an employer should be held civilly liable for such a "hostile" or "offensive," work environment, the Court created a three-tier legal framework that it succinctly summarized in both *Faragher* and *Ellerth*:

> An employer is subject to vicarious liability [liability without fault] to a victimized employee for an actionable hostile environment created by a supervisor with immediate (or successively higher) authority over the employee. When no tangible employment action is taken [which means that the complaining party did not suffer a tangible work detriment], a defending employer may raise an affirmative

defense to liability or damages, subject to proof by a preponderance of the evidence. The defense comprise two necessary elements: (a) that the employer exercised reasonable care to prevent and correct promptly any sexual harassing behavior, and (b) that the plaintiff employee unreasonably failed to take advantage of any preventive or corrective opportunities provided by the employer or to avoid harm otherwise. While proof that an employer had promulgated an antiharassment policy with complaint procedure is not necessary in every instance as a matter of law, the need for a stated policy suitable to the employment circumstances may appropriately be addressed in any case when litigating the first element of the defense. And while proof that an employee failed to fulfill the corresponding obligation of reasonable care to avoid harm is not limited to showing an unreasonable failure to use any complaint procedure provided by the employer, a demonstration of such failure will normally suffice to satisfy the employer's burden under the second element of the defense. No affirmative defense is available however, when the supervisor's harassment culminates in a tangible employment action, such as discharge, demotion, or undesirable reassignment. (*Faragher* at 807–808; *Ellerth* at 765)

Three points of this holding deserve emphasis. First, in cases where an employer can invoke the affirmative defense (supervisory harassment but no tangible job detriment), the fact that an employer did not have a complaint procedure is relevant to whether it acted reasonably, but the lack of such a procedure does not, by itself, establish the employer's legal negligence. Second, a victim's failure to take advantage of the company's "preventive or corrective opportunities" is not the only way for an employer to show that the employee acted "unreasonably," but demonstration of such a failure will "normally suffice" to establish the victim's negligence. Third, the burden of proof shifts to the victim if coworkers create the "hostile work environment." The victim must then prove that the company was negligent, rather than the company having the burden of showing that both the victim was negligent and the company was not.

Applying these standards of liability in *Faragher*, the Court held that the city of Boca Raton was civilly liable because it had not disseminated its sexual harassment policy to all of its employees, had not included within its policy a means by which victims could bypass their "harassing supervisors" if they filed a complaint, and, finally, had not monitored the activities of its "supervisors" (*Faragher* at 808–810). In contrast, the Court remanded *Ellerth* to the district court for further proceedings because Burlington Industries had not been given an opportunity to establish that it had taken "reasonable care" to prevent and correct sexually harassing behavior and that Ellerth had "unreasonably" not taken advantage of opportunities to rectify her situation (*Ellerth* at 766). The two decisions together strongly suggested that employers could shield themselves from all types of "harassment" lawsuits by employees who experienced a "hostile" or "offensive" work environment, but did not suffer any tangible job loss, if they (1) established fair and adequate procedures for employees to file harassment complaints and (2) took steps to ensure that all employees were made aware of the employer's harassment policies and procedures.

In "hostile work environment" lawsuits, what is important to realize, apart from the principles governing the civil liability of the employer, is that these cases imply that the employer is under a legal obligation to stop the harassment, whether it is harassment by a "supervisor," "manager," or "coworker." The employer has an obligation to stop such harassment, regardless of whether the victim has filed a complaint or initiated a lawsuit. Accordingly, since the Court upheld findings that both Faragher's and Ellerth's work environments involved unlawful discrimination, the respective employers could have fired the "supervisors" if they had declined to stop their harassing behavior. It would not matter that the expressive conduct was merely "offensive" in character, far removed from what would qualify as criminal harassment. Accordingly, free speech in the workplace is significantly more circumscribed than on a public street. As Q17 explains, "catcalling" on the street does not typically constitute criminal harassment, but an employer has ample incentive (fear of civil liability) to terminate the employment of any employee who engages in similar types of expression.

Unfortunately, there is not much evidence that the Court's three-tier approach to "hostile work environment" harassment has substantially eliminated "hostile work environment" harassment from the workplace. A 2016 study by the U.S Equal Employment Opportunity Commission (EEOC) reported that approximately 28,000 of the 90,000 discrimination complaints it received in 2015 included a claim of harassment, of which approximately 45 percent were on the basis of sex and 35 percent on race. In terms of sexual harassment, the report also claims that "anywhere from 25 % to 85% of women [surveyed] report having experienced sexual harassment in the workplace," depending on whether the survey left the term "harassment" undefined or if it referenced specific "sexually-based behaviors," such as "unwanted sexual attention" (60 percent of women report "yes") or the use of crude sexist terminology (also 60 percent) (EEOC 2017). These statistics suggest that workplace harassment is still a huge problem.

The rise of the Me Too Movement in late 2017 raised public awareness of the problem of sexual harassment in the workplace across American society (Almukhtar et al. 2018). Although the movement has focused to some extent on sexual assaults, it also has encouraged women across society to voice their concerns about workplace harassment. For example, professional cheerleaders have recently complained that their jobs require them to interact with fans, whether at games or at other promotional events, at which point they are often subjected to offensive sexual comments, potentially creating a "hostile work environment" (Macur 2018). How should these complaints be evaluated? Can sexist comments directed at cheerleaders by fans at NFL events create a "hostile" or "offensive" work environment? Should team owners be liable for the expressive conduct of fans? Is sexual harassment simply "part of the job" of being a cheerleader for a professional team? Courts are only beginning to struggle with these kinds of questions.

FURTHER READING

Almukhtar, Sarah, Gold, Michael, and Buchanan, Larry. "After Weinstein: 71 Men Accused of Sexual Misconduct and Their Fall from Power." *The New York Times*, February 8, 2018, available at https://www.nytimes.com/interactive/2017/11/10/us/men-accused-sexual-misconduct-weinstein.html.

EEOC, U.S Equal Opportunity Commission. "Charges Alleging Sex-Based Harassment: FY 2010–2017," available at https://www.eeoc.gov/eeoc/statistics/enforcement/sexual_harassment_new.cfm.

Feldblum, Chai R. and Lipnic, Victoria A. "Select Task Force on the Study of Harassment in the Workplace." Washington, DC: U.S. Equal Employment Opportunity Commission, 2016, available at https://www.eeoc.gov/eeoc/task_force/harassment/upload/report.pdf.

Hwang, Jamie. "Ex-Dolphins Cheerleader Files Complaint Claiming Religious and Gender Discrimination." *American Bar Association Journal* (April 20, 2018), available at http://www.abajournal.com/news/article/ex-dolphins_cheerleader_files_complaint_claiming_religious_and_gender_discr.

MacKinnon, Catherine. *Sexual Harassment of Working Women: A Case of Sex Discrimination*. New Haven, CT: Yale University Press, 1979.

Macur, Juliet, and Branch, John. "Pro Cheerleaders Say Groping and Sexual Harassment Part of the Job." *The New York Times*, April 10,

2018, available at https://www.nytimes.com/2018/04/10/sports/cheer leaders-nfl.html.

Nunez, Kate Webber. "Toxic Cultures Require a Stronger Cure: The Lessons of Reforming Sexual Harassment Law." *Penn State Law Review* 122 (2018): 463–517.

Phillips, Edward G. and Morrow, Brandon L. "The Law at Work: The Faragher-Ellerth Framework in the MeToo Era." *Tennessee Bar Journal* 54 (2018): 26–29.

Skrentny, John D. *After Civil Rights: Racial Realism in the New American Workplace*. Princeton, NJ: Princeton University Press, 2015.

Thomas, Gillian. *Because of Sex: One Law, Ten Cases, and Fifty Years That Changed American Women's Lives at Work*. New York: Picador, reprint edition, 2017.

Q19. CAN THE FEDERAL GOVERNMENT WITHDRAW FINANCIAL ASSISTANCE FROM INSTITUTIONS OF HIGHER EDUCATION IF THEY FAIL TO STOP STUDENTS FROM ENGAGING IN "HARASSMENT" OF OTHER STUDENTS BASED ON RACE, COLOR, NATIONAL ORIGIN, OR SEX?

Answer: Yes, but the First Amendment also requires public institutions of higher education to respect freedom of speech, and private institutions arguably must respect freedom of speech based on the contractual commitments they have made to their students.

The Facts: Title VI of the Civil Rights Act of 1964 broadened the federal prohibition of discrimination. It stated that no person in the United States shall, on the ground of race, color, or national origin, be "excluded from participation in, be denied the benefits of, or be subject to discrimination under any program or activity receiving Federal financial assistance." Moreover, in 1972, Congress enacted Title IX, which added sex discrimination to the preceding list of prohibited types of discrimination. One important consequence of these two laws was that all colleges and universities that receive federal funds, and the vast majority of them do receive such assistance in the form of loans or grants, had to ensure that no student was denied the "equal benefits" of an education because he or she was subjected to "harassment" that constituted "discrimination" on the basis of race, color, national origin, or sex (including sexual orientation in some states).

While Title VII covered employee-to-employee harassment (including faculty-to-faculty), Titles VI and IX extended coverage to faculty-to-student, staff-to-student, and student-to-student harassment. Regarding faculty-student harassment, a recent study has reported that harassment of this type typically involves graduate students, that 1 in 10 female graduate students at major research universities say that they have been sexually harassed by a faculty member, that the harassment typically consists of unwanted sexual contact, "ranging from groping to sexual assault to domestic abuse-like behaviors," and that "more than half (53%) of cases involved professors allegedly engaged in serial sexual harassment" (Cantalupo and Kidder 2018, 1–2). Of course, physical sexual harassment of this type is not protected by freedom of speech. To ensure equal access to the "benefits" they provide, educational institutions can impose sanctions on faculty or staff for such conduct, including termination of employment and criminal prosecution in the more serious cases, without violating freedom of speech.

Although it is hardly typical behavior, student-to-student harassment, including sexual harassment, is also a problem confronting today's universities and colleges. To address this issue, many public universities in the 1980s adopted "hate-speech codes" that prohibited any expression that creates a "hostile" or "demeaning" educational environment by "stigmatizing" an individual on the basis of race, color, national origin, or sex. However, federal courts quickly invalidated these broad prohibitions on the ground that they violated the free-speech rights of the students (see Q16). The question, therefore, became whether a public university or college could prohibit not general expressions of "hate speech" but rather student expressions that "harassed" another student or set of students on the basis of a prohibited category. More so than general expressions of "hate speech," such targeted harassment arguably violated Title VI or Title IX by "excluding" a student from participation in a college or university activity, or by "denying" a student the benefit of an education, or by "subjecting" the student to "discrimination" in the form of "harassment," comparable to the way "harassment" can constitute "discrimination" in the workplace (see Q18). For these reasons, it seemed plausible that public universities and colleges had a legal obligation to enact policies that prohibited such targeted harassment, but it was not clear how this obligation could be fulfilled without violating freedom of speech.

Even though it is a private university, Stanford University confronted this dilemma in 1990 because California law prohibited private universities from violating freedom of speech. Stanford responded with a prohibition of "harassment by personal vilification," which was defined as follows:

> Speech or other expression constitutes harassment by personal vilification if it: (a) is intended to insult or stigmatize an individual or a small group of individuals on the basis of their sex, race, color, handicap, religion, sexual orientation, or national and ethnic origin; and (b) is addressed directly to the individual or individuals whom it insults or stigmatizes; and (c) makes use of insulting or "fighting" words or non-verbal symbols. (Fundamental Standard)

The provision defined "insulting" or "fighting" words as those "which by their very utterance inflict injury or tend to incite to an immediate breach of the peace, and which are commonly understood to convey direct and visceral hatred or contempt for human beings on the basis of their sex, race, color, handicap, religion, sexual orientation, or national and ethnic origin."

Despite Stanford's decision to enact a purportedly narrow prohibition of "harassment by personal vilification," rather a general prohibition of "hate-speech," a Santa Clara County judge invalidated it, ruling that it was both overbroad and unconstitutionally content-based. Stanford's harassment policy was overbroad, in the Court's view, because it prohibited "words which will not only cause people to react violently, but also cause them to feel insulted or stigmatized" or "words that 'are commonly understood to convey' hatred and contempt on the basis of race, religion, etc." However, even if the policy was limited to true "fighting words," the Court, citing the Supreme Court's decision in *R.A.V. v. City of St. Paul* (1992) (see Q16), held that it would still violate freedom of speech because it was "an impermissible content-based regulation," one that "singles out a limited type of proscribable expression from a broad range of proscribable expression." For example, fighting words "directed toward race and the like are punishable, yet those directed toward political affiliation . . . are not" (*Corry v. Stanford*, 1995).

General discriminatory harassment policies at public universities met the same fate as Stanford's "harassment by personal vilification" policy during the 1990s. For example, in *Dambrot v. Central Michigan University* (1995), the 6th Circuit Court reviewed Central Michigan University's (CMU) Plan for Affirmative Action, which defined racial and ethnic harassment as follows:

> Any intentional, unintentional, physical, verbal, or nonverbal behavior that subjects an individual to an intimidating, hostile,

or offensive education, employment or living environment by . . . (c) demeaning or slurring individuals through . . . written literature because of their racial or ethnic affiliation; or (d) using symbols, [epithets] or slogans that infer negative connotations about the individual's racial or ethnic affiliation.

The 6th Circuit Court had little trouble finding CMU's harassment policy to be overbroad: "The language of this policy is sweeping and seemingly drafted to include as much and as many types of conduct as possible," including, for example, "unintentional" behavior, expressions that are "offensive," "demeaning," or "slurring," and slogans that have "negative connotations." "On its face," the Court concluded, "the policy reaches 'a substantial amount of constitutionally protected speech'" (55 F3d 1177, 1182 (1995)).

In addition, the 6th Circuit Court held that the policy violated freedom of speech because it was content-based since it required the university "to assess the racial and ethnic content of the speech." A major problem, according to the court, was that school officials could interpret the policy to punish "fighting words used against persons because of their racial or ethnic affiliation," but not "fighting words which could be hurled in response to a race or ethnic-based attack" (*Id.* at 1184–1185).

More than a decade later, the 3rd Circuit Court in *Dejohn v. Temple University* (2008) reviewed Temple's sexual harassment policy, which consisted of the following key language:

All forms of sexual harassment are prohibited, including the following: an unwelcome sexual advance, request for sexual favors, or other expressive, visual or physical conduct of a sexual or gender-motivated nature when . . . (c) such conduct has the purpose or effect of unreasonably interfering with an individual's work, educational performance, or status; or (d) such conduct has the purpose or effect of creating an intimidating, hostile, or offensive environment. (537 F.3d 301, 316 (2008))

The court began by noting that the policy punished a student based on motives, regardless of whether "these motives and actions had their intended effect." Second, "the policy's use of 'hostile,' 'offensive,' and 'gender-motivated' is, on its face, sufficiently broad and subjective that they 'could conceivably be applied to cover any speech' of a 'gender-motivated' nature 'the content of which offends someone,' including 'core' political and religious speech, such as gender politics and sexual morality."

Third, without a requirement "that the expressive conduct objectively and subjectively creates a hostile environment or substantially interferes with an individual's work," the policy "provides no shelter for core protected speech." The Court concluded that Temple's harassment policy was unconstitutionally overbroad unless it was "qualified with a standard akin to a severe or pervasive requirement," the standard required by Title VII for workplace harassment (*Id.* at 317–318, 319; also see *McCauley v. University of the Virgin Islands*, 2010).

Private universities and colleges are not legally obliged to respect freedom of speech because constitutional rights, including the right of free speech, only limit what government can lawfully do. In fact, the right of association, a key component of the First Amendment, grants private institutions of higher education the freedom to commit themselves to values other than freedom of speech (Sarabyn 2010). As long as the school is clear about the restrictions it imposes on speech, students who attend that institution have voluntarily accepted the restrictions and there is no violation of freedom of speech. However, the situation is arguably different if a school, in its mission statement, course catalogue, or student handbook, commits itself to free speech, as the vast majority of them do. Some courts have concluded that such explicit commitments create an enforceable contract between the school and its students (see, for example, *Havlik v. Johnson & Wales University*, 2007). Other courts have refused to characterize a school's expressed commitments to freedom of speech as constituting a contractual relationship with students on the ground that the university or college could unilaterally alter the commitments at any time (see, for example, *Pacella v. Tufts University School of Dental Medicine*, 1999). The law, therefore, remains unsettled regarding whether private universities and colleges must legally respect freedom of speech if they publicly proclaim that they will do so. However, there is no question that such schools can, if they wish, publicly implement policies that ensure their students have "equal access" to an education notwithstanding the constitutional right of free speech.

Public universities and colleges, of course, must respect both freedom of speech and, if they receive federal assistance, the requirements of Title IX, which means they cannot tolerate student-to-student harassment that indisputably constitutes discrimination, such as physical sexual assaults (see *Davis v. Monroe County Board of Education*, 526 U.S. 629 (1999)). But here too it is unsettled what the law specifically requires, in part because the Supreme Court has not yet decided a case that clearly reconciles the legal duties public universities and colleges have under Titles VI and IX with their constitutional duty to respect freedom of speech. One reason why the Court has not confronted this question is because there is broad consensus among lower federal courts that the harassment policies of public universities and colleges have leaned too far in the direction of ensuring equal student-access to their educational programs and activities and away from protecting the free-speech rights of their students. Another reason is that students who have been expelled for their expressive behavior, such as the two Sigma Alpha Epsilon (SAE) students from the University of Oklahoma who were expelled in 2014 for leading a racist chant on a bus or the female student at the University of Alabama who was expelled in 2018 for posting videos to Instagram that contained racial slurs, do not seek to protect their First Amendment rights through litigation, perhaps because they are ashamed of their behavior or because litigation is a time-consuming and expensive process (Bauer-Wolf 2018). In any case, one clear implication of the preceding decisions is that "harassing" verbal behavior does not qualify as "discrimination" under Title VI or Title IX unless it is objectively "severe" or "pervasive," which obviously excludes "isolated" and "offhand" offensive remarks. Until public colleges and universities begin to limit their harassment policies to these types of "extreme" student behaviors, there is little reason for the Supreme Court to get involved because lower federal courts have consistently invalidated such expansive harassment policies as violations of freedom of speech.

FURTHER READING

Bauer-Wolf, Jeremy. "Kicked Out for Racism." *Inside Higher Ed* (January 23, 2018), https://www.insidehighered.com/news/2018/01/23/university-alabama-may-have-violated-first-amendment-kicking-out-racist-student.

Cantalupo, Nancy Chi and Kidder, William C. "A Systematic Look at a Serial Problem: Sexual Harassment of Students by University Faculty." Volume 2018 *Utah Law Review* (2018), available at https://dc.law.utah.edu/ulr/vol2018/iss3/.

Casper, Gerhard. *The Winds of Freedom: Challenges to the University*. New Haven, CT: Yale University Press, 2014, Chapter 4.

Chemerinsky, Erwin. "Unpleasant Speech on Campus, Even Hate Speech, Is a First Amendment Issue." *William and Mary Bill of Rights Journal* 17 (2009): 765–772.

Corry v. Stanford, No. 740309 (Cal. Super. Ct. Santa Clara Co. 1995), available at https://web.archive.org/web/20050419211842/http://www.ithaca.edu/faculty/cduncan/265/corryvstanford.htm.

FIRE, Foundation for Individual Rights in Education. "State of the Law: Speech Codes," available at https://www.thefire.org/in-court/state-of-the-law-speech-codes/.

"Fundamental Standard Interpretation: Free Expression and Discriminatory Harassment." Stanford University, adopted June 1990, with Comments, available at https://web.stanford.edu/class/symsys255/Grey-Interpretation.pdf.

Grey, Thomas. "How to Write a Speech Code without Really Trying: Reflections on the Stanford Experience." *U.C. Davis Law Review* 29 (1996): 891–956.

MacKinnon, Catherine and Siegal, Reva B., eds. *Directions in Sexual Harassment Law*. New Haven, CT: Yale University Press, 2012.

Papandrea, Mary-Rose. "The Free Speech Rights of University Students." *Minnesota Law Review* 101 (2017): 1801–1861.

Sarabyn, Kelly. "Free Speech at Private Universities." *Journal of Law and Education* 39 (2010): 145–182.

Stone, Geoffrey. "Free Speech on Campus: A Report from the University Faculty Committee." University of Chicago, January 6, 2015, available at https://www.law.uchicago.edu/news/free-speech-campus-report-university-faculty-committee.

Tsesis, Alexander. "Campus Speech and Harassment." *Minnesota Law Review* 101 (2017): 1863–1917.

Q20. CAN THE STATE IMPOSE CRIMINAL OR CIVIL LIABILITY ON A SPEAKER WHO PUBLISHES PRIVATE INFORMATION ABOUT SOMEONE ELSE, PERHAPS FOR THE PURPOSE OF "HARASSING" HIM OR HER?

Answer: No. The state cannot generally impose criminal or civil liability on a speaker who publishes private information about a person—at least if the information is "a matter of public concern."

The Facts: The practice of "doxing"—the publication of a person's private information on the Internet—has recently raised, in dramatic fashion, the general question of the relationship between freedom of speech and private information. The Supreme Court first confronted the general issue of free speech and privacy in *Time, Inc. v. Hill* (1967). The case concerned a civil lawsuit against *Life Magazine* based on a 1955 article about a new Broadway play titled *The Desperate Hours*, which portrayed how

James Hill and his family were held hostage in their home outside Philadelphia by three escaped convicts for 19 hours in 1952. Both the article
and the play falsely characterized the family's experience by claiming that
the convicts beat up Mr. Hill and his son and subjected his daughter to
verbal sexual assaults. Although the article in *Life* was false, Hill could
not recover through a libel action because the article was not defamatory.
It instead depicted him acting heroically in a crisis. But even if the article was flattering, it placed unwanted public attention on his family and
therefore, he claimed, violated his right to privacy.

The majority of the Court concluded that freedom of speech barred
Hill's privacy lawsuit. Privacy was not a basis for recovery, in the Court's
view, since Hill was "a newsworthy person 'substantially without a right
to privacy' insofar as his hostage experience was involved." The decision
implied that a person could involuntarily lose rights of privacy by inad-
vertently becoming a "newsworthy" person. Neither was the fictionalized
nature of the account a basis for liability, the Court reasoned, because
"the constitutional protections for speech and press preclude . . . [liabil-
ity] to redress false reports of matters of public interest in the absence
of proof that the defendant published the report with knowledge of its
falsity or in reckless disregard of the truth," that is, unless the report met
the "malice standard" the Court had applied to libel in *New York Times v.
Sullivan* (1964) (see Q11). This rule, the Court made clear, was not confined to "political expression or comment on public affairs." Negligently
false accounts of "newsworthy persons," even if they were "private citizens," not "public officials" or "public figures," were protected by freedom
of speech so long as they were not defamatory (injurious to a person's reputation). "Exposure of the self to others in varying degrees," the majority
concluded, "is a concomitant of life in a civilized community. The risk
of this exposure is an essential incident of life in a society which places
a primary value on freedom of speech and of press" (385 U.S. 374, 386,
387–388 (1967)). Accordingly, the Court remanded the case, directing
that a jury would have to determine whether *Life Magazine* "knew" that
its article was false or published it with "reckless disregard" of its truth or
falsity.

In *Cox Broadcasting Company v. Cohn* (1975), the Court considered
whether the rule mentioned earlier should be applied to a television station that broadcast the name of a dead rape victim that a reporter had
obtained from the criminal indictment shown to him in the courtroom.
The victim's father filed a civil lawsuit against the television station,
claiming that the broadcast of his daughter's name violated his right of
privacy. The father noted that a Georgia statute made it a misdemeanor

for anyone to publish or broadcast the name or identity of a rape victim, which in his view constituted "an authoritative declaration of state policy that the name of a rape victim was not a matter of public concern." A six-justice majority recognized that there was "a zone of privacy surrounding every individual, a zone within which the State may protect him from intrusion by the press, with all its attendant publicity," but nonetheless endorsed two propositions: first, consistent with *Hill*, if the published private material was "a matter of public interest," civil liability required "knowing" or "reckless" falsehoods; second, *Hill* "saved the question whether truthful publication of very private matters unrelated to public affairs could be constitutionally proscribed" (420 U.S. 469, 475, 489, 490–491 (1975)).

Given this legal background, the Court reasoned that it should proceed with "caution," narrowing its decision to "whether the State may impose sanctions on the accurate publication of the name of a rape victim obtained from public records—more specifically, from judicial records which are maintained in connection with a public prosecution and which themselves are open to public inspection." In this narrow context, the Court concluded that the state could not impose civil liability on the television station for two reasons: first, a "great responsibility" of the news media is "to report fully and accurately the proceedings of government" and thereby help "to guarantee the fairness of trials and to bring to bear the beneficial effects of public scrutiny upon the administration of justice"; second, if there are privacy interests that should be protected in judicial proceedings, "the States must respond by means which avoid public documentation or other exposure of private information" for "[o]nce true information is disclosed in public court documents open to public inspection, the press cannot be sanctioned for publishing it" (*Id.* at 496).

More than a decade later, in *Florida Star v. B.J.F.* (1989), the Court again upheld the right of a newspaper to publish the name of a rape victim, even though the reporter obtained the name from a police incident report, not from an indictment filed with the court. To reach this result, a five-justice majority broadened its rationale beyond the right of media to publish information contained in official public records. "If a newspaper lawfully obtains truthful information about a matter of public significance," the Court argued, "then state officials may not constitutionally punish publication of the information, absent a need to further a state interest of the highest order." According to this rule, it did not matter that a "police incident record" was not one "which the public, by law, is entitled to inspect" or that the disclosure of the rape victim's name was "inadvertent" and in violation of state policy. As long as such "private"

information is "true," "of public significance," and the press obtained it
"lawfully" (in this case from the police department's pressroom), there can
never be a "need" to punish its publication "to further a state interest of
the highest order" because the state initially had the option of keeping the
rape victim's name secret. "Once the government has placed such information in the public domain, 'reliance must rest upon the judgment of
those who decide what to publish or broadcast,' and hopes for restitution
must rest upon the willingness of the government to compensate victims
for their loss of privacy and to protect them from the other consequences
of its mishandling of the information which these victims provided in
confidence" (491 U.S. 524, 534, 536–538 (1989)).

Florida Star left unresolved the question of whether a media outlet
could be held liable for publicizing private information that had been illegally obtained by a third party, but lawfully turned over to the media. The
Court addressed this question in *Bartnicki v. Vopper* (2001), a case involving the illegal recording by an unknown person of a telephone conversation between a negotiator for a teacher's union and the president of a local
union. With a possible strike in the offing, the latter said the following:

> If they're not gonna move for three percent, we're gonna have to
> go to their, their homes. . . . To blow off their front porches, we'll
> have to do some work on some of those guys. (PAUSES). Really, uh,
> really and truthfully because this is, you know, this is bad news. (532
> U.S. 514, 518–519 (2001))

The unidentified person who had recorded this conversation placed a tape
of it in the mailbox of a local citizen who opposed the union's demands.
This citizen, in turn, gave it to a local radio talk show host, who played
it on the air. The union negotiators sued the radio station and the local
citizen, claiming that federal criminal law prohibited anyone from "intentionally disclosing the contents of an electronic communication when he
or she 'know[s] or ha[s] reason to know that the information was obtained
through an illegal interception'" (*Id.* at 520).

In upholding the First Amendment right of the radio station to broadcast the illegally obtained wire communication, a six-justice majority
relied on the fact that the radio station did not participate in the illegal
interception, that the station lawfully obtained the tape of the conversation, and that the subject matter of the conversation "was a matter of
public concern" (*Id.* at 525). The only outstanding issue, according to the
Court, was whether there existed a state interest "of the highest order"
that would justify liability despite the constitutional guarantee of freedom

of speech. One relevant government interest was to deter the interception of private communications, but this interest, in the majority's view, was adequately served by punishing the initial wrongdoer, not a radio station that had only broadcast what it had lawfully received.

A second interest, the Court conceded, was the protection of privacy. Here the majority acknowledged "that some intrusions on privacy are more offensive than others, and that the disclosure of the contents of a private communication can be an even greater intrusion on privacy than the interception itself." But even if the radio broadcast was a greater intrusion of the right to privacy than the initial illegal interception, according to the Court, imposing liability on the radio station "implicates the core purposes of the First Amendment because it imposes sanctions on the publication of truthful information of public concern." Although the majority in *Bartnicki* does not go so far as to say "categorically" that truthful publications can never be "punished consistent with the First Amendment" (*Id.* at 529), it seems that the Court is edging toward this rule if the public has an interest in the private information.

How the principles of these cases should and will be applied to the relatively new phenomenon of "doxing" is not clear. All too often an evaluation of a particular case of "doxing" depends on whose information was divulged for what purpose, rather than the nature of the information itself. For example, the Wisconsin Supreme Court, based on the principle of "academic freedom," ruled in favor of John McAdams, a tenured professor of political science at Marquette University, who published a post on his personal blog that criticized Cheryl Abbate, a philosophy graduate student and instructor, because she told her Theory of Ethics Class that "everybody agrees" on "gay rights" and there was therefore "no need to discuss it." After class a student argued that gay rights should be open for discussion, but Abbate responded that the student did not have "a right in this class to make homophobic comments" and "invited" him to drop the class. Unbeknownst to Abbate, the student had surreptitiously recorded the conversation and later gave it to McAdams. In his post, which included a clickable link to Abbate's contact information and her public website, McAdams claimed that Abbate had employed a "tactic" typical among liberals: "Opinions with which they disagree are not merely wrong . . ., but are deemed 'offensive' and need to be shut up" (see *McAdams v. Marquette University*, 2018 WI 88 (July 6, 2018)).

Margaret Carlson, a columnist for *Bloomberg News*, claimed that the Wisconsin Court's decision was "another win [for the right] in adapting the First Amendment . . . to their needs to take back politically correct college campuses" (Carlson 2018). In the context of the Supreme

Court decisions discussed earlier, many legal scholars assert that Carlson's claim is at best misconceived. Rather than "adapting" the First Amendment, the Wisconsin Court's decision seems consistent with the Supreme Court's position that freedom of speech protects the publication of private information if it is a "matter of public concern." A refusal by a professor to allow discussion of a controversial topic in an ethics class would obviously be of interest to the public, especially to prospective students and their parents. This is true whether the issue is controversial from the perspective of the right or the left. On the other hand, it is indisputable that a state can punish "doxing" of private information if it is part of a "true threat," such as publishing on the Internet "dead-or-alive" posters of the names and addresses of health providers who worked at abortion clinics (see *Planned Parenthood v. American Coalition of Life Activists*, 2002, and Q9). In the same vein, "cyber-stalking" that met the criteria of "criminal harassment" (see Q17) would also not be protected by freedom of speech.

Moreover, if the "doxing" was of information that was truly private in character, such as a person's sexual orientation, medical history, social security number, nude photos of the person, or audio recordings of intimate conversations, most states provide a tort for "the public disclosure of private facts." However, this tort is available only if the public has no legitimate interest in the private information published on the Internet. Another problem is that it may be difficult and expensive to prove who posted the information on the Internet. Lastly, the line between private information and "matters of public interest" is very difficult to draw when addressing the issue of *who* published *what* about *whom*, *when*, *where*, and *how*. Any of the italicized words could trigger the public's legitimate interest in the information.

FURTHER READING

Carlson, Margaret. "Doxing Is Free Speech—If You're a Right—Wing Prof Harassing a Woman." *The Daily Beast*, July 6, 2018, available at https://www.thedailybeast.com/doxxing-is-free-speechif-youre-a-right-wing-prof-harassing-a-woman.

Carroll, Erin C. "Making News: Balancing Newsworthiness and Privacy the Age of Algorithms." *Georgetown Law Journal* 106 (2017): 69–114.

Edelman, Peter B. "Free Press vs. Privacy: Haunted by the Ghost of Justice Black." *Texas Law Review* 68 (1990): 1195–1234.

Kalven, Harry. "Privacy in Tort Law—Were Warren and Brandeis Wrong." *Law and Contemporary Problems* 31 (1966): 326–341.

Posner, Richard A. "The Right to Privacy." *Georgia Law Review* 12 (1978): 393–422.

Richards, Neil. *Intellectual Privacy: Rethinking Civil Liberties in the Digital Age*. Oxford: Oxford University Press, 2015.

Tunick, Mark. *Balancing Privacy and Free Speech: Unwanted Attention in the Age of Social Media*. New York: Routledge, 2014.

Volokh, Eugene. "Freedom of Speech and Information Privacy: The Troubling Implications of a Right to Stop People from Speaking about You." *Stanford Law Review* 52 (2000): 1–65.

Warren, Samuel D. and Brandeis, Louis D. "The Right to Privacy." *Harvard Law Review* 4 (1980): 193–220.

Q21. CAN THE GOVERNMENT PROHIBIT PHYSICAL CONDUCT THAT HAS AN EXPRESSIVE OR SYMBOLIC DIMENSION?

Answer: Yes. The government can prohibit such conduct, but only if the prohibition furthers "an important or substantial governmental interest," the interest in question is "unrelated to the suppression of free expression," and the incidental impact on free speech "is no greater than is essential to the furtherance of that interest."

The Facts: The degree to which expressive conduct is protected by freedom of speech is complicated. If the conduct satisfies the criteria of one of the unprotected categories of speech, for example, brandishing a weapon or burning a cross for the purpose of intimidation (see Q16), it is completely outside the scope of constitutional protection. On the other hand, some forms of expressive conduct, such as those that have an artistic dimension or are closely linked to speech (see Q2), are protected by the First Amendment as much as any other form of protected speech. However, there is a variety of expressive conduct that falls between conduct completely excluded from freedom of speech and conduct that is fully protected. Typically this middle category is called "symbolic conduct," and the Court has held that, though it is within the scope of freedom of speech, the government can prohibit it under certain conditions.

The Supreme Court recognized that symbolic conduct had a degree of constitutional protection as early as *Stromberg v. California* (1931), a decision that invalidated a state law that banned displaying a red flag for the purpose of opposing organized government. In a similar fashion, the Court ruled that free speech barred a state from requiring school children to "salute" the American flag in *West Virginia Board of Education v. Barnette* (1943). During the civil rights movement of the 1960s, the Supreme Court in *Brown v. Louisiana* (1966) extended the scope of free-speech protection beyond conduct involving the use of conventional symbols, such as "displaying" or "saluting" flags, by reversing a breach-of the-peace conviction of five young African American men who engaged in a "sit-in" demonstration at a public library to protest racial segregation. Three of the justices in the majority argued that the convictions should be reversed on the basis of freedom of speech. In their view freedom of speech and the right of association were "no[t] confined to verbal expression. They embrace appropriate types of action which certainly include the right in a peaceable and orderly manner to protest by silent and reproachful presence, in a place where the protestant has every right to be, the unconstitutional segregation of public facilities" (383 U.S. 131, 141–142 (1966)). Even though the plurality opinion limited its holding to "appropriate types of action," which implied that not all types of symbolic conduct were constitutionally protected, this decision became a foothold for the Court to expand constitutional protection for symbolic conduct beyond action related to conventional symbols.

A key decision in this trend was *United States v. O'Brien* (1968), where the Court confronted the question whether protestors could burn their draft cards to express their opposition to the Vietnam War. The Court unanimously upheld the ban and rejected "the view that an apparently limitless variety of conduct can be labeled 'speech' whenever the person engaging in the conduct intends thereby to express an idea" (391 U.S. 367, 376 (1968)). If conduct like burning a draft card was symbolic in nature, the Court concluded, it could yet be prohibited by government if the law passed a four-part test (the *O'Brien* test). As the Court explained, "when 'speech' and 'non-speech' elements are combined in the same course of conduct," a government prohibition is "sufficiently justified"

> [1] if it is within the constitutional power of the Government;
> [2] if it furthers an important or substantial governmental interest;
> [3] if the governmental interest is unrelated to the suppression of free expression, and [4] if the incidental restriction on alleged First Amendment freedoms is no greater than is essential to the furtherance of that interest. (*Id.* at 377)

Applying this test to draft card burning, the Court found that the ban was within the government's power "to raise and support armies"; that the government has a "substantial" interest in having draft registrants in possession of draft cards; that the government's interest was in the "noncommunicative" aspect of the conduct and "for nothing else"; and, finally, that the ban's burden on speech was no more than was necessary to achieve the "smooth and efficient functioning of the Selective Service System" (*Id*. at 377–382).

The third criterion of the *O'Brien* test—the government's interest must be "unrelated to the suppression of free expression"—became more important as the Court deepened its commitment to the proposition that government could not use its coercive authority to "take sides" in political or social debates by making "content" or "viewpoint" distinctions (see Q7). For example, one year after *O'Brien*, the Court held in *Tinker v. Des Moines Independent Community School District* (1969) that public school officials could not suspend students for wearing black armbands to school as a way to express their opposition to the Vietnam War. There was no evidence that these students disrupted school activities in any way. The Court, therefore, concluded that the "school officials banned and sought to punish petitioners for a silent, passive expression of opinion," noting that the ban did not extend to wearing political campaign buttons or Iron Crosses. "Instead, a particular symbol—black armbands worn to exhibit opposition to this Nation's involvement in Vietnam—was singled out for prohibition. Clearly, the prohibition of expression of one particular opinion . . . is not constitutionally permissible" (393 U.S. 503, 508, 510–511 (1969)). Such a content-based distinction was in the Court's view not "unrelated to the suppression of free expression" and therefore, the conduct in question was protected by free speech.

In 1974, the Court made it clear that conduct qualified as "symbolic conduct" only if the actor had an "intent to convey a particularized message" and "in the surrounding circumstances the likelihood was great that the message would be understood by those who viewed it" (*Spence v. Washington*, 418 U.S. 405, 410–411 (1974)). The Court reaffirmed this understanding of what constitutes symbolic conduct in *Clark v. Community for Nonviolence* (1984), a case addressing whether demonstrators who wanted to call attention to the plight of the homeless had a constitutional right to sleep in tents pitched in Lafayette Park and on the Mall in Washington, D.C. In reaching its decision, the Court conceded that sleeping in the parks under these circumstances was "expressive conduct protected to some extent by the First Amendment" (468 U.S. 288, 293 (1984)). Nevertheless, the Court upheld the National Park Service's prohibition of "camping" in the park or on the Mall as a reasonable time, place, and manner regulation (see Q26) or as a justifiable prohibition of symbolic conduct under the *O'Brien* test.

It was not until Gregory Johnson burned a flag at a demonstration in Dallas, Texas, to protest the policies of the Reagan administration in 1984 that the Supreme Court directly confronted the question whether burning the American flag was symbolic conduct protected by freedom of speech. Texas claimed that its law banning flag burning served two interests: "Preserving the flag as a symbol of national unity and preventing breaches of the peace." In a hotly contested 5–4 decision, the Court ruled that burning the flag was a type of symbolic conduct protected by freedom of speech. The majority quickly dismissed the state's interest in preventing breaches of the peace on the ground that the record contained no evidence of any disturbance of the peace or likelihood thereof (*Texas v. Johnson* 491 U.S. 397, 408–410 (1989)).

In resolving whether the state's interest in preserving the flag as a symbol of national unity justified the ban, the majority argued that the ban was clearly related to expression. "The State, apparently, is concerned," the majority wrote, "that such conduct [burning the flag] will lead people to believe either that the flag does not stand for nationhood and national unity, but instead reflects other, less positive concepts, or that the concepts reflected in the flag do not in fact exist, that is, that we do not enjoy unity as a Nation (*Id.* at 410). Since "Johnson's political expression was restricted because of the content of the "message he conveyed," the ban on flag burning was "content-based" and the Court had no choice but to "subject the State's asserted interest in preserving the special symbolic character of the flag to 'the most exacting scrutiny'" (*Id.* at 412), not to the *O'Brien* test. In the Court's view, Texas clearly failed to meet this demanding standard:

> If we were to hold that a State may forbid flag burning wherever it is likely to endanger the flag's symbolic role, but allow it wherever burning a flag promotes that role—as where, for example, a person ceremoniously burns a dirty flag—we would be saying that when it comes to impairing the flag's physical integrity, the flag itself may be used as a symbol—as a substitute for the written or spoken word or a "short cut from mind to mind"—only in one direction. We would be permitting a State to "prescribe what shall be orthodox" by saying that one may burn the flag to convey one's attitude toward it and its referents only if one does not endanger the flag's representation of nationhood and national unity. (*Id.* at 416–417)

The "government may not prohibit expression," the Court concluded, "simply because it disagrees with its message" and this rule "is not dependent on the particular mode [verbal speech or symbolic conduct] in which one chooses to express an idea" (*Id.* at 416). If a government's prohibition was "related to expression" because it was "content-based," then the conduct in question received as much protection under the First Amendment as verbal or written speech, not just the protection provided by the *O'Brien* test.

The Court's decision in *Johnson* was extremely controversial. In his dissent, Justice William Rehnquist claimed that flag burning was a form of "fighting words" likely to cause breaches of the peace and, for that reason, totally excluded from freedom of speech:

> As with "fighting words," so with flag burning, for purposes of the First Amendment: It is "no essential part of any exposition of ideas, and [is] of such slight social value as a step to truth that any benefit that may be derived from [it] is clearly outweighed" by the public interest in avoiding a probable breach of the peace. (*Id.* at 431)

The chasm separating the majority from Rehnquist could not be wider: the former believed that flag burning was entitled to full constitutional protection; the latter, to none at all. Public resistance to the decision was also intense. Efforts in Congress to propose amendments to the Constitution that would permit the punishment of flag burning were narrowly defeated in 1990 and 1995.

The Court's decision on flag burning, however, did not unduly broaden the scope of constitutional protection for symbolic conduct or significantly elevate the standards for determining whether prohibitions of symbolic conduct are constitutional. So long as the government's interest is not to suppress speech, it yet retains considerable latitude in prohibiting symbolic conduct under certain conditions. For example, in *Rumsfeld v. Forum for Academic and Institutional Rights* (2006), the Court considered whether a federal law could deny funds to law schools that restricted access of military recruiters to their students as a way to express their disapproval of the government's "don't ask, don't tell" policy, a policy that effectively barred openly gay, lesbian, and bisexual persons from military service. Did the free-speech rights of the law schools protect their right to deny access to the military recruiters without any loss of federal funding? The Court claimed there was no evidence that the purpose of the federal funding law was to suppress speech and made short shrift of the law schools' argument that the denial of access was a form of symbolic conduct protected by the *O'Brien* test. The Court insisted that its decisions limited constitutional protection only to symbolic conduct "that is inherently expressive," such as flag burning. In the Court's view, the

> expressive component of a law school's actions [by denying access to military recruiters] is not created by the conduct itself but by the speech that accompanies it. The fact that such explanatory speech is necessary is strong evidence that the conduct at issue here is not so inherently expressive that it warrants protection under O'Brien. If combining speech and conduct were enough to create expressive conduct, a regulated party could always transform conduct into "speech" simply by talking about it. For instance, if an individual announces that he intends to express his disapproval of the Internal Revenue Service by refusing to pay his income taxes, we would have to apply O'Brien to determine whether the Tax Code violates the First Amendment. Neither O'Brien nor its progeny supports such a result. (547 U.S. 47, 66 (2006))

In short, the Court's conclusion was that the conduct of the law schools denying access to military recruiters was not symbolic conduct at all. Congress could deny federal funds to such institutions without infringing on freedom of speech in any way.

In the context of the recent "day of rage, hate, violence, and death" in Charlottesville, Virginia, August 10–11, 2017, a day in which a militia of white nationalists and supremacists armed with semi-automatic AR-15 rifles clashed with counter-protesters, the Court's decision in *Rumsfeld* should give pause to those who currently argue that openly carrying a firearm is a form of symbolic conduct protected by freedom of speech (Yzaguirre 2017). Even if a person who openly carries a gun intends thereby to engage in political advocacy, it is not at all clear that the conduct in question is, as the Court said in *Rumsfeld*, "inherently expressive." Observers would not know if the gun bearer was "threatening" or "intimidating" someone, expressing concern about someone's safety, letting others know what dangerous times we live in, showing his fellow citizens what an expensive gun he owns, or some composite of these. After all, if a gun owner has a right based on free speech to openly carry firearms to engage in symbolic speech, would the taxpayer not also have a right to express his or her opposition to all taxes by refusing to pay income tax, which is exactly the conclusion that the Court rejects in *Rumsfeld*. In short, the idea that freedom of speech protects a person's right to carry guns openly is nothing more than a myth (Horwitz, 2016; DeBoer 2018).

FURTHER READING

DeBoer, Katlyn E. "Clash of the First and Second Amendments: Proposed Regulation of Armed Protest." *Hasting Constitutional Law Quarterly* 45 (2018): 333–371.

Ely, John Hart. "Flag Desecration: A Case Study in the Roles of Categorization and Balancing in First Amendment Analysis." *Harvard Law Review* 88 (1975): 1482–1508.

Goldstein, Robert Justin. *Flag Burning and Free Speech: The Case of Texas v. Johnson.* Lawrence: University of Kansas Press, 2000.

Horwitz, Daniel. "Open Carry: Open-Conversation or Open Threat." *First Amendment Law Review* 15 (2016): 96–120.

Kels, Charles G. "Free Speech and the Military Recruiter: Reaffirming the Marketplace of Ideas." *Nevada Law Journal* 11(2010): 92–138.

McNeal, Laura Rene. "From Hoodies to Kneeling during the National Anthem: The Colin Kaepernick Effect and Its Implications for K-12 Sports." *Louisiana Law Review* 78 (2017): 145–196.

Stone, Geoffrey. "Flag Burning and the Constitution." *Iowa Law Review* 75 (1989): 111–124.

Yzaguirre, Tyler. "Why Gun Owners Should Use the First Amendment to Protect Open Carry." *The Hill,* August 8, 2017, available at http://thehill.com/blogs/pundits-blog/civil-rights/345675-why-gun-owners-should-use-the-first-amendment-to-protect-open.

4

Regulation of Protected Speech

While Chapter 2 examined speech that is excluded from freedom of speech and Chapter 3 discussed speech within the scope of freedom of speech yet subject to sanctions under certain conditions, the present chapter will explore a third category: speech that the government cannot prohibit because of its content, but can subject it to reasonable regulations. This category of protected speech is an intelligible one even if the distinction between a legal prohibition and a legal regulation is a murky one. For instance, it is indisputable that there are legal rules identified as "regulations" that, if violated, can lead to sanctions that are equal or greater than those attached to legal "prohibitions." And not all legal "prohibitions" are criminal in character, enforced by sanctions having a punitive purpose. For example, "libel" can be either a "criminal" or a "civil" wrong: the former is a violation of a public law, and the state "punishes" it for a punitive purpose; the latter is a violation of private law, and the state "compensates" the victim for the private "wrong" done to him or her. However, whether the "libel" is criminal or civil in nature, the Supreme Court considers it a case of "wrongdoing" (see *Kokesh v. SEC* (2017)). Accordingly, one way to make sense of the distinction between a legal prohibition and a legal regulation is to say that the former generally implies some sort of "wrongdoing," while the latter does not necessarily carry that implication.

The state "regulates" speech that is not deemed generally harmful for a number of reasons: it might intrude upon rights of privacy or childraising, or it may be linked in some way to harmful conduct that the state has a duty to prevent. Because the state regulates protected speech, not because of its content, but because of these types of "incidental" or "secondary" effects, such regulations typically are narrower in scope than prohibitions of harmful speech. In effect, the state "regulates" protected expression only to the degree necessary to ameliorate or eliminate the incidental negative effects it is having on legitimate state interests. If the government attempts to expand the scope of regulation beyond that point, then the regulation violates freedom of speech. For this reason, protected speech that is subject only to regulation, not to prohibition, generally has a broader scope than either unprotected speech or speech protected conditionally.

Q22. CAN THE STATE GENERALLY PROHIBIT "INDECENT" OR "OFFENSIVE" SPEECH?

Answer: No. The First Amendment protects "indecent" and "offensive" written or verbal speech, and the government cannot prohibit it on that basis, but it can subject such expression to reasonable regulations for the protection of children and the value of privacy in the home.

The Facts: The constitutional right of a speaker to engage in "offensive" speech might seem uncontroversial, but a 2016 survey of high school students and teachers reveals that 45 percent of students reject this right for speakers in public forums and 43 percent reject it for speakers on social media (see "Future of the First Amendment"). Why this statistic is somewhat disconcerting is that the Supreme Court extended constitutional protection to offensive speech long ago, in *Cohen v. California* (1971), a case involving a defendant convicted of "willfully disturb[ing] the peace . . . by . . . offensive conduct." Cohen allegedly violated the statute by wearing a jacket bearing the words "F*** the Draft" in the Los Angeles courthouse. Although Cohen removed the jacket, holding it folded in his arms, when he entered a courtroom, he wore it, with the lettering in plain sight, when he was in the corridor where women and children were present (403 U.S. 15, 19, n.3 (1971)). Holding 5–4 that Cohen's conviction violated freedom of speech, the Court made three points: first, the statute in question was not a narrow one confined to courthouse decorum, but one "applicable throughout the entire State"; second, that Cohen's expression was not "a direct personal insult" of any individual; and, third, that there was no showing of any likelihood of violence. One relevant state interest was "to protect the sensitive from otherwise unavoidable exposure to appellant's crude form of protest," but this rationale was insufficient, according to the Court, because people offended by Cohen's expression could "effectively avoid further bombardment of their sensibilities simply by averting their eyes" (*Id.* at 19, 21).

The only other relevant state interest was based on the state's role as a "guardian of public morality," but the Court denied that the state had this role for a number of reasons. First, if states had such a role, it would be "inherently boundless," enabling government to "cleanse public debate to the point where it is grammatically palatable to the most squeamish among us," not on the basis of any "general principle," but in an ad hoc fashion, depending on the arbitrary preferences of government officials. Second, the Court noted, expression "serves a dual communicative function: it conveys not only ideas capable of relatively precise, detached explication, but otherwise inexpressible emotions as well." In the Court's opinion, the First Amendment protects this "emotive" function of expression as well as the "cognitive" one because the former is often "the more important element of the overall message sought to be communicated." Lastly, if states had the power to censor offensive words as "guardians of public morality," they might very well use it "as a convenient guise for banning the expression of unpopular views." There was no reason, the Court concluded, to run "the risk of opening the door to such grave results" (*Id.* at 22, 25–26).

Although the Court reversed Cohen's conviction, it also endorsed the government's authority to limit offensive expression to protect privacy.

> *The ability of government, consonant with the Constitution, to shut off discourse solely to protect others from hearing it is, in other words, dependent upon a showing that substantial privacy interests are being invaded in an essentially intolerable manner. A broader view of this authority would effectively empower a majority to silence dissidents simply as a matter of personal predilections. (Id. at 21)*

The government could punish offensive speech only if it intruded upon privacy interests in a "substantial" way, and it did so in a manner that was "essentially intolerable." The implication was, as the Court expressed it in *Rowan v. United States Post Office Dept.* (1970), "we are often 'captives' outside the sanctuary of the home and subject to objectionable speech" (397 U.S. 728, 738 (1970), emphasis in original).

Although *Cohen* was a closely contested decision in 1971, it quickly won broad acceptance. If substantial privacy interests or other legitimate

state interests, such as the protection of children, were not involved, freedom of speech barred any prohibition that relied exclusively on either the
"offensive" character of words or an assumption that "offensive" words
were inherently "fighting words" likely to breach the peace. A question
soon arose, however, concerning how this standard should be applied to
radio programming, especially when a New York radio station in the middle of the afternoon broadcast a 12-minute monologue by George Carlin,
one that explicitly identified the "original seven words" referring to sexual
and bodily functions that he was not allowed to use on the public air-
ways because of their vulgarity. The Federal Communications Commission
(FCC) found Carlin's monologue to be "patently offensive" and "indecent"
in violation of a federal statute. However, the FCC made it clear that its
regulations did not constitute "an absolute prohibition on the broadcast of
this type of language," but rather "channeled" such programming "to times
of day when children most likely would not be exposed to it" (*FCC v.
Pacifica Foundation*, 438 U.S. 726, 733, 751 (1971)).

The Court divided 5–4 on whether a radio station had a right under the
First Amendment to broadcast Carlin's monologue. The majority upheld
the FCC's regulation on the ground that special rules apply to broadcast
media, referring to both radio and television. First, patently offensive,
indecent material "presented over the airwaves confronts the citizen not
only in public, but also in the privacy of the home, where the individual's
right to be left alone plainly outweighs the First Amendment rights of an
intruder." Second, "broadcasting is uniquely accessible to children, even
those too young to read," enabling children to enlarge their vocabulary
"in an instant" (*Id*. at 748–749). Just as running away after the first blow
of an assault is not a proper remedy, so also, the Court argued, turning off
offensive radio or TV broadcasts was not a satisfactory solution. In the
end, the majority concluded that the FCC could "channel" or "regulate"
such offensive expression to late-night hours without violating freedom
of speech.

The Court underlined the "narrowness" of its decision in *Pacifica*,
noting that it was not deciding whether the FCC could sanction "an
occasional expletive." It also emphasized that when regulating offensive
speech "context is all-important" because, "a nuisance may be merely a
right thing in the wrong place,—like a pig in the parlor instead of the
barnyard." In the same way, a radio broadcast of Carlin's monologue late
at night might be the "right thing" in the "right" place, but when it is
broadcast at a time when many children will undoubtedly hear it, it is a
"pig in the parlor" that has no right to be there (*Id*. at 750). The Court
is implying that there is nothing inherently wrong with a radio station

broadcasting Carlin's monologue, just as there is nothing inherently wrong with being a pig. Accordingly, the government cannot "prohibit" offensive speech, but it can "regulate" it by channeling it to late-night hours for legitimate reasons, such as protecting children, just as a farmer can clearly confine his pigs to the pigpen.

In *Sable Communications of California, Inc. v. FCC* (1989), the Court addressed the constitutionality of a congressional ban on "obscene" or "indecent" sexually oriented pre-recorded telephone messages. Also known as "dial-a-porn" services, the listener had to initiate the call and the service billed the customer on a pay-per-message basis. The ban on "obscene" messages was constitutional (see Q12), but it was not clear whether the state could ban "indecent" telephone communications for the purpose of protecting minors. The Court "recognized that there is a compelling interest in protecting the physical and psychological well-being of minors," but held that the general ban was not "narrowly drawn" to serve this interest, largely because it interfered with the right of adults to receive "indecent" and "offensive" messages that were protected by the First Amendment. *Pacifica* was not controlling, the Court argued, because that case involved "channeling" offensive speech, not prohibiting it, and, unlike radio broadcasts, the "dial-a-porn" service was not "uniquely pervasive" since it required "the listener to take affirmative steps to receive the communication." Children can be sufficiently protected, the Court concluded, by requiring a credit card or a code to access the pre-recorded porn service (492 U.S. 115, 126–128 (1989)).

In *FCC v. Fox Television Stations* (2012), the Court considered whether the *Pacifica* rationale (protection of privacy and children from offensive daytime audio programming) could be extended to a new FCC regulation that sanctioned TV stations for broadcasting "occasional" or "fleeting" offensive expletives. This issue arose following a number of instances when celebrities, including Cher and Bono, used the "F-Word" when they received music awards on national television. These incidents convinced the FCC that even "isolated broadcasts" of words like the "F-Word" during daytime or prime-time hours could enlarge "a child's vocabulary in an instant" and, for that reason, such "fleeting expletives" should be channeled to late-night hours (567 U.S. 239, 247–248 (2012)).

The Supreme Court disagreed, holding that the new policy on "fleeting expletives" was unconstitutionally vague. The Fifth Amendment's vagueness doctrine required "first, that regulated parties should know what is required of them so they may act accordingly"; and "second, precision and guidance are necessary so that those enforcing the law do not act in an arbitrary or discriminatory way." In regard to the FCC's new regulation, the Court remarked, a "person of ordinary intelligence" had little to no guidance as to what words generated a "fleeting" moment of indecency and what words did not (*Id.* at 254). Although the Court in *Fox* based its decision explicitly on the Fifth Amendment, freedom of speech had a large impact on how it assessed the relevant issues. In the end, the Court refused to extend the rationale of *Pacifica* beyond the relatively narrow confines of that decision: a mid-day broadcast of a 12-minute monologue chockfull of "filthy words." The FCC could channel broadcast programming of this nature to late-night hours without violating freedom of speech, but the First Amendment, despite the contrary view of many of today's high school students, largely immunized offensive speech in other contexts, depending on whether a regulation furthered in a "narrowly tailored" way an "important governmental interest," such as privacy or the protection of children.

FURTHER READING

Bickel, Alexander. *The Morality of Consent.* New Haven, CT: Yale University Press, 1975, Chapter 1.

Calvart, Clay, et. al. "Indecency Four Years after Fox Television Stations: From Big Papi to a Porn Star, an Egregious Mess at the FCC Continues." *Richmond Law Review* 51 (1917): 329–369.

Campbell, Angela J. "Pacifica Reconsidered: Implications for the Current Controversy over Broadcasting Indecency." *Federal Communications Law Journal* 63 (2010): 195–260.

Chase, Barry. "The FCC's Indecency Jurisdiction: A Stale Blemish on the First Amendment." *Ohio Northern University Law Review* 39 (2013): 697–722.

Fairman, Christopher M. "Institutionalized Word Taboo: The Continuing Saga of FCC Indecency Regulation." *Michigan State Law Review* (2013): 567–640.

Hayes, Arthur S. *Sympathy for the Cyberbully: How the Crusade to Censor Hostile and Offensive Online Speech Abuses Freedom of Expression.* New York: Peter Lang, 2017.

Knight Foundation. "Future of the First Amendment: 2016 Survey of High School Students and Teachers." February 7, 2017, available at https://knightfoundation.org/reports/future-of-the-first-amendment-2016-survey-of-high-school-students-and-teachers.

Levmore, Saul and Nusbaum, Martha C. *The Offensive Internet: Speech, Privacy, and Reputation.* Cambridge, MA: Harvard University Press, 2012.

Richards, Robert D. and Weinert, David J. "Punting in the First Amendment's Red Zone: The Supreme Court's 'Indecision' on the FCC's Indecency Regulations Leaves Broadcasters Still Searching for Answers." *Albany Law Review* 76 (2013): 631–664.

Q23. IF FILMS, BOOKS, AND MAGAZINES CONTAIN GRAPHIC REPRESENTATIONS OF SEXUAL ACTIVITY, BUT ARE NOT "OBSCENE" ACCORDING TO THE SUPREME COURT'S DEFINITION, CAN THE GOVERNMENT NONETHELESS REGULATE THEM?

Answer: Yes. Although non-obscene representations of sexual activity are protected by freedom of speech and cannot be prohibited, they are subject to regulation by the state to further legitimate state interests that are unrelated to the suppression of such expression.

The Facts: After the Supreme Court established its definition of obscenity in *Miller v. California* (1973) (see Q12), the Supreme Court soon confronted the question of whether states could regulate non-obscene, sexually related expression in films, videos, books, and magazines. For example, in *Erznoznik v. City of Jacksonville* (1975), the Court addressed whether a municipal ordinance could prohibit owners of a drive-in movie theater from showing films containing nudity if the screen was visible from public streets. After noting that the ordinance utilized a content-based distinction to prohibit only "movies containing any nudity, however innocent or even educational," the Court quickly rejected the state's privacy-based justification for the law. "The ordinance seeks only to keep these films from being seen from public streets and places where the offended viewer readily can avert his eyes." The state's interest in protecting children fared no better. "Speech that is neither obscene as to youths nor subject to some other legitimate proscription cannot be suppressed solely to protect the young from ideas or images that a legislative body thinks unsuitable." Lastly, the Court rejected the state's claim that the ordinance was a traffic regulation to prevent the distraction of passing motorists. "There is no reason to think that a wide variety of other scenes in the customary screen diet, ranging from soap opera to violence, would be any less distracting to the passing motorist." A traffic regulation containing a content-based distinction cannot discriminate against a certain type of expression "unless there are clear reasons for the distinctions"

(422 U.S. 205, 206, 211–215 (1975)). In the Court's view, there were no such reasons for Jacksonville's ordinance.

A year after *Erznoznik* the Court addressed the question of whether municipalities could regulate adult theaters and bookstores in *Young v. American Mini Theatres, Inc.* The case concerned a Detroit zoning ordinance that dispersed adult theaters by requiring them to be located 1,000 feet from "two other 'regulated uses' [such as an adult bookstore, bar, or pawnshop] or within 500 feet of a residential area." Detroit argued that the dispersal of adult theaters was the best policy because "the location of several such businesses in the same neighborhood tends to attract an undesirable quantity and quality of transients, adversely affects property values, causes an increase in crime, especially prostitution, and encourages residents and businesses to move elsewhere" (427 U.S. 50, 52, 55 (1976)). The Court upheld the ordinance in a 5–4 decision, even though the majority could not agree on a rationale on why the ordinance did not violate freedom of speech. Justice John Paul Stevens, along with three other justices, argued that

> even though we recognize that the First Amendment will not tolerate the total suppression of erotic materials that have some arguably artistic value [and are therefore not obscene], it is manifest that society's interest in protecting this type of [sexually-related] expression is of a wholly different, and lesser, magnitude than the interest in untrammeled political debate. . . . Even though the First Amendment protects communication in this area from total suppression, we hold that the State may legitimately use the content of these materials as the basis for placing them in a different classification from other motion pictures. (*Id.* 70–71)

The four-justice plurality, therefore, accepted the view that non-obscene sexually related films were within the scope of the First Amendment, but they were of less value than political or philosophical discussions and, for that reason, the government could use content-based distinctions to regulate them for the purpose of preserving "the quality of urban life," even if this interest was not the type of "compelling" purpose that the Court has typically required to justify the government's use of content-based distinctions.

The fifth justice of the majority, Justice Lewis F. Powell, disagreed with the plurality's claim that Detroit's ordinance was content-based:

> At most, the impact of the ordinance on these interests [interest of those who wish to make and watch adult movies] is incidental and

minimal. Detroit has silenced no message, has invoked no censor-ship, and has imposed no limitation upon those who wish to view them. The ordinance is addressed only to the place at which this type of expression may be presented, a restriction that does not interfere with content. Nor is there any significant overall curtail-ment of adult movie presentations, or the opportunity for a message to reach an audience. (*Id*. at 78–79)

Since the ordinance was not content-based, Powell argued that the *O'Brien* test was the appropriate standard (see Q21) and that the ordi-nance in question met the four-part test. In particular, Powell noted, pre-serving residential and commercial neighborhoods was an "important" and "substantial" governmental interest, and Detroit was not engaged in "an effort to suppress free expression." In contrast to the ordinance the Court had invalidated in *Erznoznik*, the Detroit zoning ordinance "affects expression only incidentally, and in furtherance of governmental interests wholly unrelated to the regulation expression" (*Id*. at 80, 84).

Justice Powell's approach to the issue of zoning and adult theaters won the support of a seven-justice majority in *City of Renton v. Playtime Theatres, Inc.* (1986), a decision that upheld a municipal ordinance that concentrated, rather than dispersed, adult establishments. It did so by prohibiting them within 1,000 feet of any residential zone, church, park, or school. Although the Court's reasoning in *Renton* relied on the concept of "secondary," rather than "incidental," effects, its substantive reasoning was similar to Powell's. In the Court's opinion, the Renton ordinance was "aimed not at the *content* of the films shown at 'adult motion picture the-atres,' but rather at the *secondary effects* of such theaters on the surround-ing community." For that reason, it is "consistent with our definition of 'content-neutral' speech regulations." Moreover, the ordinance serves "a substantial governmental interest and allows for reasonable alternative avenues of communication." Preserving the "quality of urban life," as Powell argued in *Young*, is an interest "that must be accorded high respect" and the ordinance permits the location of adult theaters "in 520 acres" of the city (475 U.S. 41, 47, 48, 50, 53 (1986)).

Los Angeles followed the example of Detroit by enacting a zoning ordi-nance that dispersed "adult establishments" but amended the law to also prohibit a number of such establishments from concentrating in a single structure: a so-called adult-oriented department store. A five-justice major-ity upheld the constitutionality of the amendment in *Los Angeles v. Ala-meda Books, Inc.* (2002), but once again the majority could not agree on a rationale. A four-justice plurality denied that the ordinance was content-based since its focus was on the prevention of the "secondary effect" of increased crime, not the suppression of adult-oriented communications. In addition, the plurality agreed with the city that reducing crime was an "important" government interest and it had sufficient evidence that its regulation would achieve this purpose. Justice Anthony Kennedy agreed with the plurality that Los Angeles's ordinance should be upheld, but could not accept the plurality's claim that it was not "content-based." Instead, he argued that "zoning regulations do not automatically raise the specter of impermissible content discrimination, even if they are content based, because they have a prima facie legitimate purpose: to limit the negative externalities of land use" (535 U.S. 449 (2002)). In effect, he too agreed with the plurality that zoning regulations of sexually related expression were constitutional if their purpose was to prevent crime and not to suppress speech.

The expansion of cable television, especially adult fee-based "premium" channels, such as Playboy TV, BraZZers TV, and Cheap Thrills, provided consumers with greater access to non-obscene, sexually related programming. Although such programming entered the home, it did so over a privately owned cable, rather than over publicly owned airwaves that were subject to governmental regulation because the airwaves were public and the government had no choice but to allocate the limited number of frequencies by licensing specific broadcasters (see *Red Lion Broadcasting Co. v. FCC*, 1969). Given this major difference between public broadcasting and cable TV, the question was whether Congress could yet regulate cable companies to prevent non-obscene, sexually related programming from offending people in their homes or detrimentally affecting children?. In 1992, Congress enacted the Cable Television Consumer Protection and Competition Act (CTCPC), which (1) authorized a cable operator to exclude programming of a sexual nature from any channel if there was a "reasonable belief" that it was "patently offensive" as measured by "contemporary community standards"; (2) required a cable operator to place all such programming on channels it leased to third parties on a single channel and block it unless a subscriber requested access to it in writing, a rule that in effect gave the subscriber only an all-or-nothing option; and, finally (3) granted a cable operator the authority to exclude from "public access" channels any program that contained obscenity, sexually explicit conduct, or material that solicited or promoted unlawful conduct.

In *Denver Area Educational Telecommunications Consortium v. FCC* (1996), the Supreme Court upheld the first regulation on the ground that it was not a governmental ban, but rather a recognition that a private cable operator could use its discretion to protect children from inappropriate programming, much like a private broadcast company could elect not to carry "offensive" programming (518 U.S. 727, 743–747 (1996)). However, the Court invalidated the other two provisions of the law, largely because they were restrictive, not permissive, in character. Regarding the second regulation's blocking requirement, the Court emphasizes that it was not "narrowly tailored" to meet its "legitimate objective." For example, the government could require manufacturers to make televisions with "V-chips," which automatically identify and block sexually explicit or violent programs, or compel cable operators to provide subscribers with "lockboxes" that would permit "parents to 'lock out' those programs or channels that they did not want their children to see" (*Id.* at 755–756). Lastly, the Court invalidated the authority of cable operators over "public access" channels because they historically had no editorial control over such channels, which "are normally subject to complex supervisory systems of various sorts, often with both public and private elements." This system of supervision "would normally avoid, minimize, or eliminate any child-related problems concerning 'patently offensive' programming" and, for this reason, the measure is not "narrowly tailored" (*Id.* at 761, 764, 766).

In response to this decision, Congress passed the Telecommunications Act of 1996 with a provision that required cable operators to "scramble" or "block" channels "primarily dedicated to sexually oriented programming" or to limit such programming "to hours when children are unlikely to be viewing." In a 5–4 decision, *United States v. Playboy Entertainment Group* (2000), the Supreme Court invalidated this "content-based" provision on the ground that it was not the "least restrictive means" to protect children from "sexually related" programming on cable TV. In particular, the Court noted, cable systems "have the capacity to block unwanted channels on a household-by household basis," which would permit parents to opt out of channels if they felt it was desirable to do so to protect the sensibilities of their children. For this reason, "targeted blocking enables the Government to support parental authority without affecting the First Amendment interest of speakers and willing listeners" and "is less restrictive" than banning the channels by "scrambling" or "blocking" them or "channeling" them to late-night hours (529 U.S. 803, 815 (2000)).

The Court followed a comparable approach to Congress's attempt to ban or tightly regulate "offensive" or "indecent" expression on the Internet. In *Reno v. American Civil Liberties Union* (1997), the Court invalidated the provision of the Communications Decency Act (CDA) that prohibited "the knowing transmission of . . . indecent messages to any recipient under 18 years of age" and "the knowing sending or displaying of patently offensive messages in a manner that is available to a person under 18 years of age." In the Court's view, the CDA was different from the regulation upheld in *Pacifica* because it banned speech rather than "channeling" it to late-night hours; applied criminal rather than civil penalties; and dealt with the Internet, which required "a series of affirmative steps" to access any offensive or indecent content, unlike the radio programming addressed in *Pacifica* (521 U.S. 844, 867 (1997)). Moreover, the Court reasoned, the terms "indecent" and "patently offensive" were "vague," without "the precision that the First Amendment requires when a statute regulates the content of speech." It "effectively suppresses a large amount of speech that adults have a constitutional right to receive and to address to one another." Such a result "is unacceptable if less restrictive alternatives would be at least as effective in achieving the legitimate purpose that the statute was enacted to serve" (*Id.* at 874). Examples of such less restrictive alternatives, the Court noted, included "tagging" indecent material "in a way that facilitates parental control of material coming into their homes"; "making exceptions for messages with artistic or educational value"; "providing some tolerance for parental choice"; and, lastly, "regulating some portions of the Internet—such as commercial Web sites—differently from others, such as chat rooms" (*Id.* at 879).

Reacting to the Court's decision in *Reno*, Congress enacted the Child Online Protection Act (COPA) of 1998, which banned the "knowing" transmission for commercial purposes of any communication, including any "picture" or "image," that is accessible by minors (excluding sites that required credit or debit cards or other forms of age verification) and "obscene" in terms of their sensibilities, even if not "obscene" in terms of adult sensibilities (see Q12). In *Ashcroft v. American Civil Liberties Union* (2004), a five-justice majority found that COPA was "content-based" and not the "least restrictive means" to protect minors online. "Filters are less restrictive than COPA," the Court insisted. "They impose selective restrictions on speech at the receiving end, not universal restrictions at the source." Another advantage of a filtering regime is that "adults without children may gain access to speech they have a right to see without having to identify themselves or provide their credit card information." Lastly, much "harmful-to-minors" content comes from overseas, which is beyond the scope of COPA yet subject to any filtering system made available to parents (542 U.S. 656, 667–668 (2004)). Accordingly, filtering is not only "less restrictive" than COPA, but more effective. For this reason, unlike zoning ordinances that regulated protected adult expression based not on its substance but on its "secondary effects," or FCC regulations that "channeled" such expression to late-night hours, COPA, like the CDA, violated freedom of speech because it banned or regulated more protected speech than was necessary to protect minors from non-obscene, sexually oriented adult expression.

FURTHER READING

Bhagwat, Ashutosh. "What If I Want My Kids to Watch Pornography?: Protecting Children from 'Indecent' Speech." *William and Mary Bill of Rights* 11 (2003): 671–725.

Chris, Cynthia. *The Indecent Screen*. New Brunswick, NJ: Rutgers University Press, 2019.

Fee, John. "The Pornographic Secondary Effects Doctrine." *Alabama Law Review* 60 (2009): 291–338.

Lipschultz, Jeremy. *Broadcast Indecency: F.C.C. Regulation and the First Amendment*. New York: Routledge (Focal Press), 1996.

Ross, Catherine J. "Anything Goes: Examining the State's Interest in Protecting Children from Controversial Speech." *Vanderbilt Law Review* 53 (2000): 427–524.

Schachter, Madeleine and Kurtzberg, Joel. *Law of Internet Speech*. Durham, NC: Carolina Academic Press, 2008.

Volokh, Eugene. "Gruesome Speech." *Cornell Law Review* 100 (2015): 901–952.

Weithorn, Lois A. "A Constitutional Jurisprudence of Children's Vulnerability." *Hasting Law Journal* 68 (2017): 179–274.

Yoo, Christopher S. "The Rise and Demise of the Technology-Specific Approach to the First Amendment." *Georgia Law Journal* 91 (2003): 245–356.

Q24. IS IT CONSISTENT WITH FREEDOM OF SPEECH TO REGULATE SOME FORMS OF EXPRESSIVE NUDITY?

Answer: Yes. Although nudity in a cultural performance, such as a musical, a ballet, or an opera, is fully protected by freedom of speech, "performative" nude dancing in adult-oriented establishments can be regulated to control negative "secondary effects" even if it is within the scope of freedom of speech.

The Facts: A substantial gap exists between American public opinion and the reality of what the Supreme Court has deemed to be expression protected by the First Amendment. The Supreme Court considered the status of nudity and freedom of expression in the context of nude dancing in adult-oriented establishments in *Schad v. Borough of Mount Ephraim* (1981), which addressed whether a municipality could ban nude dancing by enacting a zoning ordinance prohibiting all live entertainment in the borough. The specific issue was whether an adult bookstore could install a coin-operated mechanism that allowed a customer to watch a live nude dancer perform behind a glass panel.

In addressing this question, the Court, citing *Joseph Burstyn, Inc. v. Wilson* (1952), insisted that "live entertainment such as musical and dramatic works, fall within the First Amendment guarantee" and that nudity alone "does not place otherwise protected material outside the mantle of the First Amendment." To substantiate this latter conclusion, the Court discussed *Southeastern Promotions, Ltd. v. Conrad* (1975), an earlier decision that held that Chattanooga, Tennessee, had violated freedom of speech by refusing to allow the use of a municipal facility for the showing of "Hair," a musical that contained group nudity and simulated sex. The implication was that nudity in musicals, ballets, and operas was fully protected by freedom of speech and that nude dancing in adult-oriented establishments was within the scope of the First Amendment, but that did not necessarily mean that the state could not yet regulate the latter form of expression.

The Court also noted in *Schad* that it had extended a degree of constitutional protection to topless dancing in *Doran v. Salem Inn, Inc.* (1975), but emphasized that the degree of protection was limited in character. For example, three years prior to *Doran*, the Court in *California v. LaRue* (1972) held that a state could use its authority under the Twenty-First Amendment to prohibit nude dancing in establishments licensed to sell liquor. Even if "some of the performances to which these regulations address themselves are within the limits of the constitutional protection of freedom of expression," the Court argued, "the critical fact is that California has not forbidden these performances across the board. It has merely proscribed such performances in establishments that it licenses to sell liquor by the drink." Such a regulation was "not an irrational one," the Court concluded, given the fact that prostitution "occurred in and around such licensed premises, and involved some of the female dancers," and "indecent exposure to young girls, attempted rape, rape itself, and assaults on police officers took place on or immediately adjacent to such premises" (409 U.S. 109, 111, 118 (1972)). The upshot was that "performative" topless and nude dancing was within the scope of freedom of speech, but it was yet subject to regulation because such dancing, when associated with alcohol use, was linked to criminal conduct that the state had a legitimate interest in deterring.

Following *Schad*, the general rule was that nude dancing was a protected form of freedom of expression, but it was subject to appropriate regulations so long as they were not so vague and broad that they captured expressive activities beyond the legitimate interests of the state. It is important to underline that even this holding was limited to nude dancing of a "performative" character. Persons who engaged in "recreational dancing" were not protected by the First Amendment because, according to the Supreme Court, this type of dancing did not qualify "as a form of 'expressive association'" (see *Dallas v. Stanglin*, 1989). The same rule obviously applied to recreational nude dancing. The state could ban such dancing with general prohibitions of public nudity. However, it was less clear whether general bans on public nudity could be constitutionally applied to performative nude dancing. *Schad* did not resolve this issue because that ordinance banned all live entertainment—a broad ban that went beyond the state's legitimate interests. Accordingly, the outstanding question after *Schad* was whether bans on public nudity were sufficiently narrow in scope to outweigh the expressive dimension of performative nude dancing.

The Court finally addressed this question in *Barnes v. Glen Theatre, Inc.* (1991), a case involving Indiana's public indecency statute, which prohibited anyone from "knowingly or intentionally" appearing "in a public place" in a "state of nudity." In deciding whether Indiana's indecency statute could be applied to "performative" nude dancing in adult-oriented establishments, the Court assumed that such expressive conduct was "within the outer perimeters of the First Amendment," even if "only marginally so," and that the Court had to "determine the level of protection to be afforded to the expressive conduct at issue . . . [as well as] whether the Indiana statute is an impermissible infringement of that protected activity" (501 U.S. 560, 566, 572 (1991)).

In addressing this latter issue, a badly divided Court decided 5–4 that Indiana's indecency statute could be applied to such dancing without infringing freedom of speech. A three-justice plurality argued that the "*O'Brien*" test controlling "symbolic conduct" should be the standard (see Q21) and that Indiana's nudity ban met this test, in part because the state did not deprive nude dancing "of whatever erotic message it conveys" by requiring "pasties" and "a G-string" (*Id.* at 567–572). Justice Scalia came to the same result as the plurality, but on different grounds. He argued that Indiana's indecency statute was directed at "all public nudity, and not just at public nude expression" and, for that reason, did not implicate free speech at all because it did not prohibit conduct "*because of its communicative attributes*" (*Id.* at 572–573, 577). Justice Souter also upheld the statute, but he did so on the ground that it served the state's legitimate interests in preventing the "secondary effects" of "prostitution, sexual assault, and other criminal activity," even though nude dancing was, in his view, "entitled to First Amendment protection" and the law suppressed speech (*Id.* at 583, 585).

Nine years later, in *City of Erie v. Pap's A.M.* (2000), the Court upheld Pennsylvania's application of a general public nudity prohibition to "performative" nude dancing in adult-oriented establishments, but once again failed to achieve complete consensus regarding the rationale. Seven justices were of the view that general nudity bans can be used to prohibit nude dancing in adult-oriented establishments if the state has adequate evidence that such prosecutions will reduce prostitution and crime or perhaps simply preserve the quality of neighborhoods or property values. In contrast, seven justices appear to grant free-speech protection to public nudity in musicals, ballets, and operas because any claim by the state that banning such nudity would reduce negative "secondary effects" is not credible or relevant. Only two justices (Scalia and Thomas) continued to exclude all forms of public nudity from the scope of freedom of speech, presumably including nudity in plays, operas, musicals, and ballets, on the ground that nudity is conduct, not speech.

Despite these rulings by the Supreme Court, some Americans continue to insist that they do in fact have a general free-speech right to appear nude in public wherever they like. In San Francisco, nudity for many years was an accepted feature of certain public events, such as the Folsom Street Fair and the Bay to Breakers, a 12K race where many of the participants run *au naturel*. However, in 2012, the city passed a new ordinance that generally prohibited public nudity. Unhappy with the new law, Oxane "Gypsy" Taub and George Davis, longtime "body freedom advocates," challenged it. The 9th Circuit Court of Appeals held on May 25, 2017, that the nudity ban was consistent with freedom of speech because it was "aimed at 'the conduct itself, rather than at the message conveyed by that conduct" (*Taub v. City and County of San Francisco*, May 25, 2017). Evidently, some myths regarding freedom of speech die hard. Even though the law is clear, there are often Americans who are ready and willing to fight for what they believe in and work to change laws they don't like.

FURTHER READING

Adler, Amy M. "Girls! Girls! Girls!: The Supreme Court Confronting the G-String." *New York University Law Review* 80 (2005): 1108–1135.

Baradaran-Robison, Shima. "Viewpoint Neutral Zoning of Adult Entertainment Businesses." *Hasting Constitutional Law Quarterly* 31 (2004): 447–496.

Blasi, Vincent. "Six Conservatives in Search of the First Amendment: The Revealing Case of Nude Dancing." *William and Mary Law Review* 33 (1992): 611–633.

Bond, Ethan. "Stripping Down a Victory for Adult Entertainment: Showtime Entertainment, LLC v. Town of Mendon." *Loyola of Los Angeles Entertainment Law Review* 36 (2016): 249–283.

Bruning, Kevin R. "Nudity and Alcohol: Morality Lies in Public Discussion." *Stetson Law Review* 29 (2000): 775–810.

Fisher, Christy A. "Nude Dancing." *Georgetown Journal of Gender and the Law* 6 (2005): 335–346.

Jacobs, Leslie Gielow. "Making Sense of Secondary Effects Analysis after Reed v. Town of Gilbert." *Santa Clara Law Review* 57 (2017): 385–451.

Leahy, Christopher Thomas. "The First Amendment Gone Awry: City of Erie v. Pap's A.M.. Ailing Analytical Structures, and the Suppression of Protected Expression." *University of Pennsylvania Law Review* 150 (2002): 1021–1078.

Q25. DOES FREEDOM OF SPEECH PERMIT THE STATE TO IMPOSE CIVIL LIABILITY ON SOMEONE WHO INTENTIONALLY INFLICTS EMOTIONAL DISTRESS ON ANOTHER BY ENGAGING IN CALLOUS AND MALICIOUS HUMOR OR EXTREMELY OFFENSIVE SPEECH THAT KNOWINGLY CAUSES PAIN AND HUMILIATION?

Answer: Yes. A state may impose civil liability on speech that is intended to inflict emotional distress—but only if the expression actually inflicts such distress, the victim is not a "public official" or "public figure," and the speech is not about "a matter of public concern."

The Facts: The tort of intentional infliction of emotional distress arose because conduct can cause not only physical infirmities or illness but also "mental distress." An early case of this type of tort was *Wilkinson v. Downton* (1897), a decision by an English court that upheld a woman's right to compensation from a man who falsely told her that her husband had broken both his legs and urged her to bring two pillows to carry him home. The Court held that the wife could recover for what was intended as a practical joke, in part because the shock to her nervous system had produced physical, emotional, and mental trauma. In the United States, an early case involved an eccentric elderly woman who was constantly digging in her backyard because she believed that a pot of gold was buried there. Knowing about her delusion, a man buried a pot in her backyard and escorted her to city hall after she found it. She then felt public humiliation when she opened the pot and found nothing of value in it. She took ill and died, but her heirs were able to recover $500 in damages (see *Nickerson v. Hodges*, 1920). In *Great A. & P. Tea Company v. Roch* (1930), a mischievous grocer was found liable for delivering a package containing a dead rat to a customer, while a leader of a mob who threatened to lynch a man unless he left town was found culpable in *Wilson v. Wilkins* (1930).

This trend of cases in the first half of the 20th century led the American Law Institute to recognize a distinct tort for intentional infliction of emotional distress in 1948 (Prosser 1956). According to the Institute, this new tort had the following requirements: (1) "outrageous conduct by the defendant"; (2) "the intention of causing, or reckless disregard of the probability of causing, emotional distress"; (3) "actual suffering of severe or extreme emotional distress"; and (4) "actual and proximate causation of the emotional distress by the defendant's outrageous conduct." A "mere insult or emotional injury" was not sufficient. In the typical case, the distress must be so egregious that a "reasonable person" would find it intolerable (see The Restatement (2nd) of Torts, § (2)(a)). Soon after the American Law Institute finished its work, state courts began to recognize the "intentional infliction of emotional distress" as an independent tort. For example, a garbage collector won a lawsuit against a defendant who threatened him with physical violence unless he paid the defendant money in *State Rubbish Collectors Ass'n v. Siliznoff* (1952). The threat was not an assault because the likelihood of violence was not imminent, but the plaintiff nonetheless recovered damages even though he suffered no physical ill effects. Also, a woman collected damages from a police officer who, in a ruse to have her involuntarily committed, falsely told her that her husband and child were injured and lying in a hospital (*Savage v. Boies*, 1954).

Intentional infliction of emotional distress and libel could overlap if a publisher knowingly published falsehoods about someone for the purpose not only of damaging that person's reputation, but also to cause emotional distress. For example, in *Goldwater v. Ginzburg* (1969), the 2nd Circuit Court upheld a libel judgment in favor of Barry Goldwater, the 1964 Republican presidential nominee, against *Fact* magazine for an article published during the campaign titled "The Unconscious of a Conservative: A Special Issue on the Mind of Barry Goldwater." The article claimed that Goldwater was "insane," "mentally imbalanced," and suffering from "mental disease." As to whether these claims were made with "malice," the Court noted that the owner and the editor of the magazine "were very much aware of the possible resulting harm," and that they carelessly used "slipshod and sketchy investigative techniques." Taken as a whole, the evidence, the 2nd Circuit Court concluded, "established with convincing clarity that the appellants were motivated by actual malice when they published these defamatory statements" (414 F.2d 324, 339 (1969)).

The 2nd Circuit Court's decision left open the question whether the state could impose civil liability if a comparable degree of malice motivated a publication of a cartoon that lampooned a public figure in an outrageous way. Such a publication could not constitute libel because it did not contain any allegation of fact, but it was an open question whether it could yet qualify as an intentional infliction of emotional distress. The Supreme Court addressed this question when Jerry Falwell, a nationally known minister and conservative commentator on politics and public affairs, sued Larry Flynt and *Hustler* magazine for its publication of a cartoon titled "Jerry Falwell Talks about His First Time." The cartoon was a spin-off of an actual Campari ad that asked celebrities when they first sampled Campari, a playful allusion to the sexual double entendre of the phrase "first times." The *Hustler* magazine cartoon presented Falwell as a celebrity whose "first time" was with his mother in an outhouse during a drunken rendezvous, which arguably undermined Falwell's public persona by depicting him as an immoral hypocrite. At the bottom of the page, in small print, there was the following disclaimer: "ad parody—not to be taken seriously."

In its decision in *Hustler Magazine, Inc. v. Falwell* (1988), the Court denied Falwell any recovery on the ground that "the heart of the First Amendment is the recognition of the fundamental importance of the free flow of ideas and opinions on matters of public interest and concern" (485 U.S. 46, 50 (1988)). In the Court's view, this principle would include opinion regarding the character of Jerry Falwell because the role of "public figures" was obviously a "matter of public concern." Even if the cartoon's depiction of Falwell was motivated by "malice," it was fully protected by freedom of speech because "in the world of debate about public affairs, many things done with motives that are less than admirable are protected by the First Amendment." If this were not the rule, "there can be little doubt that political cartoonists and satirists would be subjected to damages awards without any showing that their work falsely defamed its subject." Such cartoons are often calculated to injure the feelings of the subject of the portrayal, and they are usually "not reasoned or even-handed, but slashing and one-sided" (*Id.* at 53–54). Even if the *Hustler* cartoon of Falwell was more "outrageous" than most political cartoons, the term "outrageous," the Court argued, "has an inherent subjectiveness about it which would allow a jury to impose liability on the basis of the jurors' tastes or views, or perhaps on the basis of their dislike of a particu-lar expression." For this reason, the Court concluded, "public figures and public officials may not recover for the tort of intentional infliction of emotional distress . . . without showing, in addition, that the publication contains a false statement of fact which was made with 'actual malice,' i.e., with knowledge that the statement was false or with reckless disregard as to whether or not it was true" (*Id.* at 53, 55–56).

The upshot of the Court's decision in *Falwell* was that public officials and figures could recover for an intentional infliction of emotional dis-tress only if a libelous statement of fact caused the emotional distress. However, the Court did little in *Falwell* to clarify if and when a "private person" could recover for an intentional infliction of emotional distress caused by expressive activity. It confronted this difficult question in *Snyder v. Phelps* (2011), which addressed whether Fred Phelps and the church he founded, the Westboro Baptist Church of Topeka, Kansas, had a constitutional right to express the view that God was killing Ameri-can soldiers in combat because the United States was overly tolerant of homosexuality by picketing military funerals with signs that read "Thank God for IEDs," "Thank God for Dead Soldiers," "God Hates the USA/ Thank God for 9/11," and "You're Going to Hell." Phelps and six of his followers in 2006 carried such signs about 1,000 feet from the church where the funeral of Marine Lance Corporal Matthew Snyder was taking place and 200 to 300 feet from the funeral procession. Although the picketers complied with police instructions and did not yell or use pro-fanity, Snyder's father sued the Westboro Church and members of the Phelps family on a number of grounds, including intentional infliction of emotional distress, and won $2.9 million in compensatory damages and $8 million in punitive damages, the latter reduced by the district court to $2.1 million (562 U.S. 443, 448–449 (2011)).

The Phelps family and his church had engaged in comparable pro-tests at other funerals and comparable events around the country, in the process earning the distinction of being the subject of Louis Theroux's BBC documentary film titled *The Most Hated Family in America* and the

Southern Poverty Law Center's designation of Westboro as *"arguably the most obnoxious and rabid hate group in America"* (Southern Poverty Law Center). However, the Supreme Court ruled in favor of the free-speech rights of Phelps and the Westboro Church. According to the majority, the key to the case was whether the speech in question was "of public or private concern." The Court conceded that "the boundaries of the public concern test are not well defined," but declared that it was enough to qualify for constitutional protection if the speech in question "can 'be fairly considered as relating to any matter of political, social, or other concern to the community' or when it 'is a subject of legitimate news interest; that is, a subject of general interest and of value and concern to the public'" (*Id.* at 452–453).

The ironic implication of the Court's test is that "outrageous" speech that causes "emotional distress" gains constitutional protection to the degree that the media is attracted to covering the speech because of its "outrageous" character. In any case, although conceding that Westboro "chose to stage its picketing at . . . Matthew Snyder's funeral to increase publicity for its views," the Court found that the "content" of the Westboro Church's expression related "to broad issues of interest to society at large," such as "the political and moral conduct of the United States and its citizens, the fate of our Nation, homosexuality in the military, and scandals involving the Catholic clergy." In addition, the church "conducted its picketing peacefully . . . at a public place adjacent to a public street." The members "had the right to be where they were"; the picketing was "conducted under police supervision" and was done "out of the sight of those at the church"; and the protest "was not unruly" and "there was no shouting, profanity, or violence." The upshot, according to the majority, was "that any distress occasioned by Westboro's picketing turned on the content and viewpoint of the message conveyed, rather than any interference with the funeral itself" (*Id.* 454–457).

Based on this analysis, it did not matter that Snyder was not a "public official" or a "public figure" or that the church's speech was in fact "outrageous" and "intentionally" meant to cause "emotional distress." Any imposition of liability, the Court argued, would pose an unacceptable risk because "in public debate [we] must tolerate insulting, and even outrageous, speech in order to provide adequate 'breathing space' to the freedom protected by the First Amendment" (*Id.* at 458). In short, "outrageous" statements on "matters of public concern" that are likely to cause "extreme emotional distress" to private persons must nonetheless be protected so that others will fearlessly express "outrageous" statements on "matters of public concern" that have some degree of value. All "outrageous" statements on "matters of public concern" must be protected to ensure the necessary "breathing space" for freedom of speech. Of course, many Americans contend that this "breathing space" for outrageous statements is unnecessary or not worth the costs it imposes on the victims of "emotional distress."

FURTHER READING

Calvert, Clay. "Public Concern and Outrageous Speech: Testing the Inconstant Boundaries of IIED and the First Amendment Three Years after Snyder v. Phelps." *University of Pennsylvania Journal of Constitutional Law* 17 (2014): 437–478.

Givelber, Daniel. "The Right to Minimum Social Decency and the Limits of Evenhandedness: Intentional Infliction of Emotional Distress by Outrageous Conduct." *Columbia Law Review* 82 (1982): 42–75.

Jaffe, Elizabeth M. "Sticks and Stones May Break My Bones but Extreme and Outrageous Conduct Will Never Hurt Me: The Demise of the Intentional Infliction of Emotional Distress Claims in the Aftermath of Snyder v. Phelps." *Wayne Law Review* 57 (2011): 475–495.

Magruder, Calvert. "Mental and Emotional Disturbance in the Law of Torts." *Harvard Law Review* 49 (1936): 1033–1055.

Post, Robert C. "The Constitutional Concept of Public Discourse: Outrageous Opinion, Democratic Deliberation, and *Hustler Magazine v. Falwell*." *Harvard Law Review* 103 (1990): 603–686.

Prosser, William L. "Insult and Outrage." *California Law Review* 44 (1956): 40–64.

Smolla, Rodney A. *Jerry Falwell V Larry Flynt: The First Amendment on Trial*. New York: St. Martin's Press, 1988.

Southern Poverty Law Center. "Westboro Baptist Church," available at https://www.splcenter.org/fighting-hate/extremist-files/group/westboro-baptist-church.

Volokh, Eugene. "The Trouble with 'Public Discourse' as a Limitation on Free Speech Rights." *Virginia Law Review* 97 (2011): 567–594.

Q26. CAN THE GOVERNMENT REGULATE SPEECH THAT OCCURS ON PUBLIC PROPERTY?

Answer: Yes. The government can regulate speech that occurs on public property, but the rules vary depending on whether the public property is a "traditional public forum" (e.g., a street or a park), a "designated public forum" (e.g., a municipal theater or auditorium), a "limited public forum" (e.g., the facilities of a public university), or a "non-public forum" (e.g., a jail, a military base, or the inside of a polling station).

The Facts: Spontaneous demonstrations on public streets or in parks are not an unusual occurrence, and they arguably have given the American public the impression that they have a free-speech right to protest and express themselves on public property anytime and anywhere. This impression, however, is simply not true. In fact, late in the 19th century, the Supreme Court held that states and municipalities could exclude any and all types of speech, including political speech, from "traditional public forums," such as public streets and parks, just as a private property owner could exclude speech from his or her property (see *Davis v. Massachusetts*, 1897). The Court abandoned this absolute rule in *Hague v. Committee for Industrial Organization* (1939), a decision that invalidated a municipal ordinance that prohibited all public assemblies in the city's streets and parks without a permit from the director of safety who could arbitrarily deny it to prevent "riots, disturbances, or disorderly assemblage." The Court's justification for this ruling relied heavily on the fact that streets and parks "time out of mind, have been used for purposes of assembly, communicating thoughts between citizens, and discussing public questions." The Court conceded that this right to use streets and parks for political expression was not "absolute, but relative, and must be exercised in subordination to the general comfort and convenience, . . . but it must not, in the guise of regulation, be abridged or denied" (307 U.S. 496, 498, 516 (1939)).

The Court upheld reasonable regulations of political expression on public streets for the sake of public convenience in *Cox v. New Hampshire* (1941), a case dealing with dozens of Jehovah's Witnesses who had engaged in a political march on the public streets of a city without a license. Over 20 years later, in *Cox v. Louisiana* (1965), the Court invalidated a regulation that gave local officials no standards by which to decide whether to permit an assembly or parade, yet once again insisted regulations of "traditional public forums" were constitutional if they were "properly drawn," "'free from improper or inappropriate considerations and from unfair discrimination' . . . [and with] a 'systematic, consistent and just order of treatment, with reference to the convenience of public use of the highways'" (379 U.S. 536, 558 (1965)).

In *Kovacs v. Cooper* (1949), the Court applied these criteria to a municipal ordinance that prohibited the use of "sound trucks" on public streets, finding it clearly constitutional, even if the broadcasts were "political" in nature. However, in *Police Department of the City of Chicago v. Mosley* (1972) the Court invalidated a municipal ordinance that banned picketing on public streets near schools unless it was peaceful labor picketing. According to the Court, the "central problem" with Chicago's ordinance was

> that it describes permissible picketing in terms of its subject matter. Peaceful picketing on the subject of a school's labor-management dispute is permitted, but all other peaceful picketing is prohibited. The operative distinction is the message on a picket sign. But, above all else, the First Amendment means that government has no power to restrict expression because of its message, its ideas, its subject matter, or its content. (408 U.S. 92, 95 (1972))

That was not to say that a state could never have a legitimate interest in limiting some speech from "traditional public forums" and not others, but the state's purpose cannot be to suppress speech. Accordingly, any "justification for selective exclusions from a public forum must be carefully scrutinized." The exclusion must be "essential" to the furtherance of a "substantial governmental interest" (*Id.* at 99, 102).

During the 1980s, the Court upheld a number of laws and ordinances as legitimate content-neutral "time, place, and manner" regulations of "traditional public forums." This line of cases culminated in a three-part test for "time, place, and manner" regulations of "traditional public forums" that the Court established in *Ward v. Rock Against Racism* (1989), a decision that upheld New York City's limit on sound levels at concerts in Central Park. According to the Court, such a regulation was consistent with freedom of speech if it was (1) content-neutral; (2) narrowly tailored to serve a substantial government interest; and (3) if alternative channels for the communication of the information were left open. The Court underlined its view that the second criterion could be satisfied even if the law was not "the least restrictive or least intrusive means" of achieving the "substantial government interest." The "requirement of narrow tailoring is satisfied 'so long as the . . . regulation promotes a substantial government interest that would be achieved less effectively absent the regulation'" (491 U.S. 781, 789, 798–799 (1989)). The sound regulation was, therefore, constitutional since sound control in Central Park was an "important" interest, like the elimination of "visual clutter" in *Metromedia*, and it would be "less effectively" achieved without the sound limits than with them.

In subsequent cases, however, the Court struggled with the issue of when "time, place, and manner" regulations of "traditional public forums" were "content-neutral," especially in terms of laws that barred anti-abortion protestors from engaging in expressive activity on public streets in front of abortion facilities. In *Hill v. Colorado* (2000), a six-justice majority upheld a law that made it illegal, inside a 100-foot radius of an entrance to a healthcare facility, to "knowingly approach" within 8 feet of a person, without that person's consent, for the purpose of engaging in "protest, education, or counseling." According to the majority, this law was "content-neutral" because it was not a regulation of speech, but rather "a regulation of the places where some speech may occur"; the statute applied equally to all demonstrators, regardless of viewpoint; and, lastly, the state's interest was "to protect those who seek medical treatment from the potential physical and emotional harm suffered when an unwelcome individual delivers a message (whatever its content) by physically approaching an individual at close range, i.e. within eight feet." Justice Scalia, in dissent with Justice Thomas, claimed that the law was content-based because it "operates only on speech that communicates a message of protest, education, or counseling . . . at the entrance to medical facilities." For this reason, there was no doubt what the Colorado legislators "were taking aim at"; it was "the 'right to protest or counsel *against* certain medical procedures' on the sidewalks and streets surrounding health care facilities" (530 U.S. 703, 719, 744 (2000)).

If the Court did find that a "time, place and manner regulation" of a "traditional public forum" was content-based, it was nonetheless consistent with freedom of speech if it satisfied "strict scrutiny," that is, if it was a "necessary" means to a "compelling" governmental purpose. For example, in *Burson v. Freeman* (1992), the Court had no hesitation in finding that a federal law that prohibited distribution of campaign literature, a content-based distinction, within 100 feet of a polling place was constitutional because it was a "necessary" means to the "compelling" purpose of preventing voter intimidation.

The Court applied the same standards that it had developed to assess the constitutionality of "time, place and manner" regulations of "traditional public forums" to a new category of "designated public forums." This new type of "public forum" was not "traditional" in character, such as streets and parks, but were rather new public spaces dedicated to expressive activity, such as public theaters or auditoriums (see *Southeastern Promotions, Ltd. v. Conrad*, 1975). The government could not impose "content-based" restrictions on the use of such public facilities unless they passed strict scrutiny. Moreover, "content-neutral" restrictions were constitutional only if they were "narrowly tailored" to achieve an "important government purpose" and "other channels of communications" were left open.

During the 1980s, the Court established the category of "limited public forums" in *Widmar v. Vincent* (1981), a case that held that a public university could not allow its facilities to be used for certain types of student expression, such as political speech, and exclude other types, such as religious speech. A state had no First Amendment obligation to establish a "limited public forum," but if it did establish one, then it could not use content-based distinctions to limit access unless they were "reasonable" in character. The Court summed up its position on "limited public forums" in *Rosenberger v. Rector and Visitors of University of Virginia* (1995):

> The State may not exclude speech where its distinction is not "reasonable in light of the purpose served by the forum," nor may it discriminate against speech on the basis of viewpoint. Thus, in determining whether the State is acting to preserve the limits of the forum it has created so that the exclusion of a class of speech is legitimate, we have observed a distinction between, on the one hand, content discrimination, which may be permissible if it preserves the purposes of that limited forum, and, on the other hand, viewpoint discrimination, which is presumed impermissible when directed against speech otherwise within the forum's limitations. (515 U.S. 819, 829–830 (1995))

Accordingly, although the Court "presumes" that "viewpoint discrimination" is impermissible in "limited public forums," the Court has permitted the state to apply "content-based" distinctions, but only if they are "reasonable" given the purpose of the forum.

The complex nature of these criteria is reflected in the Court's decision in *Christian Legal Society v. Martinez* (2010), which upheld a public law school's policy of denying the use of its facilities to student groups that did not accept "all comers" to participate in the group's activities. Based on this regulation, the law school denied a student Christian group the use of its facilities because it required all members and officers to sign a statement of "faith" and renounce "unrepentant homosexual conduct." Regarding whether this procedure was constitutional, the Court concluded that the law school's policy was both "reasonable" and "viewpoint-neutral." It was reasonable because the law school was "caught in the crossfire between a group's desire to exclude and students' demand for equal access," and therefore, it "may reasonably draw a line in the sand permitting *all* organizations to express what they wish but *no* group to discriminate in membership." It was "viewpoint-neutral" because the law school applied the same policy to all student groups, not to suppress any group's viewpoint, but to discourage student groups from engaging in discriminatory conduct. Even if the policy had the "incidental" effect of burdening student groups "whose viewpoints are out of favor with the campus mainstream," it was nonetheless consistent with freedom of speech because the policy served a purpose "unrelated to the content of expression," that is the prevention of discrimination (561 U.S. 661, 694, 695–696 (2010)).

Four justices dissented, claiming that the law school's policy was not "viewpoint-neutral" because it prohibited student groups from discriminating on the basis of religion and sexual orientation, but not on other bases, such that a student environmental group could exclude students who denied global warning and animal rights groups could exclude those who favored using animals to test cosmetics (*Id.* at 724). The law school could not pick and choose what types of discrimination it would prohibit and what types it would not, according to the dissent, without engaging in "viewpoint discrimination."

Finally, apart from "limited public forums," the Court also developed a category of "non-public forums," which are public properties that the government can close to all speech activities or permit some speech if the regulations are "reasonable" and "viewpoint-neutral." An early case of this type was *Adderley v. Florida* (1966), involving trespass convictions of students who protested on the grounds of a county jail. The Court upheld the convictions, claiming that the state, "no less than a private owner of property, has power to preserve the property under its control for the use to which it is lawfully dedicated" (385 U.S. 39, 47 (1966)). The Court developed its criteria for evaluating regulations of "non-public forums" in a number of different contexts, resulting in the following frameworks: (1) a content-based regulation of a "non-public forum" was constitutional if its purpose was not to suppress a speaker's particular viewpoint and (2) a non-content-based regulation was constitutional if it was "reasonable" in terms of the purpose of the "non-public forum." Applying these rules in *Minnesota Voters Alliance v. Mansky* (2018), the Court invalidated a state ban of political apparel (e.g., a "political badge, political button, or other political insignia") inside of a polling place. Although the Court agreed that the inside of a polling place was a "non-public forum," and therefore, the state could utilize content-based distinctions (e.g., "political") if its purpose was not to suppress anyone's viewpoint; it ultimately invalidated the ban because it was not "reasonable." The term "political" was not an "objective workable standard," but rather a "subjective" one that could be applied in arbitrary ways, thereby exacerbating, rather than alleviating, partisan discord (138 S. Ct. 1876 (2018)).

The Court's standards for assessing the constitutionality of regulations of speech on public property are complicated, but it is simply not true that everyone has a free-speech right to speak on public property anytime, anywhere. The Court's fundamental premise is that the standards for assessing the constitutionality of regulations of speech on public property are different depending on whether the property is a "traditional or designated public forum," a "limited public forum," or a "non-public forum."

FURTHER READING

BeVier, Lillian R. "Rehabilitating Public Forum Doctrine: In Defense of Categories." In *Supreme Court Review*, edited by Dennis J. Hutchinson, David A. Strauss, and Geoffrey R. Stone. Chicago: University of Chicago Press, 1993, pp. 79–122.

Caplan, Aaron H. "Invasion of the Public Forum Doctrine." *Willamette Law Review* 46 (2010): 647–676.

Farber, Daniel A. and Nowak, John E. "The Misleading Nature of Public Form Analysis: Content and Context in First Amendment Adjudication." *Virginia Law Review* 70 (1984): 1219–1266.

Henslee, Elizabeth. "A Funny Thing Happened on the Way to the Public Forum: Why a Public Forum Analysis Applied to the Library Should Protect Internet Services and Delivery Systems." *Capital University Law Review* 43 (2015): 777–831.

Inazu, John D. "The First Amendment's Public Forum." *William and Mary Law Review* 56 (2015): 1159–1197.

Kalven, Harry. "The Concept of the Public Forum." *Supreme Court Review* (1965): 1–32.

Massey, Calvin. "Public Fora, Neutral Governments, and the Prism of Property." *Hastings Law Journal* 50 (1999): 309–353.

McGill, Matthew D. "Unleashing the Limited Public Forum: A Modest Revision to a Dysfunctional Doctrine." *Stanford Law Review* 52 (2000): 929–957.

Rohr, Marc. "The Ongoing Mystery of the Limited Public Forum." *Nova Law Review* 33 (2009): 299–355.

Q27. DOES A MEMBER OF AN AUDIENCE AT A PUBLIC SPEAKING EVENT OR AN ATTENDEE AT A POLITICAL DEMONSTRATION OR PROTEST HAVE A FREE-SPEECH RIGHT TO "HECKLE" A SPEAKER OR DISRUPT THE EVENT?

Answer: No. The constitutional guarantee of free speech does not protect a "heckler" at a public event who engages in disruptive expressive conduct, but it does protect non-disruptive expression if it is in compliance with lawful "time, place, and manner" regulations.

The Facts: A corollary of the constitutionality of "time, place and manner" regulations of speech (see Q26) is that a speaker who is in full compliance with these regulations cannot lawfully be "shouted down" by hecklers or "counter-protesters." Despite the widespread notion that such a heckler or "counter-protester" is simply exercising his or her rights to freedom of speech in opposition to the speaker's, any recognition of the legitimacy of what is called the "heckler's veto" is incompatible with any meaningful conception of freedom of speech. Since the right of free speech has significance only if it is a right to express controversial, not commonplace, ideas, a heckler has no right to shout down a speaker. The Supreme Court recognized this principle in two cases invalidating breach-of-peace convictions of speakers whose message offended members of their audience—*Cantwell v. Connecticut* (1940) and *Terminiello v. Chicago* (1949). The Court's rationale for rejecting the notion that a "hostile audience" has the right to "veto" the speaker's message was straightforward: "Speech is often provocative and challenging. It may strike at prejudices and preconceptions and have profound unsettling effects as it presses for acceptance of an idea" (*Terminiello v. Chicago*, 1949). Just because members of an audience do not like what they hear is no justification for imposing criminal liability on a speaker.

However, in *Feiner v. New York* (1951) the Court upheld a breach-of-peace conviction of a speaker urging African Americans to "rise up in arms and fight for equal rights." The Court distinguished *Feiner* from the earlier decisions in the following way: "It is one thing to say that the police cannot be used as an instrument for the suppression of unpopular views, and another to say that when, as here, the speaker passes the bounds of argument or persuasion and undertakes incitement to riot, they are powerless to prevent a breach of the peace" (340 U.S. 315, 319, 321 (1951)). According to the Court, a speaker who engaged in provocative speech in front of a "hostile audience" with the *intent* to incite a riot was not protected by freedom of speech.

However, three justices dissented in *Feiner*, arguing that, if a street brawl was not imminent, the police's duty was to protect the speaker from any intimidating speech by the "hostile audience." For example, Justice Black wrote that the police must make "all reasonable efforts" to protect "petitioner's constitutional right to talk," even to the extent of "arresting the man who threatened to interfere" (*Id.* at 325–327). In the same vein, Justices Douglas and Minton insisted that "an unsympathetic audience and the threat of one man to haul the speaker from the stage" was the "kind of threat" against which "speakers need police protection. If they do not receive it, and instead the police throw their weight on the side of those who would break up the meetings, the police become the new censors of speech" (*Id.* at 331). These dissents were the origin of the view that freedom of speech not only prevents the state from imposing liability on provocative speakers who are only exercising their legitimate First Amendment rights, but also imposes on the police the duty to control or arrest members of a "hostile audience" who are trying to intimidate the speaker.

During the 1960s, a majority of the Court adopted the reasoning of the dissents in *Feiner* when it overturned two breach-of-peace convictions of African Americans protesting racial segregation in front of "hostile" white audiences. In *Edwards v. South Carolina* (1963), there were 187 black students demonstrating on the State House grounds with 200 mostly white onlookers. Despite the racial tension evident at the demonstration, the circumstances were "a far cry from the situation in *Feiner*" because police protection "at the scene was at all times sufficient to meet any foreseeable possibility of disorder" (372 U.S. 229, 231–232, 236–237 (1963)). The Court came to the same conclusion in *Cox v. Louisiana* (1965). The Court conceded that the atmosphere had become "tense" and that the white crowd was "muttering," "grumbling," and "jeering," but nonetheless overturned the conviction on the ground that a contingent of 75–80 armed police officers separated the demonstrators from the "agitated" group of white citizens. In both *Edwards* and *Cox*, the Court implied that the police had a clear constitutional duty, if it was feasible, to control the "hostile audience," not to arrest speakers who were peaceably exercising their First Amendment rights.

In response to these decisions, states began charging permit fees for demonstrations in "public forums," thereby forcing speakers to help pay for the security costs that might be necessary to maintain public order. The issue was whether a state or other public entity could vary the permit fee depending on an assessment of security costs, increasing the fee if the provocative nature of the expression was thought to increase the likelihood of unlawful or violent conduct. The Court addressed this question in *Forsyth County v. The Nationalist Movement* (1992), a case dealing with a white supremacist group that wanted to demonstrate against the establishment of a Martin Luther King, Jr., federal holiday. The ordinance in question permitted an administrator "to adjust the amount to be paid in order to meet the expense incident . . . to the maintenance of public order in the matter licensed." A five-justice majority concluded that the ordinance violated freedom of speech because it vested "unbridled discretion in a government official" and because the assessed fee would "depend on the administrator's measure of the amount of hostility likely to be created by the speech based on its content" (505 U.S. 123, 127, 133–134 (1992)). Such a result was unacceptable. Freedom of speech, according to the Court, did not permit government to evaluate the provocative nature of any expression for the purpose of shifting the costs of controlling "hostile audiences" to provocative speakers who were merely exercising their First Amendment rights.

Although *Forsyth* does not prohibit governmental entities from charging a flat fee for the use of "public forums" for demonstrations, protests, rallies, or parades, the fee had to be the same whether security costs were expected to be minimal, moderate, or maximal. The result was that taxpayers must cover the security costs of provocative speakers exercising their free speech rights in "public forums." As a lower federal court argued in 1993, "Does it follow that the police may silence the rabble-rousing speaker? Not at all. The police must permit the speech and control the crowd; there is no heckler's veto" (*Hedges v. Wauconda Community Unit School District, No. 118,* 9 F.3d 1295, 1299 (7th Cir., 1993)). A different federal court came to the same conclusion in 2015: "If speech provokes wrongful acts on the part of hecklers, the government must deal with those wrongful acts directly; it may not avoid doing so by suppressing the speech" (*Santa Monica Nativity Scenes Committee v. City of Santa Monica,* 784 F.3d 1286, 1292–1293 (9th Cir., 2015)). (See also *Bible Believers v. Wayne County,* 2015.) The only exceptions to this rule was if, despite the best efforts of the police to control a "hostile audience," actual violence had broken out or was imminent or, perhaps, if the speaker was trying to incite a riot. In such circumstances, the government could perhaps arrest a speaker who refused a lawful police order to disperse, but the purpose of the order must not in any way be to suppress the speaker's message, but only to stop or prevent actual or imminent violence and disorder.

The burden of the Court's constitutional rule against the "heckler's veto" is at its height when the speaker's purpose is not simply to express his or her provocative message, but (in contrast to inciting a riot) is also to provoke a negative, possibly violent, reaction, perhaps for the ulterior motive of gaining media attention and notoriety. The weight of this burden is compounded if "counter-protesters" do not just want to "heckle" the speaker, but rather to "shut down the event" and gain media attention for their own benefit (Chait 2017). Following the vitriolic, though successful, 2016 presidential campaign of Donald Trump, these kinds of situations have arguably become more commonplace, whether at political rallies on public streets or on the campuses of public universities. One extreme example of the former is the "Unite the Right" rally held by a number of white supremacist groups, including armed militias, during August 11 and 12, 2017, in Charlottesville, Virginia. In response to this event, a network of racial activists, anti-fascists, anarchists, students, and clergy organized a counter-protest. Both sides expected violence, and their expectations were fulfilled, with the white supremacist attendees largely accountable for the resulting chaos. Dozens of people were injured in various confrontations between the two sides, and a 32-year-old woman was killed and 19 others injured when a white supremacist drove his car into a group of counter-protesters. Since the local police lost control of the situation, Virginia governor Terry McAuliffe declared a state of emergency and soon thereafter the Virginia State police declared the assembly to be unlawful. In this instance, since actual violence had erupted, it seems obvious that stopping the rally was necessary for public safety and, therefore, consistent with freedom of speech.

Recent events at public universities, which are "limited public forums" of the state (see Q26), have also strained the viability of the constitutional rule against the "heckler's veto." Berkeley University during 2017 is a case in point. In February, the university canceled a talk by right-wing commentator Milo Yiannopoulos after counter-protesters threw fireworks and rocks at police, ignited fires with Molotov cocktails, and smashed windows, injuring six persons and causing approximately $100,000 worth of damages. Berkeley blamed "150 masked agitators." In April, Ann Coulter canceled her speaking engagement at Berkeley when, for security reasons, the university shifted her scheduled talk to a later date when students would no longer be in class. Lastly, in September 2017 Ben Shapiro, a conservative political commentator, spoke at Berkeley, but nearly 1,000 counter-protesters chanted slogans outside the venue, such as "No Trump," "No KKK," and "No fascist USA." The police arrested nine of these counter-protesters, including three who were in possession of banned weapons. The university reportedly spent $600,000 on security for the Shapiro event and nearly $4 million for all outside speaking engagements of 2017.

In 2018, a Commission on Free Speech established by Berkeley's Chancellor published a report that claimed "at least some of the 2017 events at Berkeley can now be seen to be part of a coordinated campaign to organize appearances on American campuses likely to incite a violent reaction, in order to advance a facile narrative that universities are not tolerant of conservative speech" (*Report 2018*, 6). Whether this claim is true or not does not really explain why Berkeley students obstructed the expressive activities of conservative speakers. A 2017 Brookings survey of university students may help provide some insight. It found that 19 percent of all university students surveyed thought it was acceptable to use violence to stop a speaker they opposed, while 51 percent thought it was OK to disrupt such a speech by shouting so that the speaker could not be heard (Villasenor 2017). Obviously, the use of violence to stop a speaker is a criminal act inconsistent with freedom of expression. Whether "shouting down a speaker" would be consistent with freedom of speech would depend on the university's "time, place, and manner" regulations. The argument that such disruptive expressive behavior is itself protected by freedom of speech (Tushnet 2017) has not been accepted by the courts. A public university is well within its authority when it establishes reasonable regulations prohibiting disruptive expressive behavior and enforces those regulations with punitive sanctions, from warnings and suspensions to expulsions, even if "unreasonable" regulations of non-disruptive expressive conduct would be inconsistent with freedom of speech. Applying this distinction is a difficult task. A public university may very well prohibit "silent standing" inside a venue if it is "distracting" and its purpose is to disrupt a speaker's talk, but it would likely be "unreasonable" for the university to prohibit "silent standing" outside the venue because it is difficult to understand how such expression could be disruptive. Of course, in the end, since these standards are so heavily fact-dependent, no clear and fast rule can be established beforehand. Judges will have to decide in particular settings on a case-by-case basis what "time, place, and manner" regulations are "reasonable" and what expression is "disruptive" of the university's mission (Wright 2017).

The Supreme Court has not addressed the constitutional rule against the "heckler's veto" in many years, but lower court decisions strongly suggest that the rule is as valid today as it has ever been. Accordingly, despite the recent events at Berkeley and Charlottesville, it is simply inconsistent with freedom of speech to allow "hecklers" to decide which speakers can speak and which cannot. Based on the Court's rulings, it is simply not constitutionally permissible for states, municipalities, and public universities to exclude "provocative" speaking events that are arguably more likely to result in violence or disorder than "non-provocative" events. As the Court indicated in *Forsyth*, any such policy would require the state, municipality, or public university to make judgments based on the "content" of the speaker's message, which the First Amendment does not permit unless it is a "necessary" means to a "compelling" purpose. Of course, public safety is a "compelling" state objective, but banning speakers who are exercising their legitimate free-speech rights is not "necessary" to achieve this end because a state, municipality, or public university can protect public safety by providing the security appropriate to the nature of the event. Obviously, this option in particular cases can be very expensive, but no one has ever argued that protecting freedom of speech is not without its costs. The argument instead is that over the long run freedom of speech is worth more than the costs it might incur in specific cases.

FURTHER READING

Chait, Jonathan. "The 'Shut It Down!' Left and the War on the Liberal Mind." *The New Magazine*, April 26, 2017, nymag.com/daily/intelli gencer/2017/04/the-shut-it-down-left-and-the-war-on-the-liberal-mind.html.

Harmon, Rachel A. "Policing, Protesting, and the Insignificance of Hostile Audiences." *Knight First Amendment Institute at Columbia University*, *"Emerging Threats" Series* (2018), available at https://knightcolumbia.org/content/policing-protesting-and-insignificance-hostile-audiences.

Hsin, J. D. "Defending the Public's Forum: Theory and Doctrine in the Problem of Provocative Speech." *Hastings Law Journal* (2018): 1099–1145.

Leanza, Cheryl A. "Heckler's Veto Case Law as a Resource for Democratic Discourse." *Hofstra Law Review* 61 (2007): 1305–1320.

McGaffey, Ruth. "The Heckler's Veto: A Reexamination." *Marquette Law Review* 57 (1973): 39–64.

Report of the Chancellor's Commission on Free Speech, University of California, Berkeley, April 9, 2018, available at https://chancellor.berkeley.edu/sites/default/files/report_of_the_commission_on_free_speech.pdf.

Schauer, Frederick. "The Hostile Audience Revisited." *Knight First Amendment Institute at Columbia University, "Emerging Threats" Series*. (2017), available at https://knightcolumbia.org/content/hostile-audience-revisited.

Tushnet, Mark. "What the Constitution Says Berkeley Can Do When Controversial Speakers Come Knocking." *Vox*, September 23, 2017, available at https://www.vox.com/the-big-idea/2017/9/22/16346330/free-speech-week-first-amendment-constitution-bannon.

Villasenor, John. "Views among College Students Regarding the First Amendment: Results from a New Survey." *Brookings Institution*, September 18, 2017, https://www.brookings.edu/blog/fixgov/2017/09/18/views-among-college-students-regarding-the-first-amendment-results-from-a-new-survey/.

Wright, R. George. "The Heckler's Veto Today." *Case Western Reserve Law Review* 68 (2017): 159–188.

5

Free Speech and the Individual's Place in Society

Prohibitions and regulations of speech are typically justified in terms of the substantive nature of the speech in question or the circumstances under which it is uttered or published. For example, a "true" threat is a harmful type of speech that government can prohibit because it is outside the scope of freedom of speech (see Chapter 2), while unlawful advocacy is a type of expression that can be prohibited in some circumstances but not in others (see Chapter 3); other types of speech are subject to regulation because they have negative incidental or secondary effects depending on the circumstances or because the regulations only bear upon the time, place, and manner of the expression (see Chapter 4). A very different type of prohibition or regulation is one that is directed at certain individuals or persons, but not at others. This chapter will examine several examples of such prohibitions or regulations. The dispositive issue that determines whether such a prohibition or regulation is compatible with freedom of speech typically depends on the nature of the relationship that the person subject to the prohibition or regulation has with the government.

These special relationships that the government has with persons are diverse in character. One obvious instance is a student in a public secondary school. Another example is a government employee, but this category contains different subgroups, such as employees who have access to classified information or employees who have signed nondisclosure agreements with the government. Journalists working for newspapers, television stations/networks, or other media outlets constitute a very different category of persons linked to freedom of speech. It is commonly believed that journalists have special free-speech rights because the First Amendment contains a separate clause protecting the freedom of the press. Whether this claim is valid or not, the main point is that the constitutional right of freedom of speech provides varying levels of protection to different types of persons. This reality adds another layer of complexity to the topic of freedom of speech, a layer that can lead to a number of misconceptions.

Q28. DOES A STUDENT ATTENDING A PUBLIC HIGH SCHOOL HAVE THE SAME FREE-SPEECH RIGHTS INSIDE AND OUTSIDE OF THE SCHOOL?

Answer: No. Although the Court has held that students who attend a public high school do not "shed" their constitutional rights of free speech "at the schoolhouse gate," a public high school can prohibit speech inside the school for pedagogical reasons that the state could not prohibit outside of it.

The Facts: In *Tinker v. Des Moines Independent Community School District*, 393 U.S. 503 (1969), the Supreme Court upheld the right of students to wear black armbands in a public school to protest the Vietnam War (see Q21). This decision has fostered the myth that students in public school have the same free-speech rights inside or out of school, partly because the Court did insist that neither students nor teachers "shed their constitutional rights to freedom of speech or expression at the schoolhouse gate," and that, in our system,

> state-operated schools may not be enclaves of totalitarianism. School officials do not possess absolute authority over their students. Students in school, as well as out of school are "persons" under our Constitution. They are possessed of fundamental rights which the State must respect. (393 U.S. 503, 511 (1969))

This language suggests that, as "persons" under the Constitution, students inside and outside high school have the same constitutional right of free speech, which is not true. As the Court notes in *Tinker*, a student's free-speech rights extend beyond classroom hours. When a student "is in the cafeteria, or on the playing field, or on the campus during the authorized hours, he may express his opinions, even on controversial topics like the conflict in Vietnam," but the Court then added, "conduct by the student, in class or out of it, which for any reason—whether it stems from time, place, or type of behavior—materially disrupts class-work or involves substantial disorder or invasion of the rights of others is, of course, not immunized by the constitutional guarantee of free-dom of speech." But in this case, the Court emphasized more than once, the record did not contain "any facts" that might "reasonably" have led school authorities to expect that wearing black armbands would dis-rupt school activities and no such "disturbances or disorders" in fact occurred. Accordingly, in such circumstances the Court concluded, "our Constitution does not permit officials of the State to deny their form of expression" (*Id.* at 512–514).

Tinker, therefore, does not stand for the proposition that students in public schools retained all their free-speech rights. Instead it sup-ports the principle that students in public schools have no right under the First Amendment, inside or outside of class, to disrupt class work, cause "substantial" disorder, or "invade" the rights of others, presumably including fellow students, teachers, and school administrators. In *Bethel School District v. Fraser* (1986) the Court addressed the important issue of what constituted "substantial disorder." Fraser delivered a speech nom-inating a fellow student for an elective student office at a school assem-bly attended by approximately 600 students. All of the students were required to attend the assembly, one that was part of a school-sponsored program on self-government, or report to the study hall. In his speech, Fraser referred to his nominee in titillating language, emphasizing words and phrases with clear sexual double meanings.

To decide the question whether the school could discipline Fraser, the Court began with the observation that the purpose of public education was to "inculcate the habits and manners of civility as values in them-selves conducive to happiness and as indispensable to the practice of self-government in the community and the nation."

Accordingly, the Court reasoned, even if "an offensive form of expres-sion may not be prohibited to adults making what the speaker considers a political point," it did not follow that "the same latitude must be permit-ted to children in a public school." To the contrary, the Court insisted, "the constitutional rights of students in public school are not automat-ically coextensive with the rights of adults in other settings" and "it is a highly appropriate function of public school education to prohibit the use of vulgar and offensive terms in public discourse." This rule is not only applicable to the classroom. "Consciously or otherwise, teachers—and indeed the older students—demonstrate the appropriate form of civil discourse and political expression by their conduct and deportment in and out of class" (478 U.S. 675, 682–687 (1986)).

Since Fraser gave his nominating speech at a student assembly that was part of a school-sponsored program on self-government, he could not convincingly argue that his expression was private in character, unrelated to the school's official mission. But what if a public school established a student newspaper as part of its journalism curriculum? Did school officials and teachers retain the right to censor the newspaper? The Court addressed this question in *Hazelwood School District v. Kuhlmeier* (1988) by upholding the principal's decision to delete two articles from the newspaper because it was "part of the educational curriculum, and a 'regular classroom activit[y].'" The Court reached this result by distinguishing between student speech and the question "whether the First Amendment requires a school affirmatively to promote particular student speech" through "school-sponsored publications, theatrical productions, and other expressive activities." The Court argued that "educators are entitled to exercise greater control over this second form of student expression to assure that participants learn whatever lessons the activity is designed to teach, that readers or listeners are not exposed to material that may be inappropriate for their level of maturity, and that the views of the individual speaker are not erroneously attributed to the school." In effect, these student expressive activities "may fairly be characterized as part of the school curriculum, whether or not they occur in a traditional classroom setting, so long as they are supervised by faculty members and designed to impart particular knowledge or skill to student participants and audiences." The Court concluded, "The education of the Nation's youth is primarily the responsibility of parents, teachers, and state and local school officials, and not of federal judges" (484 U.S. 260, 268, 271, 273 (1988)).

The Court continued this deferential approach to public schools in *Morse v. Frederick* (2007), a case involving a school that disciplined a student who displayed, as the Olympic torch passed by the school in Juneau, Alaska, a 14-foot banner declaring "BONG HiTS 4 JESUS." Frederick unfurled his banner on the opposite side of the street from the school, but the school claimed he was on a class trip under teacher supervision and, for that reason, the banner violated the school's policy prohibiting the promotion of illegal drug use. The Court had no difficulty accepting the premise that "schools may take steps to safeguard those entrusted to their care from speech that can reasonably be regarded as encouraging illegal drug use" and that "school speech precedents" were applicable even though Frederick was off school property on a "class trip." Accordingly, the key issue was whether the banner in fact advocated illegal drug use. The Court called the banner's statement "cryptic," "no doubt offensive to some," "perhaps amusing" or meaning "nothing at all" to others." However, despite these alternative meanings, the Court concluded that the school's interpretation of the banner as advocating drug use was a "reasonable" interpretation. It did not matter to the Court that the banner would in no way constitute "unlawful advocacy" (see Q14) outside the context of a public school. In the Court's view, "schools may regulate some speech 'even though the government could not censor similar speech outside the school'" (551 U.S. 393, 397, 401–402, 406, 410 (2007)).

Against the set of precedents discussed earlier, it is difficult to assess the current controversy regarding whether high school football players have a free-speech right to protest racial injustice by kneeling during the national anthem. If *Tinker* stood alone as the only relevant precedent, the answer would arguably be "yes," but later decisions by the Court have cast the issue into doubt at a time when several public high schools have recently suspended students for engaging in such expressive conduct (Hauser 2017). *Kuhlmeier* would appear to support the constitutionality of such suspensions on the ground that schools sponsor extracurricular sporting events, just as they sponsor student newspapers. However, in *Kuhlmeier*, the school newspaper was a part of the journalism curriculum, which is not the case with football, unless a school explicitly links the sport to a curriculum dealing with leadership, team-building, or some other legitimate pedagogical goal. Moreover, compelling students to stand during the national anthem arguably triggers the constitutional rule against compelled speech that the Court announced in *West Virginia State Board of Education v. Barnette*, the 1943 decision prohibiting states from requiring students to salute the flag (see Q2). However, it is arguable that kneeling is something more than a refusal to stand for the anthem; it is a form of counter-protest that might interfere with the school's goal of instilling patriotic values, disrupt a school-sponsored event, or give the impression that the student is acting with the school's imprimatur.

The Supreme Court has yet to address the issue of high school football players kneeling during the national anthem, but the line of cases discussed earlier reflects a trend of judicial deference to local school boards, administrators, and teachers. It has also not decided whether public high schools can punish off-campus student speech, in particular that which occurs online. Currently, federal circuit courts are in sharp disagreement about how freedom of speech applies to such expression. Some circuit courts focus on whether it is foreseeable that the online student speech will have a disruptive effect on the school's mission, or they focus on the student speaker's intent; other circuit courts require a "true threat" or an "imminent likelihood" of violence (Ferry 2018). Accordingly, the current constitutional status of online student speech that occurs outside a public high school is very uncertain. It will remain so until the Supreme Court directly confronts this highly controversial issue.

FURTHER READING

Brownstein, Alan. "Bringing Order Out of the Chaos of Free Speech Cases Involving School-Sponsored Activities." *University of California Davis Law Review* 42 (2008–2009): 717–824.

Chemerinsky, Erwin. "Students Do Leave Their First Amendment Rights at the Schoolhouse Gates: What's Left of Tinker." *Drake Law Review* 48 (2000): 527– 546.

Ferry, Katherine A. "Comment: Reviewing the Impact of the Supreme Court's Interpretation of 'Social Media' as Applied to Off-Campus Student Speech." *Loyola University Chicago Law Journal* 49 (2018): 717–782.

Hauser, Christine. "High Schools Threaten to Punish Students Who Kneel during the National Anthem." *The New York Times*, September 29, 2017, available at https://www.nytimes.com/2017/09/29/us/high-school-anthem-protest.html.

LoMonte, Frank D. "Shrinking Tinker: Students Are 'Persons' under Our Constitution—Except When They Aren't." *American University Law Review* 58 (2009): 1323–1359.

McNeal, Laura Rene. "From Hoodies to Kneeling during the National Anthem: The Colin Kaepernick Effect and Its Implications for K-12 Sports." *Louisiana Law Review* 78 (2017): 145–196.

Tsesis, Alexander. "Categorizing Student Speech." *Minnesota Law Review* 102 (2018): 1147–1204.

Yudof, Mark. "Tinker Tailored: Good Faith, Civility, and Student Expression." *St. John's Law Review* 69 (1995): 365–377.

Q29. DO STUDENTS ATTENDING PUBLIC COLLEGES AND UNIVERSITIES HAVE MORE FREE-SPEECH RIGHTS THAN PUBLIC HIGH SCHOOL STUDENTS?

Answer: Yes. Students attending public colleges and universities generally have more free speech rights than high school students, but that does not mean they are equivalent to the free-speech rights of American citizens in "traditional" or "designated public forums" (see Q26).

The Facts: Public colleges and universities have the legal authority to punish speech if it is a "true threat," "libel," "fighting word," "obscenity," "criminal harassment," or "harassment" that qualifies as "discrimination" under Title VI or Title IX (see Chapters 2 and 3). Generally speaking, the rule is that the limits of freedom of speech that are applicable to the general population are applicable to students at public colleges and universities. But can public colleges and universities impose additional limitations on free speech? Some commentators argue that students at public colleges and universities have no constitutional free-speech rights, but only the right "of academic freedom." According to this view, citizens "are not students under the tutelage of the state," but students are "under tutelage of the university, which is an arena of education, not of political self-governance" (Post 2017). This point of view conflicts with the Supreme Court's ruling in *Healy v. James* (1972). In this decision, the Court held that Central Connecticut State College (CCSC) violated the constitutional right of free speech and association when it denied official recognition to a group of students who wished to form a local chapter of Students for a Democratic Society (SDS). The SDS was a national organization that had been involved in civil disobedience on college campuses during the late 1960s, including seizure of buildings, vandalism, and arson, to protest the Vietnam War.

The Court began its analysis with a strong endorsement of the view that the First Amendment applied to public campuses:

> Yet the precedents of the Court leave no room for the view that, because of the acknowledged need for order, First Amendment protection should apply with less force on college campuses than in the community at large. Quite to the contrary, "[t]he vigilant protection of constitutional freedom is nowhere more vital than in the community of American schools." The college classroom, with its surrounding environs, is peculiarly the *"marketplace of ideas," and we break no new constitutional ground in reaffirming this Nation's dedication to safeguarding academic freedom*. (408 U.S. 169, 180–181 (1972), emphasis in original)

According to the Court, CCSC's denial of recognition excluded the students from the use of campus facilities, which was enough to trigger a violation of their right of association. Even if some of the students at CCSC shared the national SDS's "philosophy of violence and disruption," that fact was insufficient to justify the denial of recognition since no "instrumentality of the State" may restrict speech or association on the ground that the views expressed are "abhorrent." The critical line is "between mere advocacy and advocacy 'directed to inciting or producing imminent lawless action and . . . likely to incite or produce such action'" (see Q14), along with, at public colleges and universities, "actions which 'materially and substantially disrupt the work and discipline of the school." In short, students at public universities and colleges had free-speech rights comparable to citizens in "traditional" or "designated public forums," but these rights, unlike the rights of citizens, did not extend to expressive activities that infringed "reasonable rules," "interrupted classes," or "substantially interfered" with the opportunity of other students to obtain an education (*Id.* at 181, 186–189).

A year after *Healy*, the Supreme Court addressed in *Papish v. Board of Curators of the University of Missouri* (UM) whether a state university could expel a student for distributing a newspaper whose cover depicted policemen raping the Statue of Liberty and the Goddess of Justice and which contained an article titled "M____f____ Acquitted," referring to the trial of a New York City youth who belonged to an organization known as "Up Against the Wall, M____f____." UM claimed that the student had violated its rule prohibiting students from engaging in "indecent conduct or speech." Addressing whether such a rule was reasonable, the Court concluded that under the principles announced in *Healy* it was unreasonable. The school expelled the student not because the distribution of the newspaper violated the UM's time, place, and manner regulations, but simply because it disapproved of its content. However, the Court concluded, "We think *Healy* makes it clear that the mere dissemination of ideas—no matter how offensive to good taste—on a state university campus may not be shut off in the name alone of 'conventions of decency'" and that "the state University's action here cannot be justified as a nondiscriminatory application of reasonable rules governing conduct" (410 U.S. 667, 667–668, 670–671 (1973)).

The Court's decision in *Papish* made it clear that public universities and colleges, just like government itself, violated freedom of speech if they utilized content-based distinctions in their regulations of the expressive activities of their students (see Q7). As the Court remarked at the end of its opinion, "The First Amendment leaves no room for the operation of a dual standard in the academic community with respect to the content of speech" (*Id.* at 671). A state university could not, therefore, have one set of regulations for decent speech and a different, more repressive set for indecent speech. In later cases, the Court applied this principle to the "limited public forums" of state universities and colleges, such as auditoriums for guest speakers. A public institution of higher education could not exclude from such an auditorium certain types of speech, for example, indecent speech or religious speech, unless the exclusion was "reasonable in light of the purpose served by the forum." In contrast to the "reasonable" use of content-based distinctions, the Court presumed that public colleges and universities violated freedom of speech if they excluded any type of speech from their "limited public forums" based on "viewpoint" (see Q26). For example, a public college or university could dedicate one of its auditoriums to serious drama, excluding all forms of comedy, but it could not allow student comedy shows in a different auditorium, but deny access to a student group that satirized Christianity.

The principle that public universities and colleges must maintain "viewpoint neutrality" arose in *Board of Regents, University of Wisconsin v. Southworth* (2000), a case involving students at the University of Wisconsin who, on First Amendment grounds, objected to paying a student activity fee that funded registered student organizations that engaged in political and ideological expression offensive to their personal beliefs. To require them to fund speech they disagreed with was, the students argued, a form of "compelled speech" (see Q2). The Supreme Court disagreed, holding that it was "unworkable" to confine student funding to programming that was "germane" to the public college or university's mission. The purpose of the extracurricular speech funded by the student activity fee was, in the Court's view, "distinguished not by discernible limits but by its vast, unexplored bounds." For this reason, to "insist upon asking what speech is germane [to the school's mission] would be contrary to the very goal the University seeks to pursue." In addition, allowing "each student to list those causes which he or she will or will not support" would be "so disruptive and expensive that the program to support extracurricular speech would be ineffective," placing the existence of the program itself "at risk" (529 U.S. 217, 232–233 (2000)).

However, the Court continued, even if public colleges or universities may use student funding to finance a vast array of extracurricular discussions of philosophical, religious, scientific, social, and political topics, it "must provide some protection to its students' First Amendment interests." In this vein, the "proper measure, and the principal standard of protection for objecting students," the Court concluded, was "the requirement of viewpoint neutrality in the allocation of funding support." What this requirement of "viewpoint neutrality" means in practice, the Court added, was "that minority views are treated with the same respect as are majority views" (*Id.* at 235).

It is not always clear how the rules regarding "reasonableness" and "viewpoint neutrality" should be applied to student speech in specific circumstances. It is clearly "reasonable" for a public college or university to punish student expressive behavior that "disrupts" its educational mission, but what exactly constitutes "disruptive behavior"? One public college disciplined a student who replied to a post on Yik Yak tagged "#blackwomenmatter" with "They matter, they're just not hot." The school justified the discipline on the ground that the speech was "abusive" behavior that constituted a "disruption of college activities" (Park 2016). The Supreme Court has yet to clarify whether such off-campus student expression is "disruptive" in the constitutional sense of that term.

Another issue arises from the fact that many educational programs at public institutions of higher learning prepare students for professional careers that have ethical codes. Is it, therefore, "reasonable" for a public college or university to sanction student expressive behavior if, in its judgment, it is not consistent with the relevant profession? For example, the University of Minnesota punished a mortuary student who posted sarcastic comments about cadavers on her personal Facebook page (Waldman 2013; Calvert 2017). Can the university justify such punishment as "reasonable" in the context of an educational program that is professional in character? The Supreme Court has not yet seen fit to resolve such questions.

The meaning of the requirement that public colleges and universities must maintain "viewpoint neutrality" is also not crystal clear. The Court has held that a public law school could deny the use of its facilities to a student group that required its members to renounce "unrepentant homosexual conduct" because the denial was based not on expression but on the discriminatory conduct of denying membership to an individual. The Court argued that the policy was "viewpoint neutral" even if it had the "incidental" effect of burdening minority student groups "whose viewpoints are out of favor with the campus mainstream" (see Q26). Recent incidents of student-athletes silently kneeling during the national anthem have dramatically highlighted the question of what is necessary for a public college or university to maintain "viewpoint neutrality." For example, state legislators threatened to cut funding to the University of Arkansas after six African American players on the women's basketball team knelt during the national anthem, but the team's coach and the university generally defended the six women on the ground of freedom of speech. A similar dispute erupted in 2016 at

East Carolina University (ECU) after members of the marching band knelt during the anthem. An ECU official later issued a press release announcing that protests of this sort "will not be tolerated moving forward" (Papandrea 2017, 1810–1811).

The ECU official's declaration may be consistent with freedom of speech because it is necessary for the marching band to maintain discipline while it is playing the anthem, but it is less clear whether the same rule can be applied to football or basketball players. Since the anthem is typically played at college football games prior to the players taking the field, it may be somewhat of an academic question to ask whether they have a free-speech right to kneel during the anthem, but it is one well worth considering. One argument in favor of banning such protests is that, even if such expressive conduct is not disruptive of the school's mission in any significant way, members of the public will gain the mistaken impression that the school is condoning such expressive conduct if it goes unpunished. However, it is not at all clear whether this kind of public misapprehension is in fact likely to occur and, even if it does, whether it cannot be solved with an appropriate disclaimer, rather than punishing the students' expressive activities. Moreover, as noted earlier, the Supreme Court has held that public colleges and universities must maintain "viewpoint neutrality." On this basis, if governments cannot, consistent with the First Amendment, require students to pledge allegiance to the flag while in public school (see Q7), then it is not at all clear how public colleges and universities can punish players who kneel during the national anthem at an intercollegiate basketball or football game. It is fair to say that a refusal to do something expressive, such as refusing to salute the flag, is only passive in character, not involving active expression, but in reality refusing to pledge allegiance to the flag in school is arguably as much a "protest" as kneeling during the anthem at a game. Since the Supreme Court has yet to address whether there is a constitutional difference between refusing to pledge allegiance to the flag and kneeling during the national anthem, this question, along with the others discussed earlier, remains unresolved.

FURTHER READING

Calvert, Clay. "Professional Standards and the First Amendment in Higher Education: When Institutional Academic Freedom Collides with Student Speech Rights." *St. John's Law Review* 91 (2017): 611–662.

Chemerinsky, Erwin. *Free Speech on Campus*. New Haven, CT: Yale University Press, 2017.

Kitrosser, Heidi. "Free Speech, Higher Education, and the PC Narrative." *Minnesota Law Review* 101 (2017): 1987–2057.

Papandrea, Mary-Rose. "The Free Speech Rights of University Students." *Minnesota Law Review* 101 (2017): 1801–1861.

Park, Michael K. "Restricting Anonymous 'Yik Yak': The Constitutionality of Regulating Students' Off-Campus Online Speech in the Age of Social Media." *Willamette Law Review* 52 (2016): 405–449.

Post, Robert C. "There Is No 1st Amendment Right to Speak on a College Campus." Vox.com, December 31, 2017, available at https://www.vox.com/the-big-idea/2017/10/25/16526442/first-amendment-college-campuses-milo-spencer-protests.

Silvergate, Harvey A. and French, David. *FIRE's Guide to Free Speech.* 2nd ed. Philadelphia: Foundation for Individual Rights in Education, 2012.

Waldman, Emily Gold. "University Imprimaturs on Student Speech: The Certification Cases." *First Amendment Law Review* 11 (2013): 382–425.

Wells, Christina E. "Free Speech Hypocrisy: Campus Free Speech Conflicts and the Sub-Legal First Amendment." *University of Colorado Law Review* 89 (2018): 533–564.

Q30. CAN A STATE OR THE FEDERAL GOVERNMENT IMPOSE LIMITS ON THE FREE-SPEECH RIGHTS OF AN EMPLOYEE ABOVE AND BEYOND THOSE IMPOSED ON THE ORDINARY CITIZEN?

Answer: Yes. As an employer, a state government or the federal government can impose relevant restrictions on the free-speech rights of its employees, but they cannot do so in a manner that unduly limits the free-speech rights of public employees. In addition, faculty at public colleges and universities have additional protections based on the principle of academic freedom.

The Facts: As an employer, the government has the authority to significantly limit the speech activities of its employees. That is not to say that the government has the power to suppress all employee speech. As early as the 1950s, the Supreme Court held that loyalty oaths as a precondition for public employment violated due process because they excluded someone from employment based on association with a proscribed group, such as the Communist Party, without any consideration of whether the individual "knew" about the group's subversive goals or methods (see *Wieman v. Updegraff*, 1952). Moreover, by 1960, the Court shifted its focus to the First Amendment when it invalidated a state law requiring teachers to file annual affidavits listing the organizations to which they belonged, concluding that "to compel a teacher to disclose his every association tie is to impair that teacher's right of free association, a right closely allied to freedom of speech and a right which, like free speech, lies at the foundation of a free society (*Shelton v. Tucker*, 1960).

The shift from due process to the First Amendment as the basis for protecting the rights of teachers at public universities and colleges continued in *Keyishian v. Board of Regents* (1967), a decision invalidating a state law that required faculty at a state university to certify that they were not Communists or members of any organization advocating the violent overthrow of organized government. The key to the Court's rationale for invalidating the law was academic freedom guaranteed by the First Amendment:

> Our nation is deeply committed to safeguarding academic freedom, which is of transcendent value to all of us, and not merely to the teachers concerned. That freedom is therefore a special concern of the First Amendment, which does not tolerate laws that cast a pall of orthodoxy over the classroom. . . . The classroom is peculiarly the "marketplace of ideas." The Nation's future depends upon leaders trained through wide exposure to that robust exchange of ideas which discovers truth "out of a multitude of tongues, [rather] than through any kind of authoritative selection." (385 U.S. 589, 603 (1967))

In the Court's view, academic freedom had three dimensions: first, the freedom of the academic community from state intrusion; second, the freedom of individual faculty members from control by the public educational institution; and, third, the free-speech rights of individual faculty members from state sanctions (Rabban 1990). In terms of the third dimension of academic freedom, the Court concluded that a public university or college could not dismiss a faculty member for belonging to an organization that advocated the violent overthrow of government. An additional requirement was that the faculty member had to have a "specific intent to further the unlawful aims of the Communist Party" (*Id.* at 610). For this reason, the free-speech rights of faculty members at public colleges and universities extended beyond those of other types of public employees.

The Court addressed the free-speech rights of high school teachers in *Pickering v. Board of Education* (1968), a case concerning a local school board that had dismissed a teacher for publishing a letter in a local newspaper that criticized the board's recent decisions. The Court's decision invalidating the dismissal rested on a distinction between expression "as a citizen" and expression "as an employee." On the one hand, the notion "that teachers may constitutionally be compelled to relinquish the First Amendment right they would otherwise enjoy as citizens to comment on matters' of public interest . . . has been unequivocally rejected in numerous decisions of this Court." On the other hand, the Court conceded, "it cannot be gainsaid that the State has interests as an employer in regulating the speech of its employees that differ significantly from those it possesses in connection with regulation of the speech of the citizenry in general." The implication was that a local school board could not impose sanctions on a high school teacher who, as a citizen, was commenting on "matters of public interest," but it could, as an employer, impose restraints on a teacher's expression if it either "impeded the teacher's proper performance of his daily duties in the classroom" or "interfered with the regular operation of the schools generally" (391 U.S. 563, 568, 572 (1968)).

In general, the Court endorsed the position that public employees, including teachers, did not give up all their free-speech rights as a condition of public employment, but they did not retain all the free-speech rights ordinary citizens have in traditional public forums. The Court considered the extent to which *Pickering* protected the free-speech rights of public employees who were not teachers in *Connick v. Myers* (1983), a case involving the firing of an assistant district attorney who, on her own authority, circulated among her colleagues a questionnaire concerning job satisfaction and internal office affairs. In a 5–4 decision, the Court rejected the argument that circulating the questionnaire was speech by Myers on a "matter of public concern." This finding proved dispositive for the Court because when "employee expression cannot be fairly considered as relating to any matter of political, social, or other concern to the community, government officials should enjoy wide latitude in managing their offices, without intrusive oversight by the judiciary in the name of the First Amendment" (461 U.S. 138, 146 (1983)).

According to the Court, whether "an employee's speech addresses a matter of public concern must be determined by the content, form, and context of a given statement, as revealed by the whole record." Applying this standard, the Court emphasized the fact that

> Myers did not seek to inform the public that the District Attorney's Office was not discharging its governmental responsibilities in the investigation and prosecution of criminal cases. Nor did Myers seek to bring to light actual or potential wrongdoing or breach of public trust on the part of [her superiors. Instead] . . . the focus of Myers' questions is . . . rather to gather ammunition for another round of controversy with her superiors. (*Id.* at 148)

The Court agreed that "public officials should be receptive to constructive criticism offered by their employees," but insisted that "the First Amendment does not require a public office to be run as a roundtable for employee complaints over internal office affairs." In the end, the Court concluded, when "matters of public concern" are not involved, "a wide degree of deference to the [governmental] employer's judgment is appropriate" (*Id.* at 149, 152).

Following *Connick*, the crucial issue was whether a public employee's expression addressed a matter of "public" or "private" concern," a distinction difficult to apply in practice. In *Rankin v. McPherson* (1987), the Court held that a public clerical employee's comment after the attempted assassination of President Reagan, "If they go for him again, I hope they get him," did address a "matter of public concern." However, in *Waters v. Churchill* (1994), the Court ruled that a nurse who complained to a coworker that their training was flawed could be fired if the public hospital "reasonably" but "mistakenly" believed that the expression was "disruptive" and addressed "a matter of private concern." Moreover, in *Garcetti v. Ceballos* (2006), the Court held that the Los Angeles district attorney could fire a deputy who claimed that a police affidavit for a search warrant contained significant falsehoods. Even if the public presumably had a legitimate interest in knowing whether police affidavits for search warrants contained misrepresentations, the deputy's memo was not on "a matter of public concern," according to the Court, because he wrote it pursuant to his official duties as a prosecutor and, for that reason, was not expressing himself as a citizen, at least not for First Amendment purposes. (See also *United States v. National Treasury Employees Union*, 1995; *City of San Diego v. Roe*, 2004; *Lane v. Franks*, 2014.)

The complexity of the law regarding the free-speech rights of public employees, however, does not undermine the underlying fact that public employees do not have the same free-speech rights that ordinary citizens typically have in traditional public forms. They may have some rights to speak out, but not if the speech is integrated with his or her official duties or if it detrimentally affects office efficiency or morale. Another important limitation on the free-speech rights of public employees is that the federal government and many state governments prohibit public employees from active political campaigning. For example, the federal Hatch Act prohibits employees of the executive branch from active engagement in partisan political activities. The Supreme Court upheld this law in *United Public Workers v. Mitchell* (1947) and reaffirmed its position in *United States Civil Service Commission v. National Association of Letter Carriers* (1973), holding that partisan activities by government employees would undermine the effectiveness and fairness of governmental operations, encourage the development of a powerful and, in all likelihood, corrupt political machine, and increase the pressure on government employees to engage in partisan politics for the purpose of currying favor with their supervisors.

However, in *Heffernan v. City of Paterson* (2016), the Court ruled that police supervisors could not demote a police officer based on a mistaken belief that he had supported a particular candidate for mayor. The police officer had picked up a campaign sign in favor of a specific candidate, but he did so not for himself, but for his bedridden mother who could not pick up the sign herself. Because the officer had been seen with the sign talking to the candidate's campaign workers, his superiors demoted him for his "overt involvement" in the candidate's campaign. The Court held that even if the facts were as the police supervisors thought them to be, they could not demote the police officer because "the Constitution prohibits a government employer from discharging or demoting an employee because the employee supports a particular political candidate." The Court assumed that support for a "particular" candidate was the basis for the demotion, but conceded that the case would be quite different if the police supervisors were acting pursuant to a "neutral policy prohibiting police officers from overt involvement in any political campaign" (136 S. Ct. 1412, 1417, 1419 (2016)). Accordingly, the Court remanded the case to determine the substance of the policy, if the supervisors were in fact following the policy, and if the policy complied with the standards of *United States Civil Service Commission*. The implication of the decision was that the demotion might have been consistent with freedom of speech if the police officer had in fact violated a neutral policy banning all forms of political partisan campaign activity.

One last issue regarding the free-speech rights of public employees concerns those who refuse to join a public union but nonetheless are required to pay the union an "agency fee." Even if such fees support the union's collective-bargaining activities, not the union's political and ideological activities, they do violate the free-speech rights of someone who opposes unions in general. The Supreme Court upheld the constitutionality of "agency fees" in *Abood v. Detroit Board of Education* (1977), but reversed itself four decades later in *Janus v. American Federation of State, County, and Municipal Employees, Council* (2018). The reversal was largely based on the Court's perception that compelled speech was especially objectionable because "individuals are coerced into betraying their convictions," which was "always [a] demeaning" experience. A public employer can require "its employees mouth a message on its own behalf," the Court insisted, because such speech would then be a part of the "employee's official duties." But it was "not easy to imagine a situation," the Court continued, "in which a public employer has a legitimate need to demand that its employees recite words with which they disagree." In other words, the government could compel speech "on its own behalf," but not (as a condition of public employment) on behalf of the union. The government's powers over employee speech, the Court conceded, "differ significantly from those it possesses in connection with regulation of the speech of the citizenry in general," but that did not mean that the Court had "to uphold every speech restriction the government imposes as an employer."

FURTHER READING

Allred, Stephen. "From Connick to Confusion: The Struggle to Define Speech on Matters of Public Concern." 64 *Indiana Law Journal* (1988): 43–81.

Finkin, Matthew W. and Post, Robert C. *For the Common Good: Principles of American Academic Freedom*. New Haven, CT: Yale University Press, 2011.

Kitrosser, Heidi. "Public Employee Speech and Magarian's Dynamic Diversity." *Washington University Law Review* 95 (2018): 1405–1422.

Norton, Helen. "Constraining Public Employee Speech: Government's Control of Its Workers' Speech to Protect Its Own Expression." *Duke Law Journal* 59 (2009): 1–68.

Rabban, David. "A Functional Analysis of 'Individual' and 'Institutional' Academic Freedom under the First Amendment." *Law and Contemporary Problems* 53 (1990): 227–301.

Roosevelt, Kermit, III. "Not as Bad as You Think: Why Garcetti v. Ceballos Makes Sense." *University of Pennsylvania Journal of Constitutional Law* 14 (2012): 631–660.

Rosenthal, Lawrence. "The Emerging First Amendment Law of Managerial Prerogative." *Fordham Law Review* 77 (2008): 33–112.

Strasser, Mark. "Pickering, Garcetti, & Academic Freedom." *Brooklyn Law Review* 83 (2018): 579–612.

Q31. IF THE GOVERNMENT PROVIDES AN EMPLOYEE WITH ACCESS TO CLASSIFIED INFORMATION, CAN THE GOVERNMENT SANCTION AN EMPLOYEE IF HE OR SHE IMPROPERLY DISCLOSES THE INFORMATION TO SOMEONE NOT AUTHORIZED TO RECEIVE IT?

Answer: Yes. The government can impose sanctions—in some cases criminal sanctions—if a current or former employee improperly discloses classified information obtained through his or her employment, especially if the employee signed a nondisclosure or a prepublication review agreement.

The Facts: Congress has enacted statutes imposing criminal liability on the disclosure of certain types of classified information, but the management of national security secrets has traditionally been a function of the executive branch. For example, in 2009 President Barrack Obama issued Executive Order 13526, which established the current system of three basic levels of classified information, each level correlated to the degree of "damage" its disclosure would cause to national security: (1) "top secret" information that would cause "exceptionally grave damage," (2) "secret" information that would cause "serious damage," and (3) "confidential" information that "reasonably" could be expected to cause "damage." An official having "original classification authority" would have to decide the level of classification. Current officials who have this "original classification authority" include the president, the vice president, agency heads, and approximately 2,000 other government officials.

One way the government prevents the disclosure of classified information is to limit access to classified information by requiring security clearances at the corresponding level. Government employees (and contractors) obtain these clearances by going through background investigations that are more intensive as one advances from "confidential" to "top secret" information and upward to "top secret—sensitive compartmented information" (TS/SCI) and so-called Special Access Programs. These investigations assess the degree to which an employee is trustworthy, honest, reliable, loyal, and not subject to blackmail. Any unauthorized disclosure by a government employee of classified information can quickly lead to the loss of his or her security clearance, which would entail loss of public employment in the national security field. In this way, the government restricts the free-speech rights of government employees with security clearances, subjecting them to dismissal for any unauthorized disclosure of classified information. The Office of the Director of National Intelligence has reported that, as of October 2015, nearly 2.9 million people had security clearances at the "confidential" or "secret" level and almost 1.4 million at the "top secret" level (ODNI Report 2016, 5).

Although employees of the federal government obviously have no free-speech right to publish classified information, it is widely assumed that former federal employees, just like ordinary citizens, can publish unclassified information whenever they wish to do so. This assumption, however, is not always correct. To provide an additional incentive to government employees not to disclose classified information, government agencies, such as the Central Intelligence Agency (CIA), require employees, as a condition for employment, to sign nondisclosure agreements (promising the government that they will not disclose classified information unless authorized to do so) or prepublication review agreements (promising the government to submit any material related to their government work for review by the relevant agency prior to publication). These prepublication review agreements require former employees to submit for government review prior to publication all their prospective writings, whether the information is unclassified or not. The existence of such prepublication review agreements is the reason why not all former federal employees have the right to publish unclassified information.

Nondisclosure agreements gave the government a contractual basis to seek a court injunction prohibiting a former employee from publishing if the government found out that he or she was about to publish classified information. Victor L. Marchetti signed such nondisclosure agreements when he joined the Central Intelligence Agency (CIA) in 1955 and when he resigned in 1969. However, in 1972, the government discovered that Marchetti was seeking to publish an article about his experiences as a CIA agent that, in its judgment, disclosed classified information concerning intelligence sources, methods, and operations. Based on this claim, the government successfully obtained an injunction against Marchetti from a federal district court, ordering him not to publish anything about the CIA or intelligence matters without prior authorization by the agency. Marchetti appealed to the 4th Circuit Court of Appeals, claiming that the injunction was an unconstitutional prior restraint (see Chapter 1).

The 4th Circuit Court disagreed with Marchetti. It conceded that the First Amendment "precludes such [prior] restraints with respect to information which is unclassified or officially disclosed," but held that such agreements are "entirely appropriate" as a way for the director of the CIA to fulfill his statutory duty to protect the confidentiality of intelligence sources and methods. The 4th Circuit Court concluded that "some prior restraints in some circumstances are approvable of course" (*United States v. Marchetti*, 466 F.2d 1309, 1313, 1316–1317 (1972)). The 4th Circuit Court's decision gave the government an option other than criminal prosecution to protect classified information. The government could now prevent the harm to national security caused by an unauthorized disclosure of classified information by seeking a court injunction—a prior restraint of speech—rather than remedy the harm in some other way after it occurred. If a current or former government employee had the temerity to disobey such an injunction, it was likely that the judge who issued the injunction would find him or her in contempt of court, subject to immediate imprisonment.

However, for the government to exercise this preventative option of an injunction, it first had to know that a CIA employee was about to publish material without prior authorization from the agency. In the case of Frank Snepp, a former CIA officer who wrote *Decent Interval*, a book about CIA activities during the Vietnam War, the government did not know it was about to be published, allegedly because Snepp "deliberately misled CIA officials into believing that he would submit the book for prepublication clearance." But what makes the Snepp case so interesting is the fact that his book did not contain any classified information. For this reason, the 4th Circuit Court held "that Snepp had a First Amendment right to publish unclassified information." The Supreme Court, however, in *Snepp v. United States* (1980) disagreed. The Court held that the government was entitled to a "constructive trust" of all the royalties Snepp earned from his book because he had breached a fiduciary obligation by not submitting the manuscript to the CIA for prepublication review. "The government does not deny—as a general principle—Snepp's right to publish unclassified information," the Court noted, but then added that, when "a former agent relies on his own judgment about what information is detrimental, he may reveal information that the CIA—with its broader understanding of what may expose classified information and confidential sources—could have identified as harmful" (444 U.S. 507, 508, 511–512 (1980)). In other words, the government was entitled to all of Snepp's royalties—not because his speech harmed national security, but rather because he did not let the CIA decide if it did or did not.

The Court argued that a constructive test was "the most appropriate remedy" for Snepp's breach of his fiduciary obligation because, "as a practical matter," actual damages were "unquantifiable," nominal damages were "hollow," and punitive damages were "speculative and unusual." These options left "the Government with no reliable deterrent against similar breaches of security." In addition, limiting the government's remedy to either a civil lawsuit or a criminal prosecution would force the government to risk disclosure of "some of the very confidences that Snepp promised to protect." In contrast, a constructive trust, the Court insisted, was not only a "swift and sure" remedy, but also one "tailored to deter those who would place sensitive information at risk." Giving the government an effective remedy for stopping people like Snepp from publishing anything about the CIA or intelligence matters without CIA approval was the Court's top priority. As the Court noted, "When the Government cannot secure its remedy without unacceptable risks, it has no remedy at all" (*Id.* at 514–515).

In 1983, President Ronald Reagan expanded and systematized the use of nondisclosure and prepublication review agreements across the federal government: all employees with access to classified information had to sign nondisclosure agreements; and those with access to TS/SCI also had to sign prepublication review agreements (see National Security Decision Directive No. 84 (March 11, 1983)). The Supreme Court indirectly endorsed the executive branch's control over who had access to classified information in *Department of the Navy v. Egan* (1988), holding that a navy employee working at the Trident Naval Refit Facility had no right of appeal after his security clearance was revoked and he lost his job. The Court's analysis rested on the premise that the president "is the Commander in Chief of the Army and Navy of the United States." Accordingly, in the Court's view, the president's "authority to classify and control access to information bearing on national security . . . flows primarily from this constitutional investment of power in the President, and exists quite apart from any explicit congressional grant." For this reason, the authority to protect classified information "falls on the President as head of the Executive Branch and as Commander in Chief." No one, therefore, "has a 'right' to a security clearance." The grant or denial of a clearance is based on a prediction of whether someone might disclose sensitive information. "Predictive judgment of this kind must be made by those with the necessary expertise in protecting classified information." It, therefore, "is not reasonably possible for an outside nonexpert body to review the substance of such a judgment" (484 U.S. 518, 527–529 (1988)). It was up to the president and his subordinates in the executive branch, not Congress or the judiciary, to decide who has access to classified information and under what conditions. In this vein, by a 1995 executive order of the president, not just federal employees, but all contractors of the federal government must sign nondisclosure agreements before they can have access to any classified information (see Exec. Order No. 12968 (August 2, 1995)).

Given the government's extensive use of prepublication review agreements, there are hundreds of thousands of former government employees who today cannot publish anything related to their governmental service, whether in a newspaper article, a blogpost, a letter to the editor, or a work of fiction, without prior approval of the government. Comparable prior restraints on speech are typically rejected as violations of freedom of speech, but in the field of national security, prepublication agreements have become the norm—a "reasonable means" of protecting classified information from unauthorized disclosure. Credible commentators have claimed that this prepublication review process is "broken," marked by vague standards, arbitrariness, and delay, with "pervasive but nearly invisible" damage to "First Amendment values" (Goldsmith 2015). President Donald Trump's August 2018 revocation of the security clearance of John Brennan, former director of the CIA, along with his threat to revoke the clearances of other national security officials (Davis 2018), is perhaps another sign that reforms of how the United States protects classified information may be needed. However, the fact that the Supreme Court has not decided a case dealing with the validity of prepublication review agreements since *Snepp* does little to promote optimism that it will soon take on this task.

Besides the loss of security clearances, the extensive use of nondisclosure agreements, and the imposition of constructive trusts to sanction violations of prepublication review agreements, the government can also try to deter the unauthorized disclosure of classified information by criminal prosecutions. But Congress has chosen not to criminalize all disclosures of classified information. It has instead limited criminal liability to those who have "reason to believe that the information is to be used to the injury of the United States or to the advantage of any foreign nation" and who disclose "information relating to the national defense" (often called "national defense information") or certain types of classified information, such as that related to communications intelligence (e.g., codes and cryptography). Until the administration of George W. Bush, prosecutions under these provisions of federal criminal law were extremely rare. However, at that point the number of prosecutions mushroomed as a way to discourage insiders from leaking information to journalists, even if the purpose of the leak was not to damage U.S. national security, but rather to make money, expose government wrongdoing, or influence public debates on important issues involving national security. For example, a navy intelligence analyst was convicted of selling classified satellite photographs of a Soviet aircraft carrier to *Jane's Defence Weekly* (*United States v. Morrison*, 1985); a former CIA officer disclosed the name of a CIA agent who had engaged in the waterboarding of an alleged terrorist (*United States v. Kiriakou*, 2012); and, finally, a CIA officer told a *New York Times* reporter about details of Iran's nuclear weapons program (*United States v. Sterling*, 2013).

In many of these cases, the defendants claimed that the criminal provisions were unconstitutionally "vague" and "overbroad" in violation of due process and the First Amendment, but to no avail. The number of leak prosecutions continues to rise, with the Obama administration pursuing at least nine cases, about "twice as many as were brought under all previous presidencies combined," while the Trump administration has recently accepted guilty pleas from two defendants who leaked information and filed charges against a former Senate Intelligence Committee staff member and a former CIA software engineer (Savage and Blinder 2018). The Supreme Court has yet to address the question of whether criminal liability for the disclosure of "national defense information" or classified information is consistent with free speech if the leaker's actual purpose is not to hurt the United States or help a foreign power, but rather to expose governmental wrongdoing or publish information the American public has a right to know. Any such decision would be a milestone regarding the relationship between national security and freedom of speech.

FURTHER READING

Casey, Kevin. "Till Death Do Us Part: Prepublication Review in the Intelligence Community." *Columbia Law Review* 115 (2015): 417–460.

Davis, Julie Hirschfeld and Shear, Michael D. "Trump Revokes Ex-C.I.A. Director John Brennan's Security Clearance." *The New York Times*, August 15, 2018, available at https://www.nytimes.com/2018/08/15/us/politics/john-brennan-security-clearance.html.

Edgar, Harold and Schmidt, Benno L., Jr. "The Espionage Statutes and Publication of Defense Information." *Columbia Law Review* 73 (1973): 929–1087.

Goldsmith, Jack and Hathaway, Oona A. "The Government's Prepublication Review Process Is Broken; The Current System for Reviewing the

Work of Former Government Employees Hurts Free Speech." *Washington Post Blogs*, December 25, 2015, available at washingtonpost.com.

Kitrosser, Heidi. "Leak Prosecutions and the First Amendment: New Developments and a Closer Look at the Feasibility of Protecting Leakers." *William and Mary Law Review* 56 (2015): 1221–1277.

Kosar, Kevin R. *Classified Information Policy and Executive Order 13526.* Congressional Research Service: R41528, December 10, 2010.

ODNI (Office of the Director of National Intelligence). *2015 Annual Report on Security Clearance Determinations*, January 2016, available at https://www.odni.gov/files/documents/Newsroom/Reports%20and%20 Pubs/2015-Annual_Report_on_Security_Clearance_Determinations .pdf.

Savage, Charlie. *Power Wars: The Relentless Rise of Presidential Authority and Secrecy.* Rev. Ed. New York: Back Bay Books, 2017, Chapter 8.

Savage, Charlie and Blinder, Alan. "Reality Winner, N.S.A. Contractor Accused in Leak, Pleads Guilty." *The New York Times*, June 26, 2018, available at https://www.nytimes.com/2018/06/26/us/reality-winner-nsa-leak-guilty-plea.html.

Vladeck, Stephen. "The Espionage Act and National Security Whistleblowing after Garcetti." *American University Law Review* 57 (2008): 1531–1546.

Q32. DOES A JOURNALIST HAVE MORE FREE-SPEECH RIGHTS THAN THE ORDINARY CITIZEN BECAUSE THE FIRST AMENDMENT PROHIBITS CONGRESS FROM "ABRIDGING" NOT ONLY "FREEDOM OF SPEECH," BUT ALSO THE FREEDOM "OF THE PRESS"?

Answer: No. Although a few justices have endorsed the view that the press has special First Amendment rights, the Supreme Court has refused to grant journalists any additional rights of freedom of speech beyond those that ordinary citizens have.

The Facts: It was Justice Potter Stewart who strongly advocated "that the Free Press Guarantee is, in essence, a *structural* provision of the Constitution," meaning that the "publishing business," as an "institution," had "explicit constitutional protection." This was the only plausible interpretation, in his view, because, "if the Free Press guarantee meant no more than freedom of expression, it would be a constitutional redundancy." Instead, this clause, according to Stewart, was meant to protect "the institutional autonomy of the press," that is, "to create a fourth institution outside the Government as an additional check on the three official branches"—a metaphorical "Fourth Estate" whose purpose was to "battle against secrecy and deception in government." For this reason, the "liberty of the press," according to Stewart, "is essential to the security of the state" (Stewart 1975, 633–636). Stewart's theory of the free press has many adherents in today's world, especially among academics, journalists, and media outlets. Their support lends credence to the notion that journalists have special rights derived from the First Amendment, but this claim is grounded more in myth than in the reality of Supreme Court decisions.

Justice Stewart undoubtedly tried to convince the Supreme Court that a "structural" understanding of the free press clause was the correct one, but a majority of the Supreme Court has never endorsed this approach. In a concurring opinion in *First National Bank v. Bellotti* (1978), Chief Justice Warren Burger explained why by underlining two major "difficulties." First, history does not establish that the framers "contemplated a 'special' or 'institutional' privilege" for the organized press; second, the task of "including some entities within the 'institutional press' while excluding others . . . is reminiscent of the abhorred licensing system of Tudor and Stuart England—a system the First Amendment was intended to ban from this country." Government could not take on this task, Burger argued, because it would require the separation of "protected" from "unprotected" speech based on "such variables as content of expression, frequency or fervor of expression, or ownership of the technological means of dissemination." Accordingly, Burger concluded that, "because the First Amendment was meant to guarantee freedom to express and communicate ideas," there was "no difference between the right of those who seek to disseminate ideas by way of a newspaper and those who give lectures or speeches" (435 U.S. 765, 798, 801–802 (1978)).

Although the Court has wavered occasionally, Burger's arguments have generally prevailed, at least in terms of whether the press has special constitutional rights of access to governmental information or special privileges to withhold information from legitimate governmental inquiries. In the 1970s, the Court decided three cases denying that the press had a special right of access to jails above and beyond the access awarded to the general public (*Pell v. Procunier* (1974), *Saxbe v. Washington Post Co.* (1974), and *Houchins v. KQED, Inc.* (1978)). Regarding the right of access to criminal trials and its relationship to the First Amendment, a key decision was *Richmond Newspapers, Inc. v. Virginia* (1980), in which the Court held 7–1 that the First Amendment protected such access, but both the public and the press equally shared the right. In the Court's view, "it would be difficult to single out any aspect of government of higher concern and importance to the people than the manner in which criminal trials are conducted," but "the First Amendment can be read as protecting the right of everyone to attend trials so as to give meaning to those explicit guarantees." However, although the Court concluded in *Richmond* that "media representatives enjoy the same right of access [to criminal trials] as the public, the Court acknowledged in passing that journalists "are often provided special seating and priority of entry so that they may report what people in attendance have seen and heard" (448 U.S. 555, 575, 573 (1980)). Here the Court derives any preference for the press from the public's right to know, not from the free press clause.

The Court extended the scope of the public's general right of access under the First Amendment to *voir dire* examinations of potential jurors in *Press-Enterprise Co. v. Superior Court* (1984) and to the transcripts of preliminary hearings of criminal cases in *Press-Enterprise Co. v. Superior Court* (1986). In the former case, the Court found the right of access outweighed any generalized right of privacy of potential jurors, while in the latter the same right transcended any concerns that pretrial publicity would risk depriving the defendant of a fair trial. But in neither case did the Court conclude that members of the press have a special right of access over members of the general public.

The Court took a comparable approach to whether members of the organized press had any special immunity from grand jury criminal investigations. In *Branzburg v. Hayes* (1972), the Court held that forcing journalists to testify before grand juries did not abridge either freedom of speech or freedom of the press. It did not matter that such coercion might deter confidential sources from furnishing valuable information to reporters "to the detriment of the free flow of information protected by the First Amendment." The "sole" issue was "the obligation of reporters to respond to grand jury subpoenas as other citizens do," keeping in mind that "neither the First Amendment nor any other constitutional provision protects the average citizen from disclosing to a grand jury information that he has received in confidence." In the end, the Court refused to "accept the argument that the public interest in possible future news about crime from undisclosed, unverified sources must take precedence over the public interest in pursuing and prosecuting those crimes reported to the press by informants and in thus deterring the commission of such crimes in the future" (408 U.S. 665, 680, 682, 695 (1972)). The Court came to a comparable conclusion regarding the legitimacy of a search warrant of a campus newspaper office in *Zurcher v. Stanford Daily* (1978), holding that it did not constitute a violation of either the First or the Fourth Amendment.

Following *Branzburg*, 40 states and the District of Columbia have enacted laws—often called "press shield" laws—that have granted a qualified privilege to journalists, one that permits them to refuse to disclose the names of confidential sources in limited circumstances, for example, when the government can readily obtain the information elsewhere. However, it is important to note that the Court has declined to rule that such privilege is constitutionally required, and that the statutory privilege varies considerably among the states, and, finally, that currently there is no federal "press shield" law. It is true that the Department of Justice has had for many years a "policy" limiting the use of grand jury subpoenas to force journalists to disclose their confidential sources, but this policy only provides limited immunity. In cases involving leaks of classified information to journalists, the Department of Justice at times has aggressively sought relevant information from journalists. For example, when Judith Miller, a reporter for *The New York Times*, refused in 2005 to disclose the name of a confidential source who had unlawfully identified Valerie Plame as an undercover CIA agent, the D.C. Circuit Court of Appeals rejected her claim of journalist privilege, and she spent 85 days in jail for contempt of court (*In re Grand Jury Subpoena: Judith Miller*, 2005).

Other leaks of classified information have raised debate about circumstances under which the federal government, consistent with freedom of speech, could criminally prosecute a reporter, a newspaper, or some other media outlet if they were involved with the publication of leaked classified information. In *New York Times Co. v. United States* (1971), the Court rejected the government's attempt at seeking an injunction against the publication of the Pentagon Papers, but two of the five justices in the majority hinted that criminal prosecution was a possibility. However, a later decision, *Bartnicki v. Vopper* (2001), cast doubt on the viability of such a prosecution by holding that a radio station could not be held civilly liable for broadcasting a private conversation illegally taped by a third party, at least not if the station acquired the tape innocently (see Q20). The disclosure of classified information by WikiLeaks in 2010 and the 2013 publication of the leaks about NSA surveillance by Edward Snowden have renewed the debate on whether reporters and media companies cross the line by knowingly publishing classified information. One possible interpretation is that reporters should lose their constitutional protection to publish classified information if they provide active assistance to the leaker, but not if they are simply the passive recipients of the information. Obviously if an ordinary citizen provided such active assistance to the leaker, he or she would likely be prosecuted on charges of "conspiracy" or "aiding and abetting" a criminal act. Since the Supreme Court has declined, in general, to give members of the media special rights under the free press clause of the First Amendment, it is possible that a journalist who gives instructions to a leaker on how, for example, to transmit to the newspaper's servers a huge electronic file of classified data or on how to hide the trail of the transmission would be criminally liable to the same degree as an ordinary citizen.

FURTHER READING

Benkler, Yochai. "A Free Irresponsible Press: Wikileaks and the Battle over the Soul of the Networked Fourth Estate." *Harvard Civil Rights-Civil Liberties Law Review* 46 (2011): 311–397.

BeVier, Lillian R. "An Informed Public, an Informing Press: The Search for a Constitutional Principle." *California Law Review* 68 (1980): 482–517.

Dyk, Timothy B. "Newsgathering, Press Access, and the First Amendment." *Stanford Law Review* 44 (1992): 927–960.

Epps, Garrett (Ed.). *Freedom of the Press: The First Amendment: Its Constitutional History and Contemporary Debate*. Amherst, NY: Prometheus Books, 2008.

Koningisor, Christina. "The De Facto Reporter's Privilege." *Yale Law Journal* 127 (2018): 1176–1268.

Stewart, Potter. "Or of the Press." *Hasting Law Journal* 26 (1975): 631–637.

Volokh, Eugene. "Freedom for the Press as an Industry, or for the Press as a Technology? From the Framing to Today." *University of Pennsylvania Law Review* 160 (2012): 459–540.

Wehbe, Alan. "The Free Press and National Security: Renewing the Case for a Federal Shield Law." *First Amendment Law Review* 16 (2018): 512–537.

6

---·❖·---

Free Speech as a Cultural Ideal

The constitutional right of free speech, as discussed in earlier chapters, protects to a degree the expressive activities of individuals from governmental sanctions, whether criminal or civil, and prohibits the government from using content or viewpoint-distinctions in favoring one ideological perspective over another. In contrast, freedom of speech as a cultural ideal does not restrict governmental action, but rather limits the degree to which Americans can morally criticize, stigmatize, or condemn other people based on what they say, write, or publish. It is, in other words, an ideal that relates to how Americans treat one another, not how the government treats them. That freedom of speech is such an ideal has already been discussed (see Q8). However, even if it is such a cultural ideal, a sizable number of Americans believe that morally condemning those who engage in unpopular or obnoxious speech is not a violation of the ideal, but rather an affirmation of it. After all, the argument goes, if a speaker has a right to engage in obnoxious speech, then *a fortiori* the righteous critic must have the right, not only to express his or her disagreement with the speaker's ideas or viewpoint, but also his or her moral opinion of the speaker. If that means a vehement and caustic attack on the speaker's humanity or moral character, then so be it. The righteous critic is simply telling others what he or she thinks of a speaker, an expressive activity arguably protected by the American cultural ideal of freedom of speech.

This interpretation of the cultural ideal of freedom of speech is a plausible one. Certainly many Americans, especially those engaged in expression in the political "arena" or the "no holds barred" world of online communications, conduct themselves in this fashion, producing a seemingly endless cycle of *ad hominem* attacks. However, it can be argued that this interpretation of the American cultural ideal of freedom of speech ignores John Stuart Mill's insight that any moral condemnation of a speaker who engages in unpopular or obnoxious speech is a form of punishment (see Q8). It is a form of punishment because it implies that the speaker is a "bad" person or, at a minimum, a person who is morally "at fault" for the substance of what he or she is advocating or asserting. In contrast, advocacy of unpopular or obnoxious ideologies of whatever type does not necessarily have this punitive dimension. If so, who has the "right" to express themselves: the obnoxious speaker or the righteous critic? Since it is illogical to claim that both have the "right," Mill argues that it must be the obnoxious speaker who has the "right" because the righteous critic is morally punishing or condemning someone for doing what he or she has a right to do, which is a form of punishing the innocent, clearly a type of wrongdoing. Since no one has a right to do wrong, the righteous critic who engages in *ad hominem* attacks of an unpopular or obnoxious speaker who has not "hurt" or "punished" anyone, but merely expressed his or her opinion, is violating the American cultural ideal of freedom of speech.

Q33. IS THERE AN AUTHORITATIVE SOURCE TO DECIDE WHAT TYPES OF EXPRESSIVE ACTIVITIES ARE PROTECTED UNDER THE AMERICAN CULTURAL IDEAL OF FREEDOM OF SPEECH AND WHAT TYPES ARE NOT?

Answer: No. Although the Supreme Court is an authoritative source to decide what expressive activities are protected under the constitutional right of freedom of speech, there is no corresponding authority to decide what types of expressive activities are protected under the American cultural ideal of freedom of speech and what types are not. However, a reasonable and coherent interpretation of this cultural ideal can be drawn from the principles that John Stuart Mill defended in his book *On Liberty* in 1859, a historically influential work that argued that the "tyranny of public opinion" was the greatest threat to freedom in the modern world.

The Facts: The Supreme Court is the ultimate authority regarding what expressive activities the constitutional right of free speech protects.

In contrast to this constitutional right, there is no ultimate authority regarding what expressive activities are protected by the American cultural ideal of free speech. There is, therefore, not as much consensus on what expressive activities are protected by the ideal. Nonetheless, there is every reason to believe that this cultural right to engage in speech is limited in character, just as the constitutional right of free speech is a limited right to engage in expression free of governmental sanctions. But where is the line to be drawn? When is it permissible, consistent with the American cultural ideal of freedom of speech, to morally criticize or condemn a speaker based on what he or she is advocating or asserting? Certainly every critic has the right to attack the substance of what a speaker advocates or asserts, but when can the critic take the additional step and morally attack the speaker? Even if the scope of protection provided by the cultural ideal is less precise than that of the constitutional right, it is yet possible to have a reasoned discussion of this subject. However, the lack of an authoritative interpreter of the cultural ideal does mean that there is no firm line between what *is* the scope of protection provided by the ideal and what *should* be the scope. Since any proposed standard cannot be defended on a *factual* basis, it must be defended on some other ground, such as its "reasonableness," "clarity," and "coherence." The reader must judge if any standard satisfies these criteria.

One obvious standard that deserves consideration is the body of Supreme Court decisions that define freedom of speech as a constitutional right. The argument would be not that these decisions are inherently authoritative as to what the cultural ideal protects, but instead that defenders of free speech as a cultural ideal simply adopt these decisions for this purpose. If this approach is adopted, then no speaker in the United States could be morally criticized, stigmatized, or condemned based on his or her expressive activities unless the federal government (or one of the state governments) could impose civil or criminal liability on the speaker. Accordingly, no one could morally condemn a speaker for insulting a person unless it constituted a "fighting word" (see Q10), for lying about another person unless it constituted libel (see Q11), for inciting unlawful action unless the unlawful action was "imminent" (see Q14), and so on. One advantage of this approach is that it has considerable clarity. The subject of the scope of the American cultural ideal of freedom of speech would instantly have the same amount of precision as the scope of the constitutional right of free speech, and critics would know immediately how to go about finding out whether they are entitled to morally blame a speaker for what he or she said or whether they must limit their criticism to the substance of what the speaker said based on their recognition of the speaker's "right" to say it. This kind of precision would provide considerable clarity. At least in a general sense, speakers would know what they could say without legitimately raising the personal ire of their fellow Americans, and critics would know how far they could legitimately go in response.

However, regardless of the clarity that would be introduced into the scope of expressive activities protected by the American cultural ideal of free speech by adopting the free-speech decisions of the Supreme Court as the standard, this approach arguably is not "reasonable." First of all, the standard for the cultural ideal of free speech must be one that most Americans "can" live with based on the fundamental principle that "ought" implies "can." There is simply no point in adopting such a rigorous standard for the cultural ideal of free speech if only a small minority of Americans would use it in their everyday social interactions. Take, for example, a speaker who deliberately tells lies about someone, but the lies do not damage the person's reputation and, therefore, do not qualify as libel. How many Americans would say that they have no right to morally criticize or condemn the speaker? Since so few Americans would abide by such a high free-speech standard, the end result would be the demise of freedom of speech as an American cultural ideal. Obviously not having a cultural ideal of freedom of speech is worse than having an ideal that is somewhat lower than the "unreasonable" one that Americans should not criticize any speaker unless his or her expressive activities could be sanctioned by the government. Accordingly, if Americans are going to continue to have a cultural ideal of free speech, that ideal must be one that is "reasonable" within the context of contemporary American society.

Although John Stuart Mill believed that oppressive public opinion (what is today called "political correctness") is the greatest danger to liberty in the modern world (see Q8), he too endorsed lowering the threshold of when social/moral condemnation was legitimate below when government could properly impose criminal or civil sanctions on conduct involving expressive activities. In his view, government could not interfere with speech unless it "harmed" another by violating the latter's legally protected interests, but he softened this standard in terms of informal social reactions to conduct, including expressive conduct. A lower standard was appropriate, he argued, because "acts of an individual may be hurtful to others or wanting in due consideration for their welfare, without going to the length of violating any of their [legally] constituted rights." In such an instance, Mill argued, the "offender may then be justly punished by opinion, though not by law." Mill elaborated his position by noting that as "soon as any part of a person's conduct affects prejudicially the interests of others [interests that are not legally protected], society [not the state] has jurisdiction over it, and the question whether the general welfare will or will not be promoted by interfering with it, becomes open to discussion" (Mill 1978, 73). Applying this standard to expressive activities, Mill's position was that, even if speech does not "harm" another's legal rights, it could yet be "hurtful" to others, or "wanting in due consideration" for the "welfare" of others, or "prejudicially" affecting the "interests" of others. If what a speaker says has any of these consequences, then it is proper, in his view, to ask whether the general welfare would be served if society interfered with it, that is, if individual members of society were free to morally criticize, stigmatize, or condemn the speaker. If it would serve the general welfare, Mill's position would be that such moral criticism and condemnation would not violate the cultural ideal of free speech.

In contrast to equating the cultural ideal of freedom of speech with the substance of the Supreme Court's free speech decisions, Mill's understanding of this ideal is more "reasonable" because it gives Americans a little more leeway to morally criticize, stigmatize, or condemn unpopular or obnoxious speakers who say "hurtful" things that prejudicially affect the "interests" and "welfare" of others in ways that do not advance the "general welfare." However, the "reasonableness" of Mill's approach is obtained, to some extent, by sacrificing a degree of clarity. Obviously, terms such as "hurtful" and the "welfare" or "interests" of others, as well as the principle of the "general welfare," are broad and vague, which makes it inevitable that reasonable people will disagree on how these terms should apply in specific cases. In effect, Mill's understanding of the cultural ideal of free speech is a "coherent" one, but it does sacrifice a degree of "clarity" for the sake of "reasonableness." Whether this trade-off is worthwhile and workable will be tested in this chapter by exploring how Mill's criterion applies to a limited number of contemporary free-speech controversies.

FURTHER READING

Alvarez, Mauricio J. and Kemmelmeier, Markus. "Free Speech as a Cultural Value in the United States." *Journal of Social and Political Psychology* 5 (2017): 707–735.

Balkin, Jack. "Cultural Democracy and the First Amendment." *Northwestern University Law Review* 110 (2016): 1053–1095.

Bloom, Lackland H., Jr. "John Stuart Mill and Political Correctness." *Louisville Law Review* 56 (2017): 1–35.

Bollinger, Lee. *The Tolerant Society*. New York: Oxford University Press, 1988.

Coleman, Franciska A. "They Should Be Fired: The Social Regulation of Free Speech in the U.S." *First Amendment Law Review* 16 (2017): 1–38.

Ho, Katherine. "Defending a Culture of Free Speech." *Harvard Political Review*, April 9, 2017, available at http://harvardpolitics.com/harvard/defending-culture-free-speech/.

Lukianoff, Greg and Haidt, Jonathan. *The Coddling of the American Mind*. New York: Penguin Press, 2018.

Mill, John Stuart. *On Liberty*. Indianapolis, IN: Hackett Publishing, 1978.

Reeves, Richard. *John Stuart Mill: Victorian Firebrand*. London: Atlantic Books, 2008.

Smolla, Rodney A. *Free Speech in an Open Society*. New York: Vintage, 2011.

Q34. IS IT CONSISTENT WITH THE CULTURAL IDEAL OF FREEDOM OF SPEECH TO MORALLY CRITICIZE A SPEAKER WHO INTENTIONALLY, RECKLESSLY, OR NEGLIGENTLY SPREADS FALSEHOODS OR SO-CALLED FAKE NEWS?

Answer: Yes. It is consistent with the cultural ideal of freedom of speech to morally criticize a speaker who intentionally, recklessly, or negligently spreads falsehoods, including speakers who unjustifiably condemn responsible journalists as propagators of "fake news"—but only if the moral criticism serves the public interest and the degree of criticism is proportionate to the culpability of the speaker's purpose and the amount of harm caused by the falsehood.

The Facts: The constitutional right of free speech does not protect speakers who intentionally or recklessly spread false statements of fact that damage another person's reputation and are for that reason defamatory (see Q11). In contrast, the constitutional right protects a speaker if the statement is one of opinion, rather than of fact; or if a statement is false, but does not harm anyone's reputation; or, lastly, if the speaker reasonably thinks the statement is true, but in fact it is false. However, the fact that non-libelous falsehoods are not subject to criminal or civil liability does not mean that the cultural ideal of freedom of speech protects such speakers from moral criticism. The latter issue is dependent on whether the statement is "hurtful" to others in the sense that it negatively affects another person's welfare or interests. If it does, and if the general welfare would be improved if such statements were discouraged, then the cultural ideal of freedom of speech would not protect the speaker. Instead, the ideal would protect the free-speech values of those who wish to morally criticize, stigmatize, or condemn the speaker, at least if the response is proportionate, and not in excess, of the "hurtfulness" of the speaker's statement.

The parody ad targeting Jerry Falwell published by pornographer Larry Flynt's *Hustler Magazine* is an example of constitutionally protected speech that would be subject to moral criticism under the cultural ideal. The ad, which was published in the November 1983 issue of *Hustler*, portrayed an inebriated Falwell having an incestuous relationship with his mother in an outhouse, but it was not libel since the ad was a parody and, therefore, not a statement of fact. Even though the ad was not libel, it was "outrageous," motivated by malice, and calculated to hurt Falwell's feelings. In addition, unlike political cartoons and satires, the ad had little to no public benefit other than increasing the notoriety of the pornographic magazine and its owner (see Q25). A similar conclusion is warranted regarding the expressive activities of Fred Phelps and his Westboro Baptist Church. The Court held that the church had a constitutional right to picket military funerals and celebrate the deaths of American soldiers to advocate their view that God was rightly punishing the United States for its toleration of homosexuality. However, it is obvious that the members of the Westboro Church, in the choice of the location for their demonstration and in the nature of their signs ("Thank God for Dead Soldiers" and "Thank God for IEDs [improvised explosive devices]"), were intentionally and deliberately "hurting" the feelings of the families of the dead soldiers as a way to increase media coverage of the church and promote its political agenda. Such speech is constitutionally protected, but not immune from moral condemnation, because the church gave no consideration to the "welfare" or the "interests" of those respectfully attending the funeral, and it is better for society to discourage such speech than to tolerate it. The cultural ideal of freedom of speech, of course, protects the church's expressive activities in other contexts, but not when its choice of time and place are calculated for the very purpose of "hurting" others.

The cultural ideal also does not protect all speakers who knowingly express factual falsehoods, even if those falsehoods are non-defamatory. It is true that the Supreme Court ruled that the constitutional right of free speech protects such falsehoods in *United States v. Alvarez* (2012). The case concerned whether Congress could constitutionally enact the Stolen Valor Act, which criminalized the making of false claims about whether one has received military medals. Alvarez had falsely claimed that he was a retired marine with 25 years of service, that he had been wounded many times, and that he had received the Congressional Medal of Honor in 1987. None of these assertions were true. Despite these lies, the Supreme Court invalidated Alvarez's conviction on the ground that falsity alone was not sufficient to place a statement outside the protection of the First Amendment. But this ruling in no way implies that ordinary Americans are not within their rights to criticize Alvarez on moral grounds for the lies he told.

The level of moral disapprobation of a liar, however, should be commensurate to the degree of culpability inherent in the purpose and consequences of the falsehood. For example, so-called white lies are not maliciously intended, and they often have positive effects, such as comforting the sick ("Granny, you look great today") or preserving a child's innocent fantasies ("Yes, Sally, Santa Claus really exists!"). Though it can be argued such innocent lies indirectly harm others by slowly eroding the societal commitment to truth, the direct benefits of such falsehoods clearly outweigh the costs, rendering moral criticism of those who utter them inconsistent with the cultural ideal of freedom of speech. Nevertheless, opinions differ on how to draw the line between "white lies" and what can be called "gray lies," those in which the speaker's motives are not clearly malicious, but are doubtful or uncertain, along with those that have both positive and negative consequences. For example, what if Alvarez claimed only that he was a retired marine for the purpose of improving his chances of getting a job? How the American cultural ideal of freedom of speech applies to such "gray lies" is indeterminate and depends on the totality of the circumstances in the specific circumstances.

Negligent lies that "hurt" the "interests" or "welfare" of others also seem to have an indeterminate status in terms of the American cultural ideal of freedom of speech. The corresponding constitutional right of free speech does not protect such lies if they are defamatory in character and relate to a private person, but it does if the lies relate to a public official or figure (see Q11). The Court's rationale for immunizing such negligent falsehoods is that it creates a "breathing space" for speakers. They can express their honestly held beliefs about public officials and figures, thereby increasing the number of true statements about the latter, even if the number of false statements also goes up. However, this type of argument seems less persuasive in terms of the cultural ideal of freedom of speech. It is doubtful that moral and professional criticism of negligent reporters and editors who publish falsehoods about public officials and figures would have the same negative effects on the "marketplace of facts" as civil or criminal liability. Moreover, such criticism would encourage media news outlets to live up to the professional standards of their craft.

However, it is generally acknowledged that the level of moral and professional criticism of reporters and editors should be proportionate to the degree of negligence and harm caused by the negligent falsehood, with gross departures from professional norms subject to harsh moral and professional criticism and minimal deviations subject to little or none.

FURTHER READING

Blitz, Jonathan. "Lies, Line Drawing, and (Deep) Fake News." *Oklahoma Law Review* 71 (2018): 59–116.

Bok, Sissela. *Lying: Moral Choice in Public Life*. New York: Vintage, 2011.

Borchers, Callum. "'Fake News' Has Now Lost All Meaning." *The Washington Post*, February 9, 2017, available at https://www.washingtonpost.com/news/the-fix/wp/2017/02/09/fake-news-has-now-lost-all-meaning/.

Burns, Eric. *Infamous Scribblers: The Founding Fathers and the Rowdy Beginnings of American Journalism*. New York: Public Affairs, 2007.

Cook, Timothy E. *Governing with the News: The News Media as a Political Institution*, 2nd ed. Chicago: University of Chicago Press, 2005.

Han, David S. "Categorizing Lies." *University of Colorado Law Review* 89 (2018): 613–654.

Levi, Lili. "Real 'Fake News' and Fake 'Fake News.'" *First Amendment Law Review* 16 (2017): 232–327.

Mansky, Jackie. "The Age-Old Problem of 'Fake News.'" *Smithsonian Magazine*, May 7, 2018, available at https://www.smithsonianmag.com/history/age-old-problem-fake-news-180968945/.

McIntyre, Lee. *Post-Truth*. Cambridge, MA: MIT Press, 2018.

Shiffrin, Seana Valentine. *Speech Matters: On Lying, Morality and the Law*. Princeton, NJ: Princeton University Press, 2016.

Q35. DOES MORAL CRITICISM OF A SPEAKER WHO ENGAGES IN SPEECH THAT "DENIGRATES" OR "STEREOTYPES" OTHERS ON THE BASIS OF RACE, SEX, ETHNICITY, RELIGION, OR SEXUAL ORIENTATION VIOLATE THE AMERICAN CULTURAL IDEAL OF FREEDOM OF SPEECH IN ALL CONTEXTS?

Answer: No. Moral criticism of a speaker who engages in speech that "denigrates" or "stereotypes" others on the basis of race, sex, ethnicity, religion, or sexual orientation is consistent with the cultural ideal of free speech if (1) the speech is calculated to "hurt" the "feelings" or the "interests" of the members of the denigrated or stereotyped group and (2) the criticism or condemnation serves the general welfare of society.

The Facts: The constitutional right of freedom of speech clearly protects speech that "denigrates" or "stereotypes" others on the basis of race, sex, ethnicity, religion, or sexual orientation unless the speech satisfies the criteria of an unprotected category of speech, such as a threat (see Q9) or a provocative fighting word (see Q10). The *cultural ideal* of freedom of speech, though, does not protect such speech to this extent. Even if such derogatory speech contains neither a threat nor a fighting word, it can in certain situations reflect such a lack of consideration for the feelings and interests of members of the targeted group that the speaker can legitimately be subject to moral ridicule. For example, in 1977, a U.S.-based Nazi organization called the National Socialist Party of America (NSPA) chose Skokie, Illinois, a suburb of Chicago with 70,000 residents, of whom approximately 30,000 were Jewish and 5,000 Holocaust survivors, as the site for a political march during which members would advocate their anti-Semitic ideology wearing Nazi uniforms and displaying the swastika. Taken all together, the verbal and symbolic speech planned for the event clearly qualified as an extreme form of "derogatory" speech, one that could only be described as "hate speech." Moreover, it was indisputable that the NSPA chose Skokie as the location for its march for the express purpose of causing Holocaust survivors to relive the trauma they experienced under Nazi rule in Europe during World War II. Their goal, therefore, was to leverage the pain their march inflicted on Holocaust survivors and other Jews to gain public attention and notoriety. Such insensitivity to the feelings and welfare of a religious/ethnic group does not contribute to, but rather detracts from, the general welfare. For this reason, there is no doubt that, even if the constitutional right of freedom of speech protected the NSPA, it was consistent with the American cultural ideal of freedom of speech to morally condemn them for what they were planning to do.

A similar conclusion is warranted for the white supremacist organizers of the "Unite the Right" rally in Charlottesville, Virginia, in August 2017. Legal scholars agree that "alt right" groups have a constitutional right to express their racist and nationalist views, and the choice of Charlottesville as the location for their rally cannot be faulted on the ground that it was selected simply to ensure that their expression hurt the feelings and sensitivities of the residents of Charlottesville. However, leaked pre-rally conversations between the white supremacists indicate that many of them planned to use the rally as a pretext for violence. In one chat supremacists joked about using a vehicle to run over counter-protesters—a scenario that sadly turned into a reality, with the death of Heather Heyer, a civil rights activist, and the injury of 19 others. After the rally, a white supremacist mocked this tragedy by posting a photo of the car from the film *Back to the Future* inserted into one of the Charlottesville crowds with the comment "Back to the Fhurer [*sic*]". Other leaked chats strongly suggest that the white supremacists planned to carry weapons at the rally and were excited at the prospect of "fighting for the white race" (Joseph 2017; Feuer 2018). Such intentions and expectations place the expressive activities of the white supremacists outside the scope of the cultural ideal of freedom of speech.

Moral criticism and condemnation of the organizers of the "Unite the Right" rally are consistent with the cultural ideal even if certain elements of the Charlottesville counter-protesters, such as the so-called anti-fa (a term used to describe a coalition of far-left groups that advocate violence and lawbreaking to combat fascism), were also morally culpable. However, there is no moral equivalency between the white supremacists and the vast majority of civil rights activists who peacefully counter-protested. The white supremacists intentionally provoked the violence, while only a small minority of the counter-protesters welcomed the opportunity to react violently. However, an implication of the blameworthy character of the white supremacists attending the Charlottesville rally is that they do have a right to hold such a rally free of moral criticism if their goal is simply to express their ideology peacefully, rather than provoke a media-frenzy through violent tactics. The cultural ideal of free speech means little or nothing unless it protects from *ad hominem* attacks those who express opinions that most Americans "hate." If all Americans have a right to their opinions, then they must have the right to express them regardless of how offensive and "hateful" they are to most of us, at least in contexts where the advocacy does not "hurt" the "welfare" and "interests" of others.

In contrast to the Nazis in Skokie, Illinois, and the "alt-right" in Charlottesville, Virginia, other forms of "derogatory" or "stereotypical" speech are fully protected by the American cultural ideal of freedom of speech because there is no evidence that the speakers intended to "hurt" the "feelings" or "interests" of others. One example of such a speaker is Dr. Charles Murray, a conservative libertarian scholar who has written a number of controversial books linking intelligence to race, poverty, and other social problems in ways that critics argue reflect "scientific racism." Despite this reputation, a student group at Middlebury College invited Murray to campus in 2017. At the talk, students who disagreed with

Murray's political ideology turned their backs on him, chanted, "Your message is hatred, we cannot tolerate it" and "Charles Murray go away." Eventually the students "shut down" the event (Beinart 2017). Such conduct is inconsistent with the cultural ideal of freedom of speech. Murray's intention was not to provoke violence or "hurt" anyone's "feelings" or "interests." He had accepted an invitation to deliver an academic talk on a controversial topic. Students had every right to disagree with the substance of Murray's assertions, but they had no right to shut down the event before it even happened. Such a moral attack of a speaker based on a perception of his beliefs is antithetical to freedom of speech as a cultural ideal. If such attacks are tolerated under the delusion that the students are simply exercising their own right to free speech, the future of freedom of speech as an American ideal, at least on college campuses, is in serious jeopardy.

Another form of "derogatory" or "stereotypical" speech that is usually protected by the American cultural ideal of freedom of speech is what is commonly called "cultural appropriation." A well-known incident of this type occurred in March 2016 at Bowdoin College. The school launched an investigation into a possible "act of ethnic stereotyping" when a group of students threw a tequila-themed birthday party for a friend and provided their guests with miniature sombreros for cultural effect. As a result of the investigation, school administrators placed the party attendees on "social probation," removed the hosts of the party from their dorm, and began impeachment proceedings against two attendees of the party who were members of student government. The student government largely sided with the administration, issuing a "statement of solidarity" that depicted the party as an act of "cultural appropriation" that "creates an environment where students of color, particularly Latino, and especially Mexican, students feel unsafe." However, since there was no evidence that the party attendees had any malicious intent toward Latinos, it is not clear why or how the party would have made Latinos feel "unsafe," especially since Bowdoin's dining hall sponsored a "Mexican night" a week after the party and many Mexican restaurants to this day encourage sombreros as suitable headgear for enjoying Mexican food (Rampell 2016). Whether the conjunction of tequila and sombreros is a form of "stereotypical" speech is subject to debate, but even if it was stereotypical expression, it was protected by the American cultural ideal of freedom of speech because it had no significant negative impact on the "feelings" or "interests" of the affected group.

It is possible for a type of "stereotypical" speech to become such a symbol of ridicule and mockery that anyone who engages in it significantly risks hurting the "feelings" of others. A speaker may not intend this harm, but the risk is so great that the speaker is morally culpable for engaging in the speech. He or she either knew or should have known the risk and is blameworthy on that basis. Wearing blackface is an example of this type of harmful stereotypical speech. In the 19th century, white actors in minstrel shows used blackface to mock and ridicule slaves and free blacks, and this tradition continued in the vaudeville era of the 1920s and 30s, with Al Jolson appearing in blackface in the popular 1927 film *The Jazz Singer* and Bugs Bunny as late as 1953 in *Southern Fried Rabbit*. Since this history is firmly rooted in American public consciousness, blackface has become a symbol of racism and bigotry. Accordingly, it is difficult to understand why a white law professor at the University of Oregon would wear blackface to an off-campus Halloween party in 2016. The professor apologized but explained that her purpose was to promote an anti-racist book written by an African American doctor. Despite this intention, the university suspended the professor with pay and eventually determined that she had violated the school's racial harassment policy (Jaschik 2017).

Although the school's sanctions are arguably an overreaction, there is reason to conclude that the law professor was morally at fault for her expression even if her intention was benign. Unintentionally insulting African Americans by wearing blackface is typically "hurtful" and ordinarily does not serve the "general welfare" of American society. At a minimum, the university determined that the law professor should have known better. Of course, it is possible to imagine contexts where blackface would not be morally objectionable: for example, if a film producer wanted to make a documentary of Al Jolson's movie career and wanted to include a few scenes of blackface for the sake of historical authenticity; or perhaps if the audience knows beforehand that blackface will be worn at a theatrical production for the purpose of capturing the degree of ridicule that African Americans endured during the vaudeville era and those who attended the event did so voluntarily. But that is not what occurred at the aforementioned Halloween party. Students felt obligated to attend the party, and they were "shocked" and "surprised" by their professor's conduct.

A more difficult case is Megyn Kelly's recent comment on her morning NBC show that wearing blackface on Halloween was "OK when I was a kid as long as you were dressing like a character" (Koblin and Grynbaum 2018). Her comment suggested that it would yet be OK to wear blackface on Halloween, which is a very doubtful claim. However, it must not be forgotten that Kelly herself was not wearing blackface, but merely talking about wearing it. The cultural ideal of freedom of speech typically protects such expression, even if the expression concerns a controversial form of symbolic conduct that has traditionally been used for the purpose of mockery and ridicule. Unless the cultural ideal protects speech about controversial topics, there is little or no reason to have it.

Other instances of stereotypical speech related to racial or ethnic minorities would also be protected by the cultural ideal of freedom of speech because they are not inherently symbols of racist bigotry. A good example of this type of expression is when an author of fiction or poetry writes in the vernacular of a racial or ethnic group different from his or her own. A recent example of this type of "cultural appropriation" is Anders Carlson-Wee's poem *How-To*, which *The Nation* published on July 5, 2018. The poem, written in black vernacular by a white poet, suggested how beggars and homeless people should get the attention of passers-by on the street. "If you're crippled don't flaunt it. Let em think they're good enough Christians to notice. . . . You hardly even there." The poem inspired an avalanche of criticism, especially on Twitter. Writer Roxane Gay tweeted, "Don't use AAVE. Don't even try it. Know your lane" (Schuessler 2018), while Randa Jarrar, a professor of English at California State University at Fresno, responded by claiming that "at some point, all of us in the literary community must DEMAND that white editors resign. It's time to STEP DOWN and hand over the positions of power" (see Flaherty).

The reaction to Carlson-Wee's poem was so intense that the poetry editors at *The Nation*, Stephanie Burt and Carmen Gimenez Smith, apologized for publishing the poem on July 24, writing that the poem contained "disparaging and ableist language" and that they were "sorry for the pain" they "caused to the many communities affected by this poem." Presumably the poem "disparaged" African Americans because it was written in black vernacular and "ableist" because the poem contained the word "crippled." Carlson-Wee also apologized, adding the additional comment that "treading anywhere close to blackface is horrifying to me" (McWhorter 2018).

Other observers, however, felt that the backlash constituted a sad reflection on the status of the American cultural ideal of freedom of speech. The poet Grace Schulman, a former poetry editor of *The Nation*, noted that she and her colleagues had never apologized for a poem because they had understood that a part of their job was "to provoke our readers" and that a "free press" and a "free society" implied "the freedom to write and publish views that may be offensive to some readers" (Jenkins 2018). And John McWhorter, professor of English and Comparative Literature at Columbia University, writes that "we end up tripping over countervailing goals" if we urge white artists to understand black "pain," "experience," and "difference," but deny them the right "to express it through their creations" (McWhorter 2018). Many members of the literary community asserted that anyone who engaged in a fair reading of Carlson-Wee's poem would understand it as a critique of the hypocrisy and the indifference of people, including white people, who "hardly see" the homeless people on the streets of American cities. Whether Carlson-Wee's poem is good poetry or not, the American cultural ideal of freedom of speech undoubtedly protects this form of expression. Free speech advocates asserted that it was unfortunate that both the magazine and the poet apologized for it. From their perspective, the poet and the magazine editors had every moral right to engage in this expression—and those who criticized them violated the American cultural ideal of freedom of speech.

FURTHER READING

Beinart, Peter. "A Violent Attack on Free Speech at Middlebury." *The Atlantic*, March 6, 2017, available at https://www.theatlantic.com/politics/archive/2017/03/middlebury-free-speech-violence/518667/.

Carlson-Wee, Anders. "How-To." *The Nation*, July 30–August 6, 2018, available at https://www.thenation.com/article/how-to/.

Feuer, Alan. "Planners of Deadly Charlottesville Rally Are Tested in Court." *The New York Times*, February 12, 2018, available at https://www.nytimes.com/2018/02/12/us/charlottesville-lawsuit-far-right-heather-heyer.html.

Flaherty, Colleen. "Controversial Professor Wants White Editors to Quit." *Inside Higher Ed*, July 30, 2018, available at https://www.insidehighered.com/quicktakes/2018/07/30/controversial-professor-wants-white-editors-quit.

Jaschik, Scott. "Oregon: Professor in Blackface Violated Anti-Harassment Policy." *Inside Higher Ed*, January 3, 2017, available at https://www.insidehighered.com/news/2017/01/03/university-oregon-finds-professor-who-wore-blackface-party-violated-anti-harassment.

Jenkins, Alan. "The Speaker vs. the Poem." *The Times Literary Supplement*, August 7, 2018, available at https://www.the-tls.co.uk/articles/public/the-nation-poem-how-to-controversy/.

Joseph, George. "White Supremacists Joke about Using Cars to Run Over Opponents before Charlottesville." *ProPublica*, August 28, 2017, available at https://www.propublica.org/article/white-supremacists-joked-about-using-cars-to-run-over-opponents-before-charlottesville.

Koblin, John and Grynbaum, Michael M. "Megyn Kelly's 'Blackface' Remarks Leave Her Future at NBC in Doubt." *The New York Times*, October 25, 2018, available at https://www.nytimes.com/2018/10/25/business/media/megyn-kelly-skips-today-blackface-nbc.html.

McWhorter, John. "There's Nothing Wrong with Black English." *The Atlantic*, August 6, 2018, available at https://www.theatlantic.com/ideas/archive/2018/08/who-gets-to-use-black-english/566867/.

Rampell, Catherine. "Political Correctness Devours Yet Another College, Fighting over Mini-Sombreros." *The Washington Post*, March 3, 2016, available at https://www.washingtonpost.com/opinions/party-culture/2016/03/03/fdb46cc4-e185-11e5-9c36-e1902f6b6571_story.html.

Schuessler, Jennifer. "A Poem in the Nation Spurs a Backlash and an Apology." *The New York Times*, August 1, 2018, available at https://www.nytimes.com/2018/08/01/arts/poem-nation-apology.html.

Sines v. Kessler, Memorandum Opinion, Case No. 3:17-cv-00072, July 9, 2018 (E.D. VA.), available at https://cases.justia.com/federal/district-courts/virginia/vawdce/3:2017cv00072/109120/335/0.pdf?ts=1531214982.

Q36. DO PRIVATELY OWNED SOCIAL MEDIA COMPANIES, SUCH AS FACEBOOK OR TWITTER, HAVE A MORAL OBLIGATION TO RESPECT THE AMERICAN CULTURAL IDEAL OF FREEDOM OF SPEECH BY EXCLUDING "FAKE NEWS" FROM THEIR COMMUNICATIONS PLATFORMS?

Answer: Yes. Privately owned social media companies, including Facebook and Twitter, have a moral obligation to respect the cultural ideal of freedom of speech by accommodating speakers who conform to the cultural ideal—and by shutting down those who do not, including speakers who intentionally spread "fake news" in the form of deceptions and outright falsehoods.

The Facts: Social media companies are privately owned and, for that reason, are not required to respect the constitutional right of free speech as defined by the Supreme Court. However, such media companies, like individual citizens, should conform their expressive activities to the demands of the American cultural ideal of freedom of speech. This moral norm requires them to deny their communications platforms to speakers who violate the cultural ideal and provide it to those who conform to it. For example, social media networks are obligated to provide their platforms to speakers engaged in offensive speech unless the speech "hurts the feelings" or harms the "interests" of Americans and does not serve society's "general welfare."

This rule is applicable to all forms of communications that travel through online social networks, including texts, photos, videos, chats, e-mails, comments, links to news or other content on the web. Perhaps in part because of the magnitude of the problem, social media companies have been reluctant to undertake the responsibility of reviewing the nature of the expressions that flow through their networks to determine what expression is consistent with the cultural ideal of free speech. The problem is especially acute in regard to what is popularly called "fake news," a category of expression consisting of intentional lies, deceptions, and falsehoods. Social media networks should do what they can to exclude such speech from their platforms because "fake news" is eroding the American societal commitment to truth, which is obviously contrary to the general welfare.

The evolution of Facebook's standards for censoring expression on its network provides a useful context for discussing how social media companies have a moral obligation to try to evaluate the types of expression their services distribute and disseminate. Founded in 2004 by Mark Zuckerberg, Facebook quickly grew to be a worldwide communications behemoth, with 12 million active users worldwide by 2006 and over 1 billion by 2012. With such rapid growth, it was inevitable that offensive and objectionable speech appeared on the network, including threats and libelous statements. Facebook initially claimed that it was a communications platform, not a publisher, and therefore, it had little or no legal or moral responsibility for the nature of the expression circulating on its network.

By 2013, this "hands-off" policy had become indefensible to many, given the size of the network and the impact Facebook had on the lives of its users. As criticism intensified, the company developed a set of internal "community standards" that restricted hate speech, bullying, threats, and harassment, but the public was largely kept in the dark about how Facebook defined these terms (Kiss and Arthur 2013). Facebook's problem with the content of the communications on its network came to a head when it became clear that the Russians had used the platform to interfere in the 2016 presidential race by spreading disinformation. In fact, on the night of the election, executives at Facebook discussed whether their company, by spreading deceptions (e.g., the false claim that Pope Francis endorsed Trump), had helped the Republican nominee win (Isaac 2016). Later in 2017, Facebook itself admitted that a Russian company linked to the Kremlin used 470 fake accounts to purchase $100,000 worth of Facebook ads as part of a propaganda campaign to elect Trump (Shane 2017).

In reaction to this scandal, Facebook published for the first time in April 2018 a 27-page version of its "Community Standards." The "Standards" banned all illegal activity from Facebook, including any forms of expression that were unlawful, such as threats, harassment, and libel. Regarding "false news," however, the "Standards" maintained that there existed "a fine line between false news and satire or opinion." For this reason, Facebook did not remove "false news," but instead reduced "its distribution by showing it lower in the News Feed." Applying this standard, Zuckerberg argued that Facebook would not exclude Holocaust denials from the network because "there are things that different people get wrong." Asked why Facebook permitted Infowars to use its platform to propagate false conspiracy theories, such as the outrageous claim that the Sandy Hook school shooting never happened, the head of Facebook's News Feed explained, "just being false doesn't violate the community standards" and Infowars simply had a "different point of view."

Facebook's position was that freedom of speech protected "fake news" from exclusion from the network, but that Facebook could "penalize" such speech by lowering its place in the News Feed, which purportedly reduced the number of users who would see it (Manjoo 2018). How freedom of speech could protect misinformation from one sanction, but not the other, was a question that Facebook never addressed. Facebook soon modified its position to permit exclusion of misinformation "that could lead to people being physically harmed," such as the violence against Rohingya Muslims that erupted in Myanmar in 2017. However, the social media company continued to frame the circulation of deliberate lies and deceptions on its platform as statements protected by free speech.

What Facebook failed to understand, according to critics, is that even though the constitutional right of free speech typically protects falsehoods from criminal or civil liability, the American cultural ideal of freedom of speech does not. Such speech is insidious and harmful to American society. Even if moral criticism of lies and falsehoods is not morally obligatory, Facebook's many critics charge that it is morally objectionable for a privately owned company to provide a service that "enables" liars and propagators of misinformation to more effectively mislead and confuse the American people. They charge that that is exactly what Facebook is doing when it does not exclude from its network those who routinely spread "news" that is obviously "fake." And it cannot remove the taint of its own moral culpability by "penalizing" these deceivers by placing the lies and deceptions lower down the News Feed.

The irony, however, is that Facebook eventually did exclude content from its network posted by Infowars and its controversial founder, Alex Jones—but it did so on the basis of its policies against "hate speech," "graphic violence," and "bullying," rather than "misinformation." Facebook defines "hate speech" as "content that purposefully targets individuals with the intention of degrading or shaming them"; "graphic violence" as "content that glorifies violence or celebrates the suffering or humiliation of others"; and "bullying" as "content that purposefully targets private individuals with the intention of degrading or shaming them." Assuming that Facebook applies these categories reasonably by only excluding from its network content that "hurts others" by "shaming" or "degrading" them, then such exclusions are consistent with the American cultural ideal of freedom of speech (Roose 2018). However, critics assert that Facebook does not seem to realize that the propagation of obvious lies, deceptions, and falsehoods can be just as damaging to American society as the circulation of the above types of speech that Facebook excludes from its network.

Twitter, YouTube, Apple, Pinterest, Mailchamp, and other social media companies also excluded Infowars from their networks, but they too did so primarily on the basis that the content was "abusive," "offensive," and "insensitive," rather than based on its obvious falsity. Accordingly, the problem of "fake news" on social media networks is far from solved. For example, following the Senate confirmation hearings of Justice Brett M. Kavanaugh in September 2018, Facebook identified 559 pages and 251 accounts controlled by Americans who had used its network to spread in a coordinated fashion false and misleading content about the woman, Christine Blasey Ford, who had accused Kavanaugh of assaulting her when they were in high school. Facebook also determined that some of the pages and accounts made money in the process by directing Facebook users to websites filled with ads. They were making money, as it were, by lying to their fellow citizens (see Frankel).

Websites on both the political right and the left have contributed to the ever-expanding amount of online lies, distortions, and falsehoods. And Facebook is right when it says that there is "a fine line between false news and satire or opinion." But critics charge that the "fineness" of this line is no excuse for Facebook and other social media companies to permit their platforms to be used to spread lies and falsehoods—especially given the reach and influence of their platforms.

FURTHER READING

Benkler, Yochai, Faris, Robert, and Roberts, Hal. *Network Propaganda: Manipulation, Disinformation, and Radicalization in American Politics.* New York: Oxford University Press, 2018.

"Community Standards." *Facebook,* available at https://www.facebook.com/communitystandards/introduction.

Frenkel, Sheera. "Facebook to Remove Misinformation That Leads to Violence." *The New York Times,* July 18, 2018, available at https://www.nytimes.com/2018/07/18/technology/facebook-to-remove-misinformation-that-leads-to-violence.html.

Frenkel, Sheera. "Facebook Tackles Rising Threat: Americans Aping Russian Schemes to Deceive." *The New York Times,* October 11, 2018, available at https://www.nytimes.com/2018/10/11/technology/fake-news-online-disinformation.html.

Gillespie, Tarleton. *Custodians of the Internet: Platforms, Content Moderation, and the Hidden Decision That Shape Social Media.* New Haven, CT: Yale University Press, 2018.

Isaac, Mike. "Facebook, in Cross Hairs after Election, Is Said to Question Its Influence." *The New York Times,* November 12, 2016, available at https://www.nytimes.com/2016/11/14/technology/facebook-is-said-to-question-its-influence-in-election.html.

Kiss, Jemima and Arthur, Charles. "Publishers or Platforms? Media Giants May Be Forced to Choose." *The Guardian,* July 29, 2013, available at https://www.theguardian.com/technology/2013/jul/29/twitter-urged-responsible-online-abuse.

Manjoo, Farhad. "What Stays on Facebook and What Goes? The Social Network Cannot Answer." *The New York Times,* July 19, 2018, available at https://www.nytimes.com/2018/07/19/technology/facebook-misinformation.html.

Roose, Kevin. "Facebook Banned Infowars. Now What?" *The New York Times,* August 10, 2018, available at https://www.nytimes.com/2018/08/10/technology/facebook-banned-infowars-now-what.html.

Shane, Scott and Goel, Vindu. "Fake Russian Facebook Accounts Bought $100,000 in Political Ads." *The New York Times,* September 6, 2017, available at https://www.nytimes.com/2017/09/06/technology/facebook-russian-political-ads.html.

Wilson, Jason. "How Rightwing Conspiracy Theorists Attacked Christine Blasey Ford's Testimony." *The Guardian,* October 5, 2018, available at https://www.theguardian.com/us-news/2018/oct/05/christine-blasey-ford-rightwing-conspiracy-theorists-burst-your-bubble.

Index